MODERN CONSPIRACY

MODERN CONSPIRACY

The Importance of Being Paranoid

Emma A. Jane and Chris Fleming

B L O O M S B U R Y

NEW YORK · LONDON · NEW DELHI · SYDNEY

Bloomsbury Academic

An imprint of Bloomsbury Publishing Inc

1385 Broadway
New York
NY 10018
USA

50 Bedford Square
London
WC1B 3DP
UK

www.bloomsbury.com

Bloomsbury is a registered trade mark of Bloomsbury Publishing Plc

First published 2014

© Emma A. Jane and Chris Fleming, 2014

Library of Congress Cataloging-in-Publication Data
A catalog record for this book is available from the Library of Congress.

ISBN: HB: 978-1-6235-6681-4
PB: 978-1-6235-6091-1
ePDF: 978-1-6235-6589-3
ePub: 978-1-6235-6431-5

Typeset by Integra Software Services Pvt. Ltd.
Printed and bound in the United States of America

CONTENTS

ACKNOWLEDGEMENTS

J – I have discovered that it takes a village not only to raise a child but to write a book (especially if one happens to find oneself child-raising *and* book-writing at the same time). An enormous, proverb-strength thank you, therefore, to some excellent villagers, whose above-and beyond-ness in relation to conjugation, charitability, compassion, consolation, cooking, company, conversation, and many other affectionate c-words, has my enduring gratitude. Profound thanks to: Nicole A Vincent, Vaishali Kashyap, Marie-Pierre Cleret, Anne Fawcett, Rachael Swain, Melanie Anderson, Kat Costigan, and Mark Rosalky (and the extended Rosalky and Ambrose clans). This is not an exhaustive list but it's a start. I am also fortunate enough to work at a university where the powers-that-be conspire to promote research; indeed this book was written, in part, with the assistance of an internal grant from the School of Arts and Media at the University of New South Wales. Gratefulness, too, therefore, to UNSW and to the many fine colleagues with whom I work there. Finally, a special thank you to Chris Fleming, for explosive intellectual generosity, for walking with me through the PhD, and for introducing me to the euphoric highs and horror lows of intellectual collaboration. I doubt we'll ever agree on semicolons; but perhaps that's for the best.

CF – much thanks to David Burchell, Jane Goodall, Michaela Davies, Sirianand Jacobs, John O'Carroll, James Gourley, and David Haggerty, whose voices and beautifully odd minds reverberate through the book in ways far greater than any mere bibliography could indicate. (I realize that sounds like a slightly muted plagiarism warning.) Sizeable and strepituous thanks are also due to my improbably large-brained co-author, without whom this book might well have remained an excited email exchange and a series of absurd jokes. I'm also deeply indebted to Malcolm Jones, Bob Vavich, and Mindy Sotiri. You each know why. Thank you.

INTRODUCTION: RUNNING DOGS AND THE 'RIGHTNESS' OF CONSPIRACY

Though this be madness, yet there is method in't.

SHAKESPEARE, *HAMLET*

'This is the age of conspiracy', Don DeLillo writes in *Running Dog* – '…the age of connections, links, secret relationships' (1989, 111). He's right. Here in the non-fiction world, hardly a day goes by without some novel revelation of a terrible new plot that would have had us all fooled – if it weren't, that is, the subject of such scandalous and continuous revelation. Thanks to the hard work of conspiracy theorists, common knowledge now has it that the World Trade Center was not destroyed by aeroplanes, but by a coordinated bomb detonation by the American government; that Paul McCartney died in a car crash in 1966 and was replaced by a body double; that Princess Diana – on the other hand – did *not* die in a car crash but was assassinated by the British monarchy (who may or may not be extraterrestrial); that fluoride controls our minds via an undetermined process of chemical alchemy that transforms human defiance into slavish obedience; that the world has been invaded by reptilian humanoids and they are already here among us; that the secret world government is run by Jews – and that, correspondingly, there *is*, in fact, a secret world government whose overarching governance passes by undetected on the basis that it is, obviously, *secret*. And so on. This allows us to supplement DeLillo's characterization of our era by adding that not only is this the age of conspiracy, it is also the age of *exposé*. Presumably, we only *know* it as the age of conspiracy because we've begun to see through it. It is thus perhaps also the age of covert connections uncovered, of public leaks to secret links, of cloak-and-dagger bonds exposed, and of shadowy meetings in basements brought to light. This is the age where potential evil schemers from this world and all others know – or soon will – that battalions of DIY detectives and suburban Fox Mulders are onto them always and already.

Exactly how many covert schemes exist outside of the conspiracist discourse invoking them is hard – indeed, perhaps impossible – to determine. Surely one of the signal reasons for our ignorance here is that, if nothing else, conspiratorial discourse is profoundly fecund: theories divide and reproduce at a startling rate and even auditing them in their totality would be work enough for Jorge Luis Borges' famous cartographers, whose tireless efforts to chart their empire in such detail resulted in a map the size of the territory which it plotted (1998, 325).[1] We will not allow this to detain us. The task here is less encyclopaedic than it is synoptic – and perhaps, eventually, diagnostic. Moreover, there's far more to account for here than supposed conspirators and conspiracists. (In all good conspiracy stories, there is of course *always* more.) Our case is that, in addition to the conspirers and those who theorize about conspirers, there is a third clan, one whose power – indeed, whose very *existence* – is mostly ignored in contemporary debate about the cultural impact of conspiracy and conspiracism. We refer, of course, to the debunkers: those armies of ardent critics who argue – often in terms strikingly similar to their targets – that all manner of catastrophes will befall us (or have *already* befallen us) because of the scourge of quasi-pathological paranoia, egregious epistemology, and ruinous irrationality accompanying the contemporary proliferation of conspiracy theorizing. As such, this is not merely the age of conspiracy and unmasked conspiracy, but the age of outraged anti-conspiracists, whose texts open, characteristically, with that 'This is the age of conspiracy' quote from DeLillo's *Running Dog*.[2]

---

[1]

In that Empire, the Art of Cartography attained such Perfection that the map of a single Province occupied the entirety of a City, and the map of the Empire, the entirety of a Province. In time, those Unconscionable Maps no longer satisfied, and the Cartographers Guild struck a Map of the Empire whose size was that of the Empire, and which coincided point for point with it. The following Generations, who were not so fond of the Study of Cartography as their Forebears had been, saw that that vast Map was Useless, and not without some Pitilessness was it, that they delivered it up to the Inclemencies of Sun and Winters. In the Deserts of the West, still today, there are Tattered Ruins of that Map, inhabited by Animals and Beggars; in all the Land there is no other Relic of the Disciplines of Geography. (Borges 1998, 325)

[2]Books on conspiracy which use this *Running Dog* quote include: David Aaronovitch's *Voodoo Histories* (2009); Thomas Melley's *Empire of Conspiracy* (2000); Peter Knight's *Conspiracy Culture* (2000); and George E. Marcus' *Paranoia Within Reason* (1999). Journal articles which use this quote are far too numerous to list here.

This book is different – if not with respect to its use of *Running Dog*, then at least in its attempt to provide a more integrated and reflexive study of conspiracy discourse, one which does not conveniently expunge its own contributions – and genre of discourse – from the field of inquiry. The bulk of scholarly literature on modern conspiracy (and there really *is* a 'bulk') focuses on only one of the constitutive groups in the aforementioned conspiracy triad: conspiracy theorists. A common theoretical refrain is that the twenty-first century's burgeoning legion of conspiracists represents a decisive rupture from a golden era of rationalism. In *Among the Truthers – A Journey Through America's Growing Conspiracist Underground,* Jonathan Kay – a Canadian journalist and fellow at the 'Foundation for Defense of Democracies' – implores readers to commit to a defence of the rationalist tradition by confronting 'the Enlightenment's enemies' – those 'shrieking prophets' who are apparently tearing 'a gaping cognitive hole' in the intellectual edifice of the rationalist project (2011, xxiii, xiii, xix). Showing himself to be his own kind of shrieking prophet, Kay's fear is that this gaping cognitive hole becomes so enormous that – having nowhere else to stand – we shall all fall into it. For Kay, without the requisite Enlightenment prophylactics, open-mindedness is a short road to vacant-mindedness.

Anti-conspiracists such as Kay tend to position themselves as lone voices in the wilderness – a fractured, post-modernist wilderness where the secular academy is busy fetishizing radical relativism rather than supporting the rational negotiation of 'a consensus truth about the way our world works' (xvi). For a supposedly silenced minority, however, debunkers are surprisingly loud, numerous, and well-represented on book store shelves. Certainly Kay's concern about the creeping conspiracist threat to the Enlightenment is one shared by many others. Damian Thompson warns that 'a pandemic of credulous thinking' – of which the *en masse* subscription to conspiracy theories is symptomatic – is threatening the great legacies of the European Enlightenment (2008, 1–3). Francis Wheen figures neo-irrationalism as a newfangled, Marx-esque opiate of the people (2004, 193), while Roger Scruton declares reason missing in action, pointing the finger at the deconstructionist 'gobbledegook' of Jacques Derrida, the pragmatic sleights of hand of Richard Rorty, and the discourse-centricity of Michel Foucault (as well as the latter's, ahem, 'rampant' homosexuality). 'Reason', Scruton writes in an essay whose tone and conclusions comport with at least two of the dictionary definitions of 'rampant', 'is now on the retreat, both as an ideal and as a reality' (1999). Then there is the London-based magazine of the Rationalist Association which boasts that it has been 'promoting reason, debate, and free thought since 1885' ('New Humanist Magazine'), but which abruptly withdraws this goodwill when the reasoning, debate, and free thought relate to those Enlightenment-terrorizing conspiracy theories. 'Rationalists have a right to feel embattled', writes *New Humanist* contributor James Gray, 'With celebrities cheerleading for bogus therapies, the internet teeming with conspiracy theories and creationists lining up to get their own schools, it can feel like the hard-won advances of the Enlightenment are unravelling before our eyes' (2012).

In this ostensible battle between the light and the dark we are in danger of equating stridency with cogency – where self-justifying panic becomes the *sine qua non* of intellectual lucidity. Contra Scruton, however, one must-have intellectual accessory missing in action in this debate is actually *nuance*. If not the end-point, a decent starting point for discussion might involve turning down the volume for a little while. Despite all the shouting, we suggest that it is ill advised to join the panic at this stage, at least in the terms Kay and thinkers of his ilk stipulate. In fact – as will be borne out in this book – rather than representing a rupture from the rationalist tradition, our case is that the contemporary cognitive mood so conducive to conspiracy thinking actually involves a certain *continuation* and *amplification* of several Enlightenment ideals, albeit often in a burlesque form. This forms one basis of our contention about the 'rightness' – or at least the formal *reasonableness* – of many of the modes of thinking utilized by conspiracists. While we may baulk at the bizarre excesses of some of their conclusions, it is harder to fault, at least in principle, their scepticism and spirit of independent inquiry. In other words, there is method in what may at first blush appear as madness.

Further – on the subject of methodological madnesses – we note that the investigative techniques and alarmism characteristic of conspiracist debunkers often bear a startling resemblance to the epistemological orientations and rhetorical armoury of those purportedly being critiqued. As we have seen in the case of Kay, critics of conspiracist thinking frequently condemn the catastrophic predictions of conspiracy theorists via equally catastrophic predictions of their own. This sort of mimetic 'doubling' is also evident in the way debunkers engage in paranoid hunts for hidden connections among ostensibly discrete conspiracist groups, in their infiltration of 'enemy' groups, and in their framing of the forces of conspiracist evil as unified, organized, personified, and driven by malevolent intent.[3]

---

[3]The idea of mimetic 'doubling' was first put forward by René Girard in *Mensonge romantique et vérité romanesque* (*Deceit, Desire and the Novel: Self and Other in Literary Structure*) (1961). In this book, ostensibly concerned with an analysis of the novel, Girard argues that antagonism is both predicated upon and generative of a kind of mirroring or 'doubling', where rivals come increasingly to resemble each other. *cf*.: Fleming 2004, 42–7.

A particularly potent example of some of the performative tensions common in debunking camps is evident in a suggestion made by the American legal scholars Cass R. Sunstein and Adrian Vermeule. Sunstein (who held the powerful government position of administrator of the White House Office of Information and Regulatory Affairs from 2009 to 2012) and Vermeule argue that the existence of domestic and foreign conspiracy theories is no trivial matter; rather, they say, it poses 'real risks' to the US government's antiterrorism policies (2008). Having warned of the 'pernicious effects' (2009, 220) associated with false, harmful, and unjustified conspiracy theories, the pair then offers a modest proposal for remedying the situation: covert 'cognitive infiltration' (224–6). This tactic, they say, could be undertaken by government agents or their allies who act either openly or anonymously in both real and virtual domains. Operatives who engage in this epistemological version of drawing poison will undermine percolating conspiracy theories by 'planting doubts about the theories and stylized facts that circulate within such groups', thereby breaking 'the crippled epistemology of conspiracy-minded groups' (219, 224, 227). While Sunstein and Vermeule admit their plan carries a risk of perverse results, they are otherwise able to maintain the writerly equivalent of straight faces – quite the achievement given the absurdity of their proposal. So the best way to rectify the fear that powerful people and institutions are engaged in conspiratorial and covert schemes designed to manipulate the gaumless masses, they suggest, is to have powerful people and institutions embark on a conspiratorial and covert scheme designed to manipulate the gaumless masses. It would be Orwellian if wasn't so Heller-esque.

Our (partial) defence of conspiracy theorists and (qualified) critique of conspiracy debunkers is not entertained for the purposes of developing a kind of *Groundwork for the Metaphysics of Madness*. In an effort to put *everyone* off side, some may now be disappointed that we are not about to endorse claims that the 1969 Apollo moon landing was faked, that giant shape-shifting reptiles live in the centre of the earth, and that Marilyn Monroe was killed by a barbiturate enema wielded by Mafia hit men in cahoots with Robert F. Kennedy and J. Edgar Hoover – most likely because she knew the real truth about UFOs and the White House whitewash. A quick walk through Conspiracy's Greatest Hits shows that the truth is not only out there – sometimes it really is *out there*. Yet, tempting as it is for the sober and sophisticated intellectual to dismiss such hypotheses – and their increasing multitude of paid-up subscribers – as all equally demented, our case is that there *are* truths to be had in even the most outlandish of conspiracy theories. But again, we must proceed carefully: these truths most often have little to do with whether or not Elvis is alive and unwell and living in Truth or Consequences, New Mexico. They are, in other words, rarely connected to the substantive claims actually *made* by conspiracy theorists. The truths to be unearthed here are far less scandalous, and usually relate to the nature – and cultural impact – of conspiracy discourse itself. Far from being meagre runner-ups to more salacious offerings, the truths conspiracism presents us turn out to be far more interesting than anything Oliver Stone – even in his darkest moments – might imagine about the CIA. One of the paradoxes of conspiracy theories is that these often tendentious breviaries of gnostic nods, winks, and prognostications, these determinedly dour discourses of secrecy and deception, offer revelations and truths *despite* themselves.

Without wishing to endorse – and so join – the Chicken Lickens, our case is that the combined force of the conspiracy triad outlined above – **conspiracy**, *exposés* **of conspiracy**, and *exposés* **of** *conspiracism* – has a potent and, yes, *at times* damaging, cultural impact. To understand this impact, we contend that it is best to avoid making *a priori* judgements about the 'rightness' or 'wrongness' of any of these three elements, but to attempt to measure individual examples along a scale – an axis of conspiracy, if you will – which ranges from 'sociopolitically beneficial' at one end, to 'sociopolitically noxious' at the other. This is in recognition of the fact, for instance, that conspiracy – the *act* of conspiring – is certainly reprehensible in a case such as Watergate, but is not *inherently* noxious. In fact, politics, business, and even family units would struggle to function in recognizable forms if they were deprived of the ability to conspire about election strategies, marketing campaigns, and birthday presents. By the same token, conspiracy theories contending Washington is in bed with cattle-mutilating and anal-probing aliens are infinitely more difficult to defend. The same *cannot* be said, however, for conspiracy theories that suggest powerful people sometimes conspire corruptly and against our best interests. (Apart from anything else this instinct drives investigative reporting and 'accountability' journalism, which function as elements of a sociopolitically beneficial 'fourth estate'.[4])

Finally, we can see that *exposés* of conspiracism – that discourse which presents itself as a rational corrective to the dangerous delusions of the

---

[4]The term 'fourth estate' was originally used to contrast the press to the Lord Spiritual, the Lords Temporal, and the Commons. It is now used to contrast the press with the legislative, executive, and judicial arms of government. More generally, 'fourth estate' is used to refer to a social, or political, force whose influence is not consistently or officially recognized.

masses – may sometimes deliver on this promise. Equally, however, such putative correctives can *sometimes be as one-eyed, agenda-driven, and immune to counterevidence as the conspiracy thinking they condemn.* The dearth of scholarly analysis and critique of these scholarly critics is problematic. Far from being solely helpful (or even solely neutral) commentary which is located outside its field of inquiry, the discourse of debunking is deeply invested in and imbricated with conspiracist discourse, to the point where a hostile mimetic escalation can be observed occurring between these two ostensible opposites. Thus the authors of debunking texts who insist their sole *motivation* is to pose solutions to the social problem of conspiracy thinking, may still produce discourse whose primary *function* is to exacerbate putatively pathological forms of thinking rather than mitigate them. Our hope is that this book offers an analysis of conspiracy-related discourse which is more successful at transcending this mimetic double bind – if only because it acknowledges that such ambitions invariably traverse an asymptotic path, pursuing a goal which may be strived for, but will likely never be reached. (Perhaps a precondition of any form of critique is a rigorous commitment to the logic of the discourse that provides the subject of analysis, even if this relationship is oppositional – maybe *especially* if it is oppositional. Much more will be said about the idea of 'critique' in later chapters.)

In Chapter 1, 'Powerful Secrets', we provide a brief history of conspiracies, conspiracy theories, and conspiracist critiques. We acknowledge the desirability, and also the impossibility, of furnishing a single, one-size-fits-all definition of conspiracism – one that would provide us, for instance, with an algorithm to allow us to neatly separate the reasonable from the unreasonable conspiracy theory. Ultimately, however, we conclude that, in addition to the sorts of criteria we will indicate, 'banality' is as reasonable a litmus test as any. As we shall see, even the schemers behind Watergate were less grand planny Dr Evils than shambolically humdrum Professor Screw-Ups.

Chapter 2, 'Impossible Things', narrows the lens on one of our objects of analysis by offering a detailed examination of the evidential structure of conspiracy theories – those characteristics and 'logics' which render the unbelievable *impregnable*, and which have transformed outsider paranoia into popular gospel. Special attention is given to the common conspiracist view that the absence of proof *is* the proof, to the plausibility possibilities offered by the Internet, and to an unfortunate condition that has been labelled 'death by footnote'.

In Chapter 3, 'A Short History of an Epistemic Ambience', we move from the 'whats' of conspiracy discourse to the 'whys' by offering a novel explanation for the contemporary proliferation of conspiracists and their theories. In it, we avoid the sort of technological determinism which points the finger at the rise of those media technologies enabling mass communication. While media channels such as the Internet are indeed exceedingly conspiracy theory-friendly, they provide only one way into an understanding of the object at hand. Our argument is that in imagining conspiracy theory to be irreducibly contemporary means we will fail to see the signal conspiratorial moments in early modern thought. (We are not the first to attempt to make this point, although relatively few have.[5])

Neither do we subscribe to the popular view that conspiracy thinking is first and foremost a kind of *en masse*, post-traumatic shock response to individual political catastrophes such as the Kennedy assassination in 1963 or the al-Qaeda strike on America in 2001. Without wishing to downplay the social, political, and philosophical significance of such monumental calamities, our case is that conspiracy thinking is better understood by considering the emergence of a paradigmatic – and consummately modern – *epistemic ambience* whose signal characteristics are doubt, scepticism, and ultimately paradoxical relationships with institutional authority and the truth (often called Truth, with the capitalization signifying a certain Platonic gravitas). Conspiracy thinking can also be considered in the context of the Internet's radical DIY-ification of just about everything. While the printing press revolutionized what John Hartley has called 'read only' literacy, the rapid expansion of the cybersphere has involved a mass uptake of 'read-write' uses of multimedia (2009, 17). Conspiracy thinking

---

[5]We are heirs, in the West, to the formation of the modern republic of secular sovereignty that received its first major realization in the French Revolution. As a small but significant selection of historians have argued, conspiratorial discourse was the organizing rhetoric behind the paranoid excesses of Jacobinism, which saw widespread executions of Hébertists and Dantonists. Indeed, both Jean-Paul Marat and Maximilien de Robespierre forged their political education to a conspiratorial vision of revolutionary politics – an obsessive search for uncovering 'plots'. John Farrell has argued, for instance, that Jean-Jacques Rousseau's seminal theory of the origin of private property and civil society is explicitly conspiratorial in its outlook (2006, 261–78). And Rousseau is not alone among thinkers of his era to accord epistemological privilege to conspiracist theories of society. Voltaire's famous slogan about the church, "Ecrasons l'infame" [let's crush the infamous], is predicated on a view of religion – and its institutional representatives – as fundamentally engaged in a collective repression of ordinary people for the purposes of gaining social and cultural advantage – of religion as a 'more or less pernicious delusion concocted by priests' (Gans 2011, 75. *cf.*: Girard 1987, 70). Also valuable is the collection edited by Barry Coward and Julian Swann (2004); the essays therein examine the historical role in conspiracies and conspiracy theory in the early modern period.

is similar in that it involves a democratization of epistemology – with all of democracy's messiness, blunt instrumentation, and odd outcomes.

Chapter 4, 'Pleasures, Sorrows, and Doubling' continues these explanatory narratives by examining the common sociopsychological and etiological factors tied to both conspiracy thinking and conspiracy theory debunking. This leads us, inevitably, to a detailed discussion of the uncanny resemblances between the rhetorical style and methodology of these two declared enemies, a discussion which makes use of the work of, among other thinkers, the French cultural theorist René Girard. In this chapter, we also begin examining the counterintuitive appeal of paranoid thinking. Paranoia, we're often told, is if not a debilitating illness then at least a deeply unpleasant state. It may poison our relations with others, and sour our outlook on the world. Yet both conspiracy theorizing and conspiracy theory debunking appear to *delight* its participants, filling them with a powerful sense of private knowledge, laboriously arrived at by their own resources in defiance of the bovine credulity of others. Given that much conspiracy discourse seems to be thoroughly paranoiac in manner and method, how can both these things be true at once? Here we show that the opposition is too simple by half and the contradiction is only apparent.

Chapter 5, 'Cultural Ramifications and Reflections', supports the debunkers' case that an excess of certain kinds of conspiracy discourse can be dangerous, but figures debunking as it usually appears as a significant part of the problem, not least because of its key role in the escalating symmetry of antagonisms discussed in Chapter 4. Here we argue that treating conspiracy theories as epistemological errors means that debunkers are caught in a dialectical game where they are forced to debate on the same terrain as their opponents, exchanging evidence and counter-evidence, questioning sources, and attempting to infirm the rival's arguments. Part of a comprehensive understanding of conspiracy discourse involves allowing that not only do conspiracies occur (and often in such banal form that we fail to register them *as* conspiracies), but that *actual* conspiracies also often occur as a result of conspiracy *theories*. We should be loathe to deny an actual conspiracy against the Jews, for instance, on the basis that we reject the accuracy of *The Protocols of the Elders of Zion*. Further, we need to understand the ways in which the cognitive and explanatory styles associated with conspiracy theorizing have a far wider ambit than what we usually accept. This is indeed the age of conspirators, of conspiracists, *and* of conspiracist debunkers: all groups whose central concern, one way or another, relates to powerful truths and who knows about them.

Chapter 6, 'Conspiracy and Theory', takes a mildly baroque theoretical detour in order to ask what conspiracy theory reveals about what it means to analyse society and culture more generally: what is it we think we're doing when we undertake the task of comprehending the world we live in, including comprehending something we call 'conspiracy theory'? How do we go about doing this? And how might we respond to what we've discovered? On the way we will have reason to raise certain questions concerning Richard Hofstadter's thesis about 'the paranoid style' (1964) – not its *existence*, but its *provenance*. It may turn out that, as a cognitive style, paranoia has many more adherents than simply those who believe their neighbour may be an upwardly mobile reptile. Furthermore, we argue that the temptation to dismiss all forms of conspiracism as 'paranoia' is not only uncritical and un-self-reflective; it tends to miss precisely what would be encouraged: that one of its sources is the reticence to accept uncritically someone else's conception of a universal good or an unquestionable truth (*cf.*: Melley 2000, 13).

Our overall conclusion – cleverly and conspiratorially concealed in that section of the book called 'Conclusion' – asks 'Where to Now?' We could say more, but then we'd probably have to kill you. In fact, if you insist on turning the page, we must first ask you to solemnly vow – via a series of secret handshakes and gesticulations too secret to have even been devised yet – that you, dear and also most untrustworthy reader, will keep *all* information contained in this book to yourself.

1 POWERFUL SECRETS

I shall not today attempt further to define the kinds of material I understand to be embraced within that shorthand description; and perhaps I could never succeed in intelligibly doing so. But I know it when I see it, and ... this case is not that.

POTTER STEWART, US SUPREME COURT JUDGE

There are known knowns; there are things we know we know. We also know there are known unknowns; that is to say, we know there are some things we do not know. But there are also unknown unknowns – the ones we don't know we don't know.

DONALD RUMSFELD, FORMER US SECRETARY OF DEFENSE

'Is he a tall grey bio-android or what?'

Like many conservative American political groups, the goals of the RR Movement United include preserving family values, upholding the US constitution, and acting in the role of 'media watchdog'. It accepts prayer requests, and sells T-shirts, tote bags, aprons, and dog clothes with slogans to help promote its campaign to ensure concerned patriots are 'awake to the truth' ('Welcome to the RR Movement United'). There is, however, a conspicuous point of difference between RR and comparable organizations: alongside its relatively unexceptional conservative social activist agenda is a bellicose declaration of violent, castration-centric war against the demonic reptilian hybrids that have apparently infiltrated the highest levels of government along numerous timelines in multiple dimensions. 'WE DO NOT CARE IF YOU ARE A CHRISTAN, MUSLIM, OR JEWISH, A PAKI, A POLICE OFFICER, A RICH PIG A ORGANIC PORTAL, A CHEMTRAIL SHILL, A DEBUNKER KING, A NSA SHILL, A CIA AGENT OR A DEMON WHORE SLAVE BITCH', the unnamed founder and CEO of Reptilian Resistance announces in oddly inclusive invective on the movement's website. 'IF YOU ARE HARVESTING REPTILIAN GENES AND YOU ARE IN A POSITION OF INFLUENCE FOR YOUR SPECIES THERE IS A GREAT POSSIBILITY THAT YOU WILL BE TERMINATED ... [and] ... TRANSFERRED TO OUR PERSONAL TORTURE AND RESEARCH LABORATORY' ('Reptilian Resistance', emphases in original).[1]

As alarming as it may be to learn that drug usage, sexual perversions, and senseless shootings at day care centres and postal facilities may all be the work of Multidimensional Reptilian Demon Lords, the Reptilian Resistance movement seems an implausible candidate for mainstream media attention and high level political intervention. Yet, in early 2013, the group made international headlines when it posted what it claimed was high-definition video evidence that a member of President Barack Obama's security team was also a 'shape shifter alien humanoid'. The Reptilian Resistance broadcast was based on footage shot during the president's 2012 address to the American Israel Public Affairs Committee at the Washington Convention Center. It used a computerized voiceover with an English accent to draw viewers' attention to the unusual appearance and 'creepy movements' of a suited member of Obama's security brief who restlessly scans the crowd in front of the president:

> pay close attention to how his head features suddenly change. His ears, his nose, his chin, cheek bone, jaw and mouth are no longer looking human at all. Matter of fact now he has a blatant, non-human face, so what just happened? Did his shape shifting device fail during Obama's speech in the middle of an amphitheater crowded with people? Is he an actual reptilian humanoid? Is he one of the Annunaki?[2] Is he a tall grey

---

[1]We have decided against using 'sic' after grammatical, spelling, and other errors in online material in recognition of the informalities of expression commonly found in these contexts.

[2]In their essay on the 'reptoid hypothesis', Tyson Lewis and Richard Kahn refer to the conspiracist view that, rather than having evolved according to Darwinian natural selection, humans are the result of genetic experimentation carried out by a race of reptilian aliens called the Anunnaki (2005, 51).

bio-android or what? Is that video evidence that the Illuminati elitism is in bed with at least one ancient extraterrestrial race, hidden in plain sight and pulling the strings of mankind? ('Obama's Reptilian Secret Service Spotted AIPAC Conference 3 Angles [HD]').

Debate raged in the cybersphere. Many viewers posting comments below the clip on *YouTube* were mocking. They pointed out that the security guard's odd change in appearance was most likely due to precisely what the Reptilian Resistance voiceover urged viewers to ignore: 'the distortions and image artifacts caused by post-editing zooming'. Some wondered why a reptoid smart enough to invade the upper echelons of government undetected was unable to prevent itself shapeshifting in front of millions of people on television. Others, however, took the claims quite seriously: 'American Government is full of motherfucking reptilians or reptilian-human hybrids', one person posted, 'and as long as there are sheeple,[3] they will hide in plain sight like this' (2trancentral commenting on Obama's Reptilian Secret Service Spotted AIPAC Conference 3 Angles [HD]). Elsewhere, commentators said they found the reptile conspiracy theory convincing because of their own experience with supernatural forces: 'ive made eye contact with these beings that appeared for a few moments then vanished without making a sound … its funny how its so easy for u to speculate when u have no personal background with the unexplained u illuminati faggot' (XAntichristX13 commenting on LifeLibertyNow 2013).

A significant sub-sector of correspondents did not accept Reptilian Resistance's account of high-level shapeshifter infiltration, but were sympathetic to the idea in general. (In other words, their position could be summed up as: 'we subscribe to reptile conspiracy theories – just not this one'.) Many were unimpressed with the patronizing and insulting tone of the disbelievers. Consider the responses to a *YouTube* video claiming it would not only debunk but 'destroy' the Reptilian Resistance case. 'My god, what an arrogant asshole', read one, 'I bet this asshole has a room totally devoted to his degrees and certificates and probably admires and dusts them off on a

---

[3]'Sheeple', a colloquial portmanteau of 'sheep' and 'people', is used to refer to the herd-like mentality of those people who do what they are told and accept received wisdom without question. Urban Dictionary defines 'sheeple' as, 'People unable to think for themselves. Followers. Lemmings. Those with no cognitive abilities of their own' (Naegling 2003). To put it in a somewhat glib, zoomorphic idiom, we might say that conspiracy theory tends to figure society as constituted by a bunch of sheep, owned by wolves, policed by pigs - and, more often than not, threatened by reptiles.

daily basis and then pats himself on the back for his better then anyone else narcissistic intellect' (Tiberiusduck commenting on ibid.). Another thought it was 'stupid to spend time to make a 9 min video just to say "some people are stupid"' (nikko Chatzisomething commenting on LifeLibertyNow 2013). Someone else wondered whether Skeptic the Destroyer's next move would be to debunk pro-wrestling (ChildrenoftheGorn commenting on LifeLibertyNow 2013).

As the arguments became increasingly heated and as various postings and re-postings of the original Reptilian Resistance video approached what is known as 'viral' status on the Internet, mainstream media outlets began reporting the story. It was picked up by, among others, conservative US commentator Glenn Beck (whose own tendency to circulate conspiracy theories has resulted in the creation of a humorous Glenn Beck conspiracy theory generator which promises to deliver 'Fair and Balanced Paranoia' on demand). Then, extraordinarily enough, the White House weighed in. In a wry comment to *Wired* magazine, Caitlin Hayden, the chief spokeswoman for the National Security Council, dismissed alien bodyguards as too expensive in an era of budgetary cut-backs: 'I can't confirm the claims made in this video, but any alleged program to guard the president with aliens or robots would likely have to be scaled back or eliminated in the sequester. I'd refer you to the Secret Service or Area 51 for more details' (cited in Beckhusen 2013). *Wired* journalist Robert Beckhusen joked that he was journalistically obliged to observe that this wasn't a flat denial. Conspiracy theorists, on the other hand, read the White House comments very differently. After all, it was an *admission* of sorts, wasn't it? A common claim was that such 'HIT-PIECES' were evidence that the 'Controllers' were on the run: '(WE) the "Truthseekers" are really starting to gain real traction & (WE) are forcing the MSM's[4] hand. (WE) really (ARE) starting to make an (IMPACT) and starting to reach (Critical-Mass) so much so (WE) are … Starting to (WIN) the InfoWar' (UfoDisclosure 2012). And so it goes – odd capitalizations, twitchy bracketing, and all.

Such allegations of Obama-endorsed shapeshifters are obviously located at the more florid end of the conspiracy theory spectrum (as well as at the most ornate end of the punctuation gradient). Yet this conspiracy narrative – as well as the mass of responses, counter-responses, and counter-counter-responses that follow – illustrates many key characteristics of contemporary conspiracy discourse. We can see, for instance, that Reptilian Resistance makes a number of energetic contentions about

---

[4]'MSM' in this context refers to 'mainstream media'.

conspiratorial activity at the zenith of free world governance, yet feels under no obligation to actually prove any of them. This, we are told, is simply the nature of theories.[5] Conspiracists *do* acknowledge the notion of what is called in epistemology the 'burden of proof',[6] but this is conveniently – and radically – shifted to the debunkers. 'It's not our job to prove there's a lizard in the White House' is the conspiracist message here. 'It's your job to prove there *isn't*.'[7] In addition to reversing the usual legal maxim of *semper necessitas probandi incumbit ei qui agit* (which translates roughly as 'the necessity of proof always lies with the person who lays charges' (Saha 2010, 196)), the Reptilian Resistance case study illustrates a second critical conspiracist rhetorical move which, if accepted, would render conspiracy theories – as a genre – immune to rebuttal. As we have seen, the mere fact that a debunker engages with a conspiracy theory is paraded by conspiracists as indubitable 'proof' of the truth of the original conspiracy theory (as well as of conspiracy theories in general). Thus the most meticulously argued and rationally irresistible debunking enterprise renders itself null and void simply because it exists.

The evidential structures of conspiracy theories will be discussed in detail in Chapter 2. For the time being, we confess to finding ourselves in unlikely – and slightly uncomfortable – partial agreement with Reptilian Resistance. As we have seen, conspiracists often claim that conspiracy theories wouldn't generate such heated opposition if they weren't – to put it in colloquial terms – a 'thing'. This is where we concur, at least in principle. Examined in isolation, the original shapeshifter claim seems intellectually and perhaps even psychiatrically marginal. Yet we can note two points about this. First, the conspiracist hypothesis is *meaningful*; indeed, one cannot refute – even in principle – a conjecture that is *de facto* meaningless. Second, something about the conspiracist hypothesis calls forth an almighty reaction across a remarkable range of contexts. Clearly, all this constitutes a 'thing'. Where we diverge with

[5]This attitude is obvious elsewhere on the Reptilian Resistance site. Under a blog on the 'Altered Vibrational Frequency' of Multidimensional Reptilian Demon Lords, for example, the author notes that: 'In The Absence Of Further Evidence We Will Merely Report These Theories And Not Speculate On Their Validity' ('Multidimensional Reptilian Demon Lords').

[6]See: Epstein 1973/74 (esp. 558–9).

[7]The angry responses to 'Obama Reptilian Secret Service Conspiracy DEBUNKED and DESTROYED!' (and its snide references to 'reptilian Jew nazis') are also revealing in this respect. 'I need ACTUAL proof that they dont exist and until you can provide that, you have debunked nothing', reads one (MrSolax202 commenting on LifeLibertyNow 2013).

the conspiracists, however, is in our diagnosis of, or emphasis on, what this 'thing' might be. Our case is that what is being exposed – at least in this instance – is not (we very much hope) an evil *über* lizard, but a striking cultural phenomenon that involves the discursive contributions of conspiracists, as well as those of debunkers, mockers, and sombre scholarly analysts.[8]

Some aspects of this phenomenon are undoubtedly associated with fear, suspicion, paranoia, and genuinely unhappy concern, but a sizeable chunk involves humour, irony, entertainment, and the various pleasures to be gained from derision. Quite frankly, often it is hard to tell which is which – to identify who is joking and who is not. Little wonder, therefore, that so many analysts of conspiracy and conspiracy theories are so spectacularly unsuccessful in reaching agreement about what this thing called conspiracy discourse might be. To borrow from the Reptilian Resistance material at the beginning of this chapter, compare one text on conspiracy with another and pay close attention to how the narratives suddenly change. The view on conspiracy is no longer consistent at all. What just happened? Is conspiracy thinking harmless silliness or an Enlightenment-threatening menace? Is the danger alien reptiles, rhetoric about alien reptiles, or what? As we are about to discover, the real shapeshifter here is the concept of conspiracy itself.

Shit happens. (And so do conspiracies)

Despite extensive experience in retail taxonomy, Amazon.com – the world's largest e-store – does not seem entirely sure about how best to classify those texts belonging to the conspiracy canon. It categorizes books on conspiracy and conspiracism in its 'History' and 'Politics & Social Sciences' sections, as well as in 'Health, Fitness & Dieting'. Likewise, in the domain of scholarship, conspiracy-related issues are addressed by thinkers from an eclectic range of disciplines including philosophy, politics, history, media and cultural studies, literary criticism, and psychology. Within these fields, conspiracies and conspiracism are examined through a kaleidoscope

---

[8]To assert this is not equivalent to holding *a priori* that conspiracies do not occur, an issue we will take up shortly. Rather, the point is that we need to make a priority of reflecting not merely on the substantive issues raised by conspiracists and their detractors, but to examine carefully the discursive contours and the cultural relevance of the 'thing' that we call conspiracy theory.

of conceptual lenses, including those relating to moral panic,[9] the 'cultic milieu',[10] and 'popular knowledge'.[11] Conclusions drawn from such studies are then deployed to support various positions in broader arguments such as those relating to historical revisionism and the so-called culture wars,[12] as well as the endless debate about the mindless idiocy – or the inexhaustible wisdom – of the masses.

As such, a significant sub-genre of the conspiracy canon contains texts purporting to critique and debunk public misunderstandings by reasserting an incontrovertible version of the 'real'. Examples include Wheen's *How Mumbo-Jumbo Conquered the World: A Short History of Modern Delusions* (2004); Thompson's *Counterknowledge: How We Surrendered to Conspiracy Theories, Quack Medicine, Bogus Science, and Fake History* (2008); and Harry G. Frankfurt's notorious 2005 essay on bullshit called … *On Bullshit*, in which he concludes that one of the most salient features of our culture is that there is so much bullshit, due in part, to 'various forms of skepticism which deny that we can have any reliable access to an objective reality and which therefore reject the possibility of knowing how things truly are' (64). On the subject of the *word* 'bullshit', we can see that the topic of conspiracy has an

---

[9]'Moral panic' is the theory that agents and institutions of control, including the media, exaggerate and amplify forms of deviance in order to justify the control of those portrayed as 'deviant' (Cohen 2002). Knight suggests moral panic as an 'alternative theory of conspiracy theories which does not rely on a psychoanalytic premise of repressed desires' – rather public outbursts of anxiety can be seen as having been engineered by those in power to 'justify their own devious policies' (2000, 18–19). Also relevant here are Melley's observations that, in relation to the 'agency panic' he associates with conspiracy thinking, 'many of our most radical encounters with the decentered subject are presented to us in the mode of panic, by terrified characters and worried cultural critics' (2000, 201).

[10]British sociologist Colin Campbell uses the term 'the cultic milieu' to refer to a cultural space in which 'cultic beliefs like astrology and witchcraft have "hitched a ride" on the developing counterculture and spread themselves more widely throughout society' (2002, 12). Jeffrey Kaplan and Heléne Lööw describe the cultic milieu as oppositional by nature because it 'is a zone in which proscribed and/or forbidden knowledge is the coin of the realm … The sole thread that unites the denizens of the cultic milieu – true seekers all – is a shared rejection of the paradigms, the orthodoxies, of their societies' (2002, 3–4).

[11]In *Knowledge Goes Pop: From Conspiracy Theory to Gossip*, Clare Birchall locates 'popular knowledges' on 'a continuum of popular cognitive practices that deny scientific rationalism and justified true belief as the only criteria for knowledge', arguing that the best entry point to understanding popular knowledges is one that 'moves beyond the truth or falsity of statements produced by a particular knowledge' and instead inquires as to 'why people might choose to invest in them' (2006, 1, xii).

[12]This is especially true with regards to the internecine academic battles still raging over postmodernism and deconstruction.

intriguing tendency to incite profanity from academics (a breed not normally known for producing writing containing a proliferation of colloquial colour and movement). Several scholars note, for instance, that in the absence of the coherent causality contained in conspiracist explanations, all that remains is the excruciating absurdity of 'shit happens' (*cf.*: Keeley 1999; Mandik 2007). David Coady, meanwhile, sums up the work of Karl Popper and his 'disciples' as seeking to replace 'the conspiracy theory of society'[13] with 'the cock-up theory of society' (2006, 5). Popper's view is that the odds that there exist huge malevolent plots fabricated by sinister, powerful despots are so low that we should have a rational preference for a version of 'shit happens' over conspiratorial accounts, which are closer to – to paraphrase the slogan of the National Rifle Association – '*shit* doesn't happen – *people* do'.

Moving away from unexpected expletives, we can see that most theorists writing on these topics agree on the need to differentiate the *conspiracy* from the *conspiracy theory*. Here, however, the consensus tends to end. To grossly simplify decades of scholarly debate, the primary bone of contention relates to the fact that (like defecation) conspiracies happen. Furthermore, in addition to *happening,* conspiracies are regarded by many as politically, socially, and ethically unforgivable. Thus to be concerned – even to have *theories* – about conspiracies does not seem in and of itself unreasonable. How then, to settle on a definition able to separate reasonable, rational, and sociopolitically responsible conspiracy theories, from those other ones about, say, politically ambitious reptiles? While many have set their minds to this task, progress has been limited. In *Of Conspiracy Theories*, for instance, Brian Keeley wonders whether it might be possible to do with conspiracy theories what David Hume did with miracles: to 'show that there is a class of explanations to which we should not assent, *by definition*' (1999, 111, emphasis in original).[14] Keeley goes to lengths to define what he

---

[13]The 'conspiracy theory of society' is a term Popper coins in the second volume of *The Open Society and Its Enemies* (1966). He goes on to argue that the conspiracy purview is a primitive replacement for theism which assumes that all bad outcomes are intended, planned, and executed by sinister cabals rather than flowing from the unintended and unwanted consequences which are an inevitable fact of life (2006, 13–15).

[14]The issue of whether Hume's arguments in *Dialogues Concerning Natural Religion* are decisive has been the basis of much debate in philosophy, which is far from settled. In any case, Keeley misconstrues Hume's central argument, which is not concerned with a *definitional* proscription of miracles, but one concerning empirical 'matters of fact' and issues concerning a certain conception of probability. (If it were the case that Hume wound up ruling out certain events *a priori* – that miracles are impossible precisely because they are miraculous – then his argument would be vulnerable to charges of begging the question.)

calls Unwarranted Conspiracy Theories or UCTs – with special emphasis being paid to various classes of errant data (116–18). Eventually, however, he decides that – despite the strong, common intuition that it is possible to delineate the warranted from the unwarranted conspiracy theory – there is nothing straightforwardly analytic that permits us to distinguish between good and bad conspiracy theories. 'The best we can do', he concludes with resignation, 'is track the evaluation of given theories over time and come to some consensus as to when belief in the theory entails more skepticism than we can stomach' (1999, 126).

Like Keeley, many other thinkers are unable to offer much beyond the old adage – originally used by an American judge in relation to a pornographic film[15] – that while we may struggle to *define* an unreasonable, irrational, and sociopolitically loopy conspiracy theory, we're pretty sure we know one when we see one on *YouTube*. This sort of qualified discernment, of educated clairvoyance, is invoked by David Aaronovitch in *Voodoo Histories: The Role of the Conspiracy Theory in Shaping Modern History*, when he argues that, even though the understanding of history is fraught, 'those who understand history develop an intuitive sense of likelihood and unlikelihood' (2009, 7). One problem with this approach to conspiracy busting is that the marshalling and interrogation of facts associated with claims about a particular conspiracy or conspiracy theory comes second to an assessment of the worth of the claimsmakers. Is she or he a reliable intuitor or an absolute nut job? More importantly, do they really *understand* history? If we somehow allow that Aaronovitch's argument doesn't beg the question ('Those who understand develop an intuitive sense of understanding' – or perhaps, 'An intuitive sense of understanding is possessed by those who understand'), it is harder to excuse its *ad hominem* basis, reinscribing as it does the dubious notion that 'the truth' and 'the real' are accessible only to an elite, bullshit-resistant minority. Daniel Pipes takes no prisoners in this regard. 'This', he writes of his work in *Conspiracy: How the Paranoid Style Flourishes and Where It Comes From*, 'is the opposite of a study in intellectual history. I deal not with the cultural elite but its rearguard, not with the finest mental creations but its dregs' (1999, 49). We should take seriously Pipes' claim that he is not writing history – that

---

[15]In 1964, the US Supreme Court was asked to determine whether the French film *The Lovers* was obscene. Of hard-core pornography, Potter Stewart, one of the judges hearing the case, said: 'I shall not today attempt further to define the kinds of material I understand to be embraced within that shorthand description; and perhaps I could never succeed in intelligibly doing so. But I know it when I see it, and the motion picture involved in this case is not that' (US Supreme Court).

much is certain. What is less certain is the validity of his classificatory system. There is good reason to be cautious of those who draw definite distinctions between humanity's finest specimens and its dregs, given that such taxonomies rarely result in the taxonomist relegating her or himself to the ignominy of the latter. And, as we shall soon see, the reckoning of Pipes himself is also critiqued as being on the draff-ish side. (Differently inclined taxonomists are always waiting in the aisles.)

A second, near insurmountable snare for scholarly theorists of conspiracy lies in the fact that the objects of analysis involve *secrets*. How, then, can the debunking inquirer ever know that they have access to all the knowledge they need to know? Unless proceeding from the questionable assertion that *all sociopolitically significant conspiracies have been exposed* and *only sociopolitically insignificant conspiracies remain unexposed*, this 'thing' called conspiracy is radically unknowable. Coady's neat point here is that, 'since secrecy is essential to the success of conspiracies, the ones that we know about will tend to be the unsuccessful ones' (2006, 5). Of course, there are parallel problems for those constructing the conspiracy theories: the refrain of 'Well, *of course* we don't have that kind of evidence – it's a *secret*' risks making a flat *absence* of evidence into volitional *absenting* of evidence. When considering the impact of actual conspiracies, therefore, we find ourselves having to make a decision about whether to restrict our focus to *known knowns* (those conspiracies we are sure have actually occurred), or whether to entertain the possibility that there are also *known unknowns* (conspiracies involving conspirators who have thus far been able to cover their tracks) – and also which kinds of unknowns are knowable. Add to this problem those *unknown unknowns* (which, let's face it, could involve any number of totalitarian trans-dimensional reptilia) and, once again, we find ourselves in a vortex of epistemological uncertainty that threatens to reach Rumsfeldian proportions.[16]

We will attempt to deal with some of these thorny epistemological issues later; for now we can note the fact that because conspiracies and conspiracy theories vary so dramatically in their believability, scale,

---

[16]Asked at a press conference about the absence of evidence linking the government of Iraq with the supply of weapons of mass destruction to terrorist groups, Donald Rumsfeld, then the US Secretary of Defense, replied: 'Reports that say that something hasn't happened are always interesting to me, because as we know, there are known knowns; there are things we know we know. We also know there are known unknowns; that is to say we know there are some things we do not know. But there are also unknown unknowns – the ones we don't know we don't know. And if one looks throughout the history of our country and other free countries, it is the latter category that tend to be the difficult ones' (2002).

and impact, they sometimes have the quality of Rorschach ink blots. Different analysts look into them and see very different things. Pundits are also able to pick and choose historical examples to support almost any conspiracy-related proposition. Want to argue that conspiracies are both real and deadly serious? Simply cite the Dreyfus Affair, the Tuskegee Syphilis experiment, Watergate, and Reagan's Iran-Contra scandal. Prefer to make the case that conspiracies are banal and mostly harmless? Go no further than the fact that, in any given December, millions of parents the world over conspire to convince children of the existence of a magical fat man with a thing for baubled consumerism, flying reindeers, and worker elves.

Similar options are available when arguing about conspiracy theories. To contend that such things have the potential for unspeakable evil point readers (as Aaronovitch does) to conspiracy theory–driven catastrophes such as Stalin's show trials, McCarthy's anti-Communist witch-hunts, and Hitler's genocide (Aaronovitch 2007); or – more recently – the estimated 330,000 deaths in South Africa linked to that country's conspiracist embrace of AIDS denialism (Thresher-Andrews 2013, 7). If you would prefer, however, to frame conspiracy theorizing as nothing but non-toxic slapstick, all manner of wacky popular theses are available for fun poking: Kentucky Fried Chicken is a Ku Klux Klan plot to make black men impotent! The Wingdings font in Microsoft Word contains secret 'kill kill' messages! The Early Middle Ages in Europe did not actually exist! (In a plea for funds to further interdisciplinary research into the latter, Dr Hans-Ulrich Niemitz of Berlin admits the theory 'contradicts all basic knowledge' and attacks historians' self-respect, but urges potential sponsors to nevertheless be patient, benevolent, and open to the radically new idea that a phantom period of approximately 300 years was inserted between 600 AD and 900 AD either by accident or deliberate falsification (2000, 1).)

While it is perfectly reasonable for analysts to focus on only one end of the conspiracy and conspiracy thinking spectrums, any general theories of these subjects – if this is even possible – must endeavour to incorporate the contradictory extremes. Furthermore, it would seem a risky proposition to attempt to argue that conspiracies or conspiracy theorizing are either – or even mostly – *all good* or *all bad*. Let us examine, however, several definitional rubrics adopted by authors who press on and prosecute such arguments anyway. The work of Pipes – he of the fine mental creations and dislike of dregs – is anchored firmly in the 'conspiracy theories are all bad' camp, not least because he contends that conspiracy theories are also all imaginary. Pipes' definition is that conspiracies belong to the realm of the real, in that they involve conspirators jointly and secretly aiming to achieve prohibited goals (1998, 9), while conspiracy theories are never anything more than epiphenomena of paranoid perception; they are 'the fear of a nonexistent conspiracy' (1999, 21). Sunstein and Vermeule agree, nominating conspiracy theories as 'a subset of the larger category of false beliefs' (2009, 206). Others say it is actually these *views* on conspiracy theories which are false. In *Empire of Conspiracy*, for example, Timothy Melley dismisses Pipes' definition as 'absurd' because it means that no actual conspiracy could ever be theorized 'except by a paranoiac' (2000, 205).

At the other end of the spectrum in the 'conspiracy theories are mostly all good' zone, is Coady – one of the few unashamed academic cheerleaders for conspiracy theorizing. Coady makes his case in multiple places in slightly different ways (*cf.:* 2003; 2006; 2007, esp. 195–6; 2008; and 2012), but his broad argument can be sketched as follows: (1) political life is filled with temptations to dishonesty and we know that politicians have often succumbed to these temptations; (2) in democracies, it is desirable for political conspiracies to be exposed; (3) most citizens don't have the time, skills, or inclination to embark on this activity so they outsource it to, among others, conspiracy theorists; (4) conspiracy theorists are those people who are unusually willing to investigate conspiracy, partly because they are unusually reluctant to believe 'official stories' (2003); and (5) the latter are, therefore, performing an important task on behalf of the community and should be lauded rather than stigmatized.

Reversing the usual line of argument, Coady – whose work will be discussed at greater length in Chapter 6 – goes on to claim that the contemporary treatment of those accused of being conspiracy theorists is 'an intellectual witch hunt', and that it is the *decrease* of conspiracism and conspiracy thinking which is deplorable (2012, 110, 111). In fact, he goes so far as to accuse those who are unwilling to entertain conspiracy theories as being guilty of 'an intellectual and moral failing' (2003, 197). Coady's vision is for a world in which the term 'conspiracy theorist' is reclaimed, and in which criticism is directed not towards conspiracy theorists but towards 'coincidence theorists', those people 'who fail, as it were, to connect the dots; who fail to see any significance in even the most striking correlations' (2012, 127):

A hardened coincidence theorist can watch a plane crash into the second tower of the World Trade Centre without thinking that there is any connection between this event and the plane which crashed into the other tower less than an hour earlier. Similarly, a coincidence theorist could be aware that all 175 editors of Rupert Murdoch's publications around the world endorsed the invasion of Iraq, without seeing any connection between their expressed views and those of their boss ... The errors of the conspiracy theorist ... tend to be less dangerous than the errors of the coincidence theorist. The conspiracy theorist usually only harms himself. The coincidence theorist can harm us all by making it easier for those in power to conceal their conspiratorial machinations. (2008)

Alarming diagnoses, we can see, are offered by both the critics and the champions of conspiracy thinking. In the anti-conspiracist camp, we have the – not particularly novel – suggestion that the great unwashed masses are a bunch of dupes and chumps, mindless dudgeons whose small capacity for cogitation and large appetite for sensation have them shrieking 'alien shapeshifter!' at the slightest video pixilation. (In other words, people are democracy-endangering fools because they don't trust the authorities enough.) In the pro-conspiracist camp, politics is depicted – in true conspiracist fashion – as a place of relentless scheming, where even constant vigilance is never quite enough. (In other words, people are democracy-endangering fools because they trust the authorities *too much*.) While this book does canvas the potentially serious ramifications of conspiracy thinking, our case is that many commentators are inclined to pass absolute judgement prematurely. A better way to proceed, at least initially, is to inquire what – and why – conspiracies and conspiracy theories *are*, before moving on to the thornier issue of whether these things constitute a problem which requires solving. To do this, we move away from the sort of short-term thinking which conceptualizes the contemporary proliferation of conspiracism as – first and foremost – the result of twentieth- or twenty-first-century developments. Instead, we look back to conspiracy thinking's unlikely link with an age when rational citizens believed that reason, scepticism, and scientific thought would put an end to superstition, intellectual immaturity, and odd thinking once and for all.

Live reptiles, dead kittens, and powerful secrets

In 2013, Public Policy Polling asked Americans for their views on twenty popular conspiracy theories. The results are enlightening – and astounding. Apparently 28 per cent of voters believe a secretive power elite with a globalist agenda is conspiring to rule the world; and more than half of Americans are convinced that a larger conspiracy was involved in the JFK assassination. One in five Republican voters believes Barack Obama is the 'anti-Christ'; and nearly one in 10 citizens are certain fluoride is added to the water supply for sinister reasons. Furthermore, of the people surveyed:

- 14 per cent believe in Bigfoot;
- 15 per cent say the government or the media adds mind-controlling technology to TV broadcast signals;
- 5 per cent think exhaust seen in the sky behind aeroplanes is actually chemicals sprayed by the government for malevolent purposes; and
- 15 per cent are fairly sure the medical industry and the pharmaceutical industry 'invent' new diseases to make money.

Last (but by no means least, given the White House-high hullabaloo over shapeshifters), 4 per cent of voters believe 'lizard people' control society by gaining political power ('Conspiracy Theory Poll Results' 2013). Little wonder America calls itself *the home of the brave*. With so many diabolical enemies supposedly engaging in such an assortment of ghastly underhandedness, it's amazing so many denizens feel able to struggle out of their bunkers. The citizens of other nations seem to believe themselves similarly under siege: a full quarter of the UK population, for instance, is convinced that Princess Diana was assassinated (Thresher-Andrews 2013, 5), while an equal number of Britons believe the Apollo 11 mission was a hoax ('Apollo 11 hoax: one in four people do not believe in moon landing' 2009). A handful even think Buzz Lightyear (a character from the children's movie *Toy Story*) was the first person on the moon (ibid.). Certainly it does seem to suggest that – as DeLillo and all those conspiracy books which keep quoting him put it – this is indeed the age of conspiracy.

Yet, as current as our fascination with conspiracies seems to be, many of their signal features – and the correlative anxieties aroused by the closed informational circuit – can be traced directly to the formation of the modern scientific mind. In the late seventeenth century, English philosopher Thomas Hobbes was embroiled in an intellectual brawl with Robert Boyle – whose kitten-extinguishing air pump proved a palpable hit in the invitation-only parlours of the Enlightenment *cognoscenti*. For Boyle, the future of natural philosophy lay in the creation of scientific 'events', staged in front of a select group of – usually fifty – qualified observers. (Boyle even kept lists of the names of his expert witnesses along with their 'patents of nobility' (Kuhn

1977, 45).) The Royal Society of London, of which Boyle was a member and which he helped found, shared this view of the getting of wisdom as an elite, invitation-only affair. But Hobbes did not think it possible that a select group of gentlemen watching a mysterious machine could procure the universal assent he saw as essential both to effective civil rule and the proper acquisition of knowledge. Of Boyle and his 'Fellows of Gresham', Hobbes wrote: 'They display new machines, to show their vacuum and trifling wonders, in the way that they behave who deal in exotic animals, which are not to be seen without payment. All of them are my enemies' (cited in Shapin & Schaffer 1985, 112).

It is not our task to attempt any detailed adjudication of the debate between Hobbes and Boyle[17] – assuming it could be done in the first instance – but merely to note that some of the defining features and issues we have come to associate with the debates around knowledge and public access to it are not unique to our era. Without flattening out – or attempting to minimize – the cultural gulf that separates our age from that of the seventeenth century, it is nonetheless instructive to see current arguments about conspiracy theory as channelling certain substantive political and epistemic issues that reach back at least to the Enlightenment. Centuries before Julian Assange and Generation Hactivist, Hobbes seems to have subscribed to the oh-so-Internet slogan that 'information wants to be free'. The claim has ample precedent. In *Dialogus Physicus,* for instance, Hobbes addresses Boyle thus: 'Why do you speak of fifty men? Cannot anyone who wishes come, since as I suppose, they meet in a public place, and give his opinions on the experiments which are seen, as well as they?' Boyle responds unequivocally: 'Not at all' (cited in Shapin & Schaffer 1985, 113). It is important to stress that the crux of the matter here concerns not just the proper, epistemically adequate acquisition of knowledge; it concerns equally the social ethics of knowledge production, the relationship of science to civil society and the democratic participation in its construction.[18]

These debates about whether knowledge should be safely contained in private spaces or allowed to circulate democratically offer a way towards

---

[17]The most comprehensive account of the debate between Boyle and Hobbes has been provided by Steven Shapin and Simon Schaffer in *Leviathan and the Air-Pump* (1985). See esp. 110–54 & 232–44. Christopher Norris, on the other hand, takes a more dim view of Shapin and Schaffer's account – and the intellectual basis of 'strong sociology' more generally (1997, 265–324).

[18]Arguably the most recent and cogent analysis of science's relation to democracy has been provided by Bruno Latour in *Politics of Nature* (2004a).

formulating a working definition of the conspiracy as a particular kind of 'powerful secret'.[19] Using this definition, it is clear that the conspiracy can operate in a vast range of domains and has a history as long as speech communication itself; presumably even very early hominids elected to share certain confidential declarative grunts and ostensive growls with some members of their group and not others.[20] While secret plans and covert actions may be benign (the surprise birthday party) or noxious (assassination), it is difficult to deny the centrality of their roles in social and political life. Centrality, however, is not the same as ethical neutrality.

Debates about the ethics of conspiracy focus primarily on their use and function in politics, particularly in democracies where we would hope to encounter a maximum of transparency and accountability, and a minimum of diabolical scheming. That said, there has, at times, been a high degree of public tolerance – even public enthusiasm – for state secrecy. As Christopher Hodapp and Alice Von Kannon point out, the US government routinely hid secret missions and programs (as well as military failures) during World War II as part of the war effort and as per the 'Loose lips sink ships' propaganda posters: 'It was vital to keep the national mood focused on winning. And the general belief of Americans was that government secrecy was a good thing... Secrecy was patriotic. The government and military were *supposed* to be keeping secrets' (2008, 14, emphasis in original).

The contemporary mood in this regard is very different. While there is a battle-weary acceptance that conspiracy in government is inevitable, this is framed as being an affront rather than a favour to the well-being of the populace. Consider Assange's take on the subject in *Conspiracy as Governance*. In this terse, 2000-word manifesto, the former hacker argues that conspiratorial interactions and 'collaborative secrecy' are key to the maintenance and strengthening of even the most putatively democratic and supposedly transparent manifestations of political power (2006).[21] Drawing on the work of the sixteenth-century Florentine political advisor and writer Niccolò Machiavelli (whose philosophy of

---

[19]The logical relation here, between conspiracies and 'powerful secrets', is irreflexive – the former is a proper subset of the latter. We are obviously not claiming that every 'powerful secret' is a conspiracy.

[20]For speculations along this line, see for instance, Piazza and Bering (2010).

[21]Assange has an ally here in the form of Carl Oglesby, a sixties radical who went on to publish a book advancing a conspiracist version of the JFK assassination (1992). 'Clandestinism is not the usage of a handful of rogues', Oglesby writes, 'it is a formalized practice of an entire class in which a thousand hands spontaneously join. Conspiracy is the normal continuation of normal politics by normal means' (1976, 15).

political influence is contained in his short treatise *The Prince* (2005)), Assange's avowed fatalism is contained in his citation of Machiavelli's assertion that by the time substantive political evils become visible to the masses, 'there is no longer any remedy to be found' (cited in Assange 2006).

The Prince of WikiLeaks then writes casually of the untenable demand on resources required to assassinate conspirators (apparently quite literally; there is no indication that the term 'assassinate' here involves any metaphorical displacement). He goes on to suggest instead that conspiracies be dismantled by attacks on communication flows. Assange presents these contemporary conspiracies via a flurry of mixed metaphors – they are figured as connected graphs; computing or cognitive devices; inanimate, machine-like power units (which are somehow both cleavable and throttle-able); beasts vulnerable to having their blood stupefyingly thickened; and randomly hammered board nails snarled by twine of various gauges. Of whatever coherent network and emergence theory *can* be extracted from this conceptually and rhetorically erratic polemic, Peter Ludlow notes that Assange's purview of conspiracies may involve conspirators who don't even realize they are *part* of a conspiracy (Saunders & Ludlow 2011). Membership of such secret societies is not secured via surreptitious handshakes or shibboleths, but simply via the exchange of very important information between persons who may be completely unaware of their VIP status. It's an exclusive club where membership is granted to the member unnoticed (although, given the extraordinarily expansive nature of this version of the conspiracy, perhaps the most exclusive club is the one containing citizens who discover they are *not* part of any conspiracy). Assange's conceptualization of conspiracy as an accidental and quotidian possibility of information exchange *simpliciter* reminds us a little of Molière's *Le Bourgeois Gentilhomme* (1670), whose title character realizes, with considerable satisfaction, that he has been talking 'prose' for forty years without realizing it.[22] It is also reminiscent of the 'vast, Kafkian' conspiracies imagined by William Burroughs in which 'it is difficult to know what side anyone is working on, especially yourself.

---

[22]The bourgeois gentleman is informed by his tutor that '*Tout ce qui n'est point prose, est vers; et tout ce qui n'est point vers, est prose*' ('All that is not prose is verse; and all that is not verse is prose'), to which the gentleman exclaims, with considerable satisfaction, '*Par ma foi, il y a plus de quarante ans que je dis de la prose, sans que j'en susse rien.*' ('My goodness! For more than forty years I have been speaking prose without knowing it') (Molière 1670, Act II, Scene IV).

Agents continually infiltrate to work on other side [*sic*] and discredit by excess of zeal; more accurately, agents rarely know which side they are working on' (1993, 269, 307).[23]

Retreating somewhat from Assange's idea that any political party is a conspiracy *per se*, we know there are any number of 'classic' conspiracies that are historically indubitable. But there is a key difference, structurally speaking, between these uncontested conspiracies and those which are the subject of conspiracy theories: proven conspiracies very often involve a banality and institutional disorganization that is conspicuously missing from the average conspiracy theory, in which countless numbers of conspirators from multiple organizations are able to march in evil lockstep *ad infinitum*. While a sturdy commitment to Rumsfeldianism precludes us from absolute certainty on such issues, it seems reasonable to conclude that the grand conspiracy enjoys its greatest success in the rhetoric of conspiracists rather than in the events of the real world. Popper – in line with his subscription to fallibilism and the notion of the inevitability of 'unintended consequences' – notes that conspiracies never, or hardly ever, turn out as intended (2006, 13). Even Machiavelli concedes that 'while there have been many conspiracies, few of them have succeeded' (2005, 84).[24]

The banal conspiracy, if we may call it such, may seem very different in kind to the grand conspiracy of Watergate; however, when we look more closely, we see that even the Watergate conspiracy had an emergent quality – that it wasn't conceived *in toto* and then executed according to a scheme existing at the outset. While the precise rationale for the 17th June break-in at the Democratic National Committee headquarters at the Watergate office complex in Washington in 1972 remains murky, much of the available evidence suggests it was not part of some Nefarious Grand Plan so much as one of many ill-considered and opportunistic acts undertaken as a result of the dysfunctional culture of political corruption

---

[23]Also apposite here are the sorts of decentralized conspiracies posed in D. M. Thomas' fictional account of the Kennedy assassination:

> There are two kinds of conspiracy … There's the kind that is kept to just two or three reliable people; it appears to be impenetrable; but if someone finds just one clue the whole thing unravels. The other kind involves dozens of people, most of whom don't know each other and don't know *of* each other. They know only the small part they've been asked to play. The whole thing is messy, there seem to be innumerable clues; but almost all of them turn out to be red herrings, and they simply draw people deeper into a maze that has no exit. (1992, 17, emphasis in original)

[24]See also Aaronovitch, who notes that 'true conspiracies are … in reality seemingly dogged by failure and discovery' (2009, 9), and Pipes, who agrees that '[f]amiliarity with the past shows that most conspiracies fail' (1999, 39).

and 'siege mentality' extant in the White House under the paranoid Nixon (Genovese 1999, 10). It may be perversely disappointing to discover that one of the biggest political scandals in American history was not carefully pre-planned by evil geniuses but was more likely a coalescence of political blunders flowing from one man's prosaic insecurity.[25] Furthermore, if the leader of the most powerful nation on earth could not even manage 'to get a few incriminating tapes wiped clean' (Aaronovitch 2009, 9), what hope would less elevated conspirators have at seeing a grand plan through to completion?

Additionally, the scope and significance of the Watergate scandal was not something which existed before it was uncovered, but grew and took shape alongside and *partly as a result of* the efforts expended to expose it. Michael A. Genovese reminds us that Watergate actually involved three separate – albeit interconnecting – conspiracies: the 'Plumbers conspiracy',[26] the 'reelection conspiracy',[27] and the 'cover-up conspiracy' (1999, 4). The latter – designed to contain criminal charges and protect Nixon – began only after the Watergate burglars were caught. It was deliberate, but 'poorly organized' and 'almost instinctive' (ibid.) – a response to the actions of various law enforcement bodies and the investigative journalism of *Washington Post* reporters Bob Woodward and Carl Bernstein. Once again, conspiracy theorists may be disheartened to be reminded of the fact that the Watergate cover-up was not laid bare by the efforts of a coven of conspiracy busters but by a pair of maverick cub reporters from the *Post's* police beat.

That said, the conspiracy-minded can take heart in the fact that those dogged citizens determined to uncover powerful political secrets may have unexpected avenues of influence. Watergate began as a minor break-and-enter that was committed, as far as we know, by men operating without the

---

[25]Many accounts of Watergate marvel at how 'someone as intelligent and experienced' as Nixon could have behaved 'so stupidly' (Genovese 1999, 4). Thus, speculative answers are offered not only in the literature of political science but in the form of a 'psychobiography' which cites Nixon's narcissism, paranoiac character, and inflated sense of entitlement as explanations for his irrational decision to connive in a 'petty cover-up scheme' during an election that 'for all intents and purposes had already been won' (Volkan et al. 1997, 3–5).

[26]The 'plumbers conspiracy' refers to break-ins and illegal wiretapping carried out by members of Nixon's staff as partisan vendettas during the president's first term (Genovese 1999, 4).

[27]The 'reelection conspiracy' grew out of lawful endeavours to re-elect the president but 'degenerated into illegal efforts to extort money; launder money; sabotage the electoral process; spy; commit fraud, forgery and burglary; play "dirty tricks"; and attack Democratic front-runners' (Genovese 1999, 5).

knowledge of President Nixon. But more than the initial act itself, it was the scale of the subsequent *cover-up* that made the scandal so momentous. This may have only occurred because Woodward and Bernstein began asking questions – about whether the Watergate burglary really was just another local crime story, and so on.[28] As David Greenberg observes, 'Woodward and Bernstein's work shaped the way Watergate unfolded' (2003, 162). Obviously this is not to suggest that the journalists were in any way to *blame* for the scandal; merely that truth-seeking and conspiratorial covering-up do not necessarily exist as discreet phenomena operating only in opposition to each other. Instead they may intertwine and engender each other symbiotically.

Returning to those distinctions which *are* evident between the conspiracy and the conspiracy theory, we note that while actual conspiracies tend to involve the frailty of the personal, rather than the grand planning of the political, conspiracy *theories* almost always relate to large sociopolitical arenas – and the exercise of power within these domains. It is true that – at their most baroque extreme – conspiracy theories envisage the force wielded by creatures from other planets or dimensions; but the agendas of such beings are usually said to involve the nefarious manipulation, domination, and/or annihilation of earth. As such, the exercise of sociopolitical power characteristic of conspiracy theories is still evident, even if it happens to involve aliens and inter-cosmic reptiles (though perhaps a better term here is 'sociopolitico-extraterrestrial power').

Conclusion

In summation, we will reiterate two of the key conclusions reached thus far – as minimal as they may seem: (1) conspiracies happen; and (2) conspiracies involve powerful secrets. In principle, therefore, it would seem both reasonable and rational to be a conspiracy theorist in the sense that one may have theories about the fact that, in addition to those conspiracies that have already been exposed, other conspiracies may have occurred or may be occurring without the knowledge of the general public. Moreover we concur – albeit reluctantly – with Peter Knight's view that there is

---

[28]While opinions vary on the role the media played in uncovering Watergate and ousting Nixon, Greenberg's case is that – had it not been for media pressure – the FBI may not have pursued crimes beyond the initial break-in: 'If the *Post* hadn't kept Watergate alive, it's not certain that the bureau, or the Senate would have kept digging' (2003, 162).

limited benefit in attempting to measure conspiracy theories against 'a gold standard of rationality' and of trying to disprove ostensibly 'weird' beliefs by dogmatic insistence on the proper version of events (2000, 11, 13). A foolproof formula for separating the reasonable from the unreasonable conspiracy theory would obviously be enormously useful. But, as embarrassing as it is to admit failure at a task as ostensibly straightforward as offering an algorithm to determine whether or not lizard people walk among us, we have, indeed, failed at this particular project.

This is not all that can be said, however. History – although it doesn't neatly divide populations into 'the idiots' and 'the wise' – does tend to show that the real life conspiracy has a number of distinguishing characteristics which often, if not always, set it apart from the overblown and implausible conspiracy theory. These include the qualities of chaos, emergence, and banality – as well as a tendency for plots to fail sooner rather than later. Humans, it seems, are better at finding things out than at covering things up for any length of time. We acknowledge that these modest findings are entirely academic, and likely to have little, if any, traction, within the ranks of conspiracists. Conspiracy debunking has been around as long as conspiracy thinking and – if Public Policy Polling's research is anything to go by – has been monumentally unsuccessful. More inquiry is necessary, therefore, into the resilience of conspiracy theories, into why conspiracy thinking is so astoundingly resistant to the usual modes of critique and correction.

2 IMPOSSIBLE THINGS

Alice laughed. 'There's no use trying,' she said, 'one can't believe impossible things.' 'I daresay you haven't had much practice,' said the Queen. 'When I was younger, I always did it for half-an-hour a day. Why, sometimes I've believed as many as six impossible things before breakfast.'

LEWIS CARROLL, *THROUGH THE LOOKING-GLASS*

A great deal more is known than has been proved.

RICHARD FEYNMAN, NOBEL PRIZE–WINNING PHYSICIST

The world of lies is the real world.

KAZUO SAKAI AND NAKANA IDE, *THE ART OF LYING*

Perpetual fidelity

The conspiracist idea that the Nazis had a secret moon base, built fully functioning space ships from alien technology, and are still controlling our tides from their secret underground headquarters in Antarctica may seem entirely unbelievable. Yet, in their own terms, conspiracy theories possess characteristic patterns of argument and series of evidential premises and supports, albeit idiosyncratic ones. As such, we turn now to the evidential structure of conspiracy theories – those characteristics and modes of reasoning designed to render the implausible as plausible. Let us begin by considering, by way of example, the conspiracist case that NASA (the National Aeronautics and Space Administration) and multiple other organizations faked the Apollo 11 moon landing in 1969. At first blush, the evidence that Neil Armstrong and Buzz Aldrin both travelled to and indeed walked on the moon seems overwhelming. Certainly in terms of reasoning, it is possible to assemble the contexts and the arguments for the visit both in advance of the journey and afterwards. The evidence in an empirical sense is also strong, and can be assembled in a way that furnishes sufficient warrant to back the hypothesis that American astronauts *did* set foot on the moon in 1969.[1] At the risk of banality are the following: (1) eyewitness accounts of the blast-off; (2) heterogeneous video footage of the exit and entry events; (3) a large and variegated monitoring team at Houston that appeared to include media representatives; (4) an extended period of data analysis at the time; (5) the testimony of the astronauts themselves; and (6) the contestatory dimension of the space-war which led to close scrutiny on each side of the other's claims. Furthermore, no one seems to be disputing that the Soviet Union's Sputnik missions took place into space, and it is generally acknowledged that considerable technology existed, albeit with high risk, that supported the possibility of an American moon visit.

How then can it be claimed that humanity did not go to the moon? Put to the acid test of actual witness-experience, few of us can claim to have experienced it or seen it sans mediation.[2] We are, therefore, beholden to government, media, and other institutional sources for our information – and their penchant for spinning self-interested fictions is well established. (All six lunar landings did, after all, occur during the reign of President Nixon. Could it be mere coincidence that Apollo 11's high-definition telemetry data tapes also went 'missing'? (Macey 2006).) It is left to the truth-seekers, therefore, to examine and test the space claims in search of evidence and motive for deceit. A common conspiracist construction reverses the Cold War's race for space supremacy into a context in which, having realized the impossibility of the giant leap enterprise, the United States decides to fake it rather than risk failure. Typical claims made by conspiracists include: (1) the flag pitched on the moon was waving, but should have been motionless given the lack of air; (2) when the module blasted off from the moon, it kicked up no dust; (3) it was unlikely that the air-conditioning units in the astronauts' suits would have worked; (4) someone in Australia thought she saw a soft drink bottle while watching live footage of the event; and (5) the light in the photographic images of

---

[1]Despite his hectoring tone, Philip C. Plait in *Bad Astronomy* (2002) presents the most convincing counter to moon-landing-sceptics.

[2]Indeed, anyone who might attempt to corroborate the veracity of the official account by offering that they knew it was possible because *they had also been to the moon* would, in so doing, undermine it.

the moon looked odd, and may have been mocked-up in Hollywood (likely with sponsorship from Walt Disney and direction by Stanley Kubrick). Furthermore, the large number of NASA personnel who have died since 1969 have all been murdered as part of the ongoing cover-up.

Here it is interesting to note that – despite professing a deep distrust of traditional institutions of authority such as governments – conspiracy theories actually reveal an extraordinary *faith* in the organizational aptitude and institutional discipline of such bodies. Consider the scheming, forward planning, and perpetual fidelity to an agenda that would be required for governments and/or military operations to prosecute an effective conspiracy. Surely the effort involved in a four-and-a-half-decade intergovernmental ruse required to fake the Apollo 11 moon landing would dwarf the cost and organization of a moon landing itself. The conspiracy would be, in many ways, a grander accomplishment than the space exploration it purportedly fabricates. (Then again, perhaps the conspiracist counter is that the substantial sums once diverted to NASA are now being allocated to government programs designed to fake all levels of space exploration…)

It is easy and, as we have conceded, more than a little enjoyable to mock. But – as we have also pointed out – such counter-hypotheses are taken very seriously by a significant portion of the population. According to the Public Policy Polling survey discussed in Chapter 1, 7 per cent of American voters believe their nation did not send astronauts to the moon: that is to say, more than twenty-two million people in the United States contend seriously that the country did not ever go there ('Conspiracy Theory Poll Results' 2013). This seems like a very large number of Americans. Yet it is only a fraction of the 250 million US citizens – the nearly four in five people – who believe the government is keeping information about UFOs a secret (Bucci 2012). Clearly conspiracists can no longer be dismissed as an asymmetrical *minority* standing in quirky opposition to an apparent common sense; rather, on an increasing number of contemporary issues, they constitute a deafeningly vocal *majority*. As Knight observes, conspiracy theories have become a regular feature of everyday political and cultural life, 'not so much an occasional outburst of counter-subversive invective as part and parcel of many people's normal way of thinking about who they are and how the world works' (2000, 2). Centuries into the age of reason, many of us are following the example set by the White Queen by believing six impossible things before breakfast. The natural question here is, why? Why – in an age where (we are told, at least) science offers more evidence-based explanations than ever before – are so many of us so willing to embrace a mode of thinking from a Lewis

Carroll *mundo bizarro* where the monarchs are giddy from the strain of remembering things before they have occurred?

How not to explain things with words: Or, *just sayin'*...

As foreshadowed in the previous chapter, the nature of conspiracy theories is captured in their name: they are *theories*. What's more – because of their very clandestine nature – they are mostly theories that are beyond the realm of proofs and refutations.[3] Michael Barkun's conclusion from this is that belief in conspiracy theories is ultimately a matter of faith rather than proof (2003, 7). Yet there is good evidence that – in line with definitions of 'theorise' in lay contexts[4] – many conspiracists see their task as one involving *speculation* rather than *proving* – or even *believing*. Faith, therefore, may not even enter the equation. Further, as we have stated, some conspiracies have occurred – and there is no indication that their time has passed. As such, we can identify a certain reasonableness about subscribing to conspiracy theories, albeit a reasonableness often inflected by a dogged pursuit of an *idée fixe* which can produce what we could call a tendency to *a priori*-ism: an epistemological orientation whereby the conspiracy theorist always-already knows the meaning of yet-uncovered evidence and awaits it with her or his categories pre-fabricated. Nonetheless, as lopsided as it is, few conspiracy theorists are epistemological fideists – people for whom evidence *per se* is unimportant, whose commitment is a form of self-confessed faith.

As we have seen in the case of Reptilian Resistance, a common conspiracist move is to simply posit a conspiracy theory and then stand by for reaction, apparently on the presumption that all requisite work in the theorizing process is complete. Such conspiracists often wrap up their

---

[3]The idea of falsifiability as an element of any genuine non-analytic hypothesis owes itself to the work of Popper's *The Logic of Scientific Discovery* (1968). Popper's scientific epistemology is not without its problems – as Thomas Kuhn and Paul Feyerabend later showed (1975) – but the basic idea of being able to infirm empirical claims is one criterion which usually constitutes part of their rigour. That is, if any ostensibly empirical claim is able to accommodate every possible criticism within its own terms then it is difficult to see in what sense we could distinguish *corroborations* of the conjecture from *criticisms* of it.

[4]Merriam-Webster's online dictionary defines 'theorize' as to form or propose as a theory or to 'speculate' ('theorize').

presentations with a comment such as 'just sayin'' or 'just putting it out there' – a strategy which (in addition to deferring the heavy lifting of actually testing a thesis) works to cast the speaker as innocently curious rather than, say, outrageously anti-Semitic. The *Dearborn Independent* was a weekly newspaper published by the US industrialist Henry Ford in the early decades of the twentieth century. In 1919, it began campaigning against what it called 'The International Jew: The World's Foremost Problem'. This dreadful crusade ran for ninety-one weeks, was eventually published in various book forms, and is said to have inspired Hitler. Yet, as Aaronovitch observes, its starting point was a 'folksy "just askin" stance' (2009, 30).

This point is illustrated in the preface to one of the book versions of the *Dearborn Independent* articles, where Ford writes, 'Why discuss the Jewish Question? Because it is here' (2011, iii). The king of the assembly line then proceeds to show he was skilled in the mass production of ideology, as well as of automobiles. Sweetly denying that his 'little book' is the result of prejudice or antagonism, he maintains that, 'The motive of this work is simply a desire to make facts known to the people … We give the facts as we find them; that of itself is sufficient protection against prejudice or passion' (iii–iv). These 'facts' include a close reading of *The Protocols of the Elders of Zion* – an anti-Semitic hoax which outlines a Jewish plan for world domination and which historian Norman Cohn says was used by Hitler as a 'warrant for genocide' (1996).[5] In his own, down-home anti-Semitic project, Ford pays special attention to the way 'the International Jew and his satellites' (casually referred to as the conscious enemies of civilization) are hard at work menacing and frivolizing people's minds with social poisons such as musical jazz, moving pictures, cheap jewellery, luxurious non-essentials, and corruptive sports attire – not to mention those 'centers of nervous thrills and looseness' such as Coney Island: 'It is possible to take the showy young man and woman of trivial outlook and loose sense of responsibility, and tag them outwardly and inwardly, from their clothing and ornaments to their hectic ideas and hopes, with the same tag, "Made, introduced and exploited by a Jew" ', (2011, iv, 102–4). Nope, nothing but harmless questioning and indisputable fact presentation, there.

For a more recent example of 'just sayin'-ism', consider former Venezuelan president Hugo Chávez's 2011 suggestion that Washington might be the Dr Evil behind a wave of cancer among Latin American heads of state. 'I am not accusing anyone', Chávez said the day after

[5]*cf.*: Rauschning 1939; Herf 2006; Weikart 2009, 63, 86–7; and Aaronovitch 2009, 17–48.

Argentina's president Cristina Fernández de Kirchner announced she had been diagnosed with thyroid cancer and would undergo surgery. 'I am simply taking advantage of my freedom to reflect and air my opinions faced with some very strange and hard to explain goings-on' (de Kirchner cited in Phillips 2011). Reiterating that he had absolutely no proof to support his cancer-as-a-secret-military-weapon claim, Chávez still went on to publically wonder: 'Wouldn't it be weird if [the US] had developed a technology for inducing cancer and nobody knows up until now?' (cited in Minaya & Luhnow 2013). Well, yes, it *would* be weird. Then again, the president wasn't saying it was true; he was just taking advantage of his freedom to put it out there. He was *just sayin'*. (Two years later, when Chávez himself died of pelvic cancer, Venezuelan vice president Nicolás Maduro *just said* some more, suggesting that in the future it would emerge that the country's historic enemies had also 'attacked' Chávez with the illness (cited in Minaya & Luhnow 2013).) Once again, we can see that the *just sayin'* move allows the conspiracy theorist to frame themselves as a harmless – yet also righteous – questioner, a sort of speculative whistle-blower. The accused, meanwhile, finds themselves in an impossible bind. Answering such questions with silence implies a guilty 'no comment' – yet so does answering such questions with answers. After all, what's the big deal? Why make such a fuss in the face of simple curiosity if you don't have something to hide? A claim, often even only a *hint*, of conspiracy is all that's required. The claimant can then parade his or her open-mindedness through a kind of ongoing pattern of statement, followed by disclaimers.

The right-wing US broadcaster Rush Limbaugh, for instance, suggested during the 2012 US presidential election campaign that a pro-Obama liberal media conspiracy might have been responsible for naming the villain in the Batman movie *Dark Knight Rises* 'Bane' because 'brain-dead people … the pop culture crowd' would conflate it with Bain Capital – the company of Republican candidate Mitt Romney: 'You may think it's ridiculous. I'm just telling you this is the kind of stuff the Obama team is lining up' (cited in Finocchiaro 2012). In other words, Limbaugh wasn't saying 'the Obama team' *had* lined this up – merely that what the team was lining up was *this kind of stuff*. Similarly, Limbaugh's conviction that Obama is some sort of secret Muslim radical easily accommodates the president's role in the killing of Osama bin Laden … *perhaps*. He asks, 'What if Ayman al-Zawahiri and other al-Qaida leaders gave up Osama bin Laden for the express purpose of making Obama look good? Giving Obama stature, political capital … Do you think the militant Islamists will be as hopeful of getting rid of Israel with a Republican president or with a Democrat president? Just throwing it out there' (cited in Seitz-Wald 2012). Another American media master of just throwing things out there is, of course, Glenn Beck. Tying together bond market volatility, a photographer killed attempting to capture an image of the Californian tsunami, Libyan unrest, and a Japanese earthquake, he states,

> We can't see the connections here. Now look, I'm not saying God is, you know, causing earthquakes. Well – I'm not saying that he – I'm not not saying that either. God – what God does is God's business, I have no idea. But I'll tell you this: whether you call it Gaia or whether you call it Jesus – there's a message being sent. And that is, 'Hey, you know that stuff we're doing? Not really working out real well. Maybe we should stop doing some of it.' I'm just sayin'. (cited in Dimiero 2011)

Validity by association

To a certain extent, the *fact* of high-level political conspiracies such as Watergate have been used to validate the *fiction* (or at least the fiction-esque nature) of the florid conspiracy theories that have followed in their stead. To mangle a well-known phrase, it's a case of *validity by association*. A similar case has been made – quite convincingly – in a number of historical texts arguing that the United States is particularly susceptible to conspiracy theories because of the political collusion and deception associated with the founding of the Republic itself. Both conspiracy and conspiracy thinking were evident within the ranks of the British and the leaders of the American revolution. As Bernard Bailyn puts it,

> The colonists … saw about them, with increasing clarity, not merely mistaken, or even evil, policies violating the principles upon which freedom rested, but what appeared to be evidence of nothing less than a deliberate assault launched surreptitiously by plotters against liberty both in England and in America … The opponents of the Revolution – the administration itself – were as convinced as were the leaders of the Revolutionary movement that they were themselves the victims of conspiratorial designs. (1992, 95, 150)

David Brion Davis wonders whether the circumstances of the Revolution have 'conditioned Americans to think of resistance to a dark subversive force as the essential ingredient of their national identity' (1972, 23), while Knight observes that American history 'has seen more than its share of nativist demonology, as citizens have sounded the alarm about the threat to God's chosen nation, conjuring up tales about subversive forces ranging from Catholics to Communists, and from the Masons to the militias' (2000, 2).

The extravagance of speculative conspiracy theories has connections with quotidian realities in other ways. In his highly influential analysis, *The Paranoid Style in American Politics*, Hofstadter announces enthusiastically that his use of the term 'paranoid' is intended to be pejorative (1964, 77). Yet he concedes that paranoid writing begins with certain broad defensible judgements. There was, he concedes, something to be said for the anti-Masonic movement in America in the late nineteenth century: 'After all, a secret society composed of influential men bound by special obligations could conceivably pose some kind of threat to the civil order in which they were suspended' (86). Aaronovitch agrees, at least in principle. 'A fantasy with the faintest glimmer of truth' is his conclusion about the theory that there had been a gargantuan conspiracy to destroy Stalin and his Soviet Union (2009, 68). On this point, it would certainly be foolish to deny that there *were* people who wanted Stalin's defeat and who conversed together in secret (if only because such meetings could not have been staged openly). But, as Aaronovitch continues, 'there is an immense gap between agitating against a dictator and a conspiracy on the scale described at the show trials' (69). Extending our discussion of the inconvenient truth that *conspiracies happen*, therefore, we can see that, like a convincing lie, a convincing conspiracy theory is often anchored in partial or incontrovertible facts.

Another hallmark of conspiracy thinking canvassed in the previous chapter (and also evident in the *just sayin'* tactic) concerns the conspiracist's unorthodox approach to the burden of proof. Of the 'logic' of conspiracists, for example, Ted Goertzel's case is that most groups do not attempt to prove the truth of their view, so much as to identify supposed flaws in the case of the other side. The argument, therefore, becomes a matter of accumulation rather than persuasion (cited in Schwartz 2009). As such, the conspiracy needn't be argued for in the final instance because it is the only hypothesis still standing. Returning to American political history, note Senator Joe McCarthy's infamous declaration in relation to the supposed Communist infiltration of the United States: 'How can we account for our present situation unless we believe that men high in this government are concerting to deliver us to disaster? This must be the product of a great conspiracy, a conspiracy on a scale so immense as to dwarf any previous such venture in the history of men' (cited in Hodgson 2005, 42). Such abductive reasoning is reminiscent of the gumshoe methods of Sherlock Holmes. 'How often have I said to you', the great detective says, shaking his head at his dear Dr Watson, 'that when you have eliminated the impossible, whatever remains, however improbable, must be the truth' (Doyle 2003, 125).

Another common type of conspiracy case-making does not make a plausible case for the truth of any particular conspiracy theory, so much as to render – via various manoeuvres – such theories unfalsifiable *ex ante*. Barkun, for example, identifies a 'closed system' of information which renders conspiracy theories non-falsifiable, because every attempt at falsification is dismissed as a ruse (2003, 7). He argues that conspiracist reasoning typically runs in the following way: because the conspiracy is so powerful, it controls virtually all of the channels through which information is disseminated – the media, universities, and so forth. Given that the conspiracy desires at all costs to conceal its activities, the belief is that it will use its control over knowledge production and dissemination to mislead those who seek to expose it. Hence information that appears to put a conspiracy theory in doubt must have been planted by the conspirators themselves in order to mislead. We could supplement to this: any appeal to institutional authority or the consensus of experts simply 'proves' the validity of the conspiracy; unanimity here is evidence that alternate points of view are pre-emptively dismissed *tout court* and the absence of the professional representatives of alternate hypotheses signifies a kind of epistemological star chamber.

Furthermore, we can see that the propositional content of conspiracy theories is resolutely immune to counter-evidence, endlessly able to subsume alternative views and even contradictory evidence into its expositional edifice. An example is the American 'birther'[6] movement whose members claim that US president Barack Obama is not a natural-born citizen of America and is therefore ineligible to hold office. Once again, this is not the bugged out paranoia of a vocal fringe group. Polls conducted in 2010 show that more than a quarter of the American public continue to have doubts about the president's citizenship (Travis 2010). In addition to being an alien in the citizenship sense, conspiracists also claim the president is a crypto-Muslim, that he took the oath of office on a Koran, that he refuses to say the Pledge of Allegiance, and that his full secret name includes either Muhammed or Mohammed. (On the plus side for Obama, two in three Americans *do* believe he would be better suited than Mitt Romney to deal with alien invasion (Bucci 2012).)

Sceptics – as in those sceptical about these conspiracy theories rather than those suspicious about the leader of the free world's free-world-citizen status – might wonder how the birther beliefs could have survived Obama's

---

[6]The word 'birther' parallels the term 'truther' which is used to describe those who doubt the official description of the 9/11 attack as being the result of terrorism (McGovern 2011).

production of his birth certificate in 2008. For the conspiracists, however, this was just another 'gotcha' moment. 'Ah-ha!' came the cry. 'It's a fake! And why produce false "evidence" unless you have something to hide?' The certificate, it continues to be claimed, lacks the requisite embossed seal and registrar's signature. Moreover, its colour shade is wrong, it has no crease from being folded and mailed, and is 'clearly Photoshopped and a wholesale fraud' (Hollyfield 2008). Birthers also question birth announcements printed in Honolulu's two major newspapers in 1961, raising the extraordinary possibility that Obama's grandparents may have planted these phony notices as part of an elaborate pre-emptive plan to enable their grandson to eventually become president.

The conspiracist claim that disconfirmation amounts to confirmation (just as lack of proof *is* the proof) can be read in relation to the notion of 'protesting too much' – a phrase used by Shakespeare to suggest that a vehement denial may indicate a disavowed opposite (1992, 196).[7] It is true that such a dynamic *may* exist. Once again, however, the contention that strong denial *always* represents a conscious or unconscious lie raises the ridiculous – and potentially extremely dangerous – scenario of an accused person's guilt being established regardless of whether they agree with, remain silent about, or dispute a charge. Consider Hitler's conclusions about media denunciations of *The Protocols of the Elders of Zion*:

> How much the whole existence of this people is based on a permanent falsehood is proved in a unique way by 'The Protocols of the Elders of Zion', which are so violently repudiated by the Jews. With groans and moans, the FRANKFURTER ZEITUNG repeats again and again that these are forgeries. This alone is evidence in favour of their authenticity. What many Jews unconsciously wish to do is here clearly set forth. It is not necessary to ask out of what Jewish brain these revelations sprang; but what is of vital interest is that they disclose, with an almost terrifying precision, the mentality and methods of action characteristic of the Jewish people and these writings expound in all their various directions the final aims towards which the Jews are striving. The study of real happenings, however, is the best way of judging the authenticity of those documents. If the historical developments which have taken place within the last few centuries be studied in the light of this book we shall understand why the Jewish Press incessantly repudiates and denounces it. For the Jewish peril will

[7]The exact quote is from *Hamlet* and reads: 'The lady doth protest too much, methinks' (Shakespeare 1992, 196).

be stamped out the moment the general public come into possession of that book and understand it. (Hitler 2002)

In addition to the 'protesting too much' argument, Hitler seems to be saying that the best test of the authenticity of such documents are whether they accord with our take on happenings in the world around us; in other words, whether they accord with – or can be poisonously pretzel-ed so that they accord with – our prejudices.

The Internet and death by footnote

A common approach to understanding conspiracy theories involves looking at those twentieth century–developed media of mass communication which amplify what might otherwise circulate in micro-communities as whispered gossip (indeed the etymology of the word comes from the Latin *con + spirare* – to breathe together). We do not subscribe to the sort of simplistic media determinism which might frame the Internet as somehow *causing* conspiracy theories (although we *do* note that the anthropomorphic imagining of an organization or structure as having a will, an agency and a nefarious agenda is precisely the sort of narrative which is very attractive to contemporary conspiracists). It would, however, to be equally facile to dismiss the Internet as having *no significance at all* in the proliferation of modern conspiracy theories given its increasingly central role in the sociocultural context in which we moderns live. A better way forward is to acknowledge the non-determining but nevertheless entirely real influence, in relation to conspiracism, of contemporary communications media and the social facilities available for communications in general.

The Internet contributes to the development, circulation, and uptake of conspiracy theories in two significant ways. Firstly, its status as an open-access and self-publishing medium means that public opinion, popular knowledge, gossip, and rumour are able to circulate at unprecedented speeds and volumes. As Thompson observes, 'a rumour about the Antichrist can leap from Goths in Sweden to an extreme traditionalist Catholic sect in Australia in a matter of seconds' (2008, 11). Secondly, the Internet has the effect of aggregating opinion in a highly visible manner, thus providing persuasive 'proof' for those (non-Socratics) who equate *plausibility* with *popularity*. In 2006, for example, the French politician Christine Boutin was asked in a media interview whether she thought President George W. Bush might have been behind the 9/11 terrorist attacks. She replied, 'I think it is possible ... I know that the websites that speak of this problem are websites that have the highest number of visits ... And I tell myself that this expression of the masses and of the people cannot be without any truth' ('French official suggested Bush was behind September 11' 2007). Similarly, for many believers, the sheer number of conspiracy theories in circulation is seen as an evidentiary accumulation which supports the veracity of such beliefs themselves (Lee 2011, x).

Apposite here is Peter Berger's discussion of 'plausibility structures', by which he means the sociocultural contexts in which particular utterances are given their meaning and from which they derive their putative legitimacy (1967, 45–51; 123–70).[8] The Internet itself gives rise to particular plausibility structures that borrow from earlier forms. A notable – perhaps even *footnote-able* – example concerns the academic convention of referencing. The open source online encyclopaedia *Wikipedia* requires that reliable, verifiable sources be cited via inline citations and academic-style endnotes in order to 'improve the credibility of *Wikipedia*' ('When and why to cite sources'). But *Wikipedia's* relatively strict rules on what is and is not a reliable source ('Sources that are usually not reliable') are not necessarily shared by other Internet users. *Conservapedia* – an evangelical Christian corrective to *Wikipedia* whose motto is 'The Trustworthy Encyclopedia' – cites no less than 201 references to support a page claiming that atheists are more likely to be obese than those who are religious ('Atheism and obesity'). Many of these, however, refer to biblical or religious blogs rather than scholarly texts, while four link conveniently back to *Conservapedia's* own pages – providing a neat exemplar of what Jean Baudrillard called 'the logic of the simulacrum' (2006, 56). Of course if it's truly the 'trustworthy encyclopedia' (and who could claim to be against 'trustworthiness'?), then *why cite anything else*?

Such circular citation is loudly deplored by debunkers who shake their collective heads at the tendency for conspiracists 'to quote each other so as to suggest a wide spread of expertise lending support to the argument' (Aaronovitch 2009, 12). To a certain extent, however, debunkers engage in similar behaviour themselves. Consider the glowing recommendation on the cover of Thompson's *Counterknowledge* which describes the debunking-themed book as: 'An invigorating trumpet blast against the monstrous regiment of twenty-first-century quacks, flat-earthers, and mumbo-jumbo merchants, loud enough to wake reason from its sleep.' This warm quote is provided by Wheen – debunker extraordinaire and author of *How Mumbo-Jumbo Conquered the World*. Pipes provides a similarly

---

[8] *cf.*: Berger 1969, 34–44.

enthused endorsement on the back cover of *Among the Truthers*, where he describes Kay's 'sparkling but serious account of his immersion in the world of post-9/11 American conspiracy theorists' as both erudite *and* wise (cited in Kay, 2011). Book cover blurbs are hardly pin-ups for fully blind peer refereeing, yet there is still a degree of performative contradiction on display in such cases. Knight identifies a similar circularity in descriptions of people or cultural artefacts as 'paranoid' simply because they gesture towards a hidden agenda: 'It seems that labeling a view paranoid has now become an empty circular description with a gloss of scientific rigor: the paranoid is someone who (amongst other things) believes in conspiracy theories, and, conversely, the reason that people believe in conspiracy theories is that they are paranoid' (2000, 15).

The uncanny 'doubling' evident between conspiracists and conspiracy theory debunkers will be discussed at length in Chapter 4. Returning to the topic at hand, we note the way hyperlinking on the Internet allows for another contemporary adaptation of the academic referencing process, where anything can attain a patina of legitimacy by virtue of the dignity of links. *The Majestic Documents* is a website whose mission is to 'aggressively' bring forth the 'overwhelming truth of the UFO/ET reality' while exposing 'information withheld by all inside sources' (*The Majestic Documents – Evidence That We Are Not Alone*). The authors of this site make good use of the aura of authentication afforded by hyperlinks which offer, among other things, access to 'document authentication' and 'document sources'. One staff member provides an academic-style list of publications (which includes two listings in the *MUFON UFO Journal*) while the site's call for outstanding researchers who specialize in 'forensic linguistics and stylistics' is also couched in quasi-scholarly terms ('Contact Us/We Need Your Help').

Other examples of this phenomenon can be found on the website of the Thrive Movement run by the conspiracy theorist Foster Gamble. Gamble maintains, among much else, that there is a pattern – a 'donut-shaped toroidal vortex' – by which nature sustains a healthy system, and that this code is being suppressed by a small cabal of families who are not only working towards global governance, but who plan to kill much of humanity (cited in Wile 2012). In an article entitled 'Diversity in the World of Extra-Terrestrials', he writes that 'as a scientist' it makes complete sense to him that just as Earthlings have differing skin pigmentation, eye colour, and body hair depending on ancestral habitats, 'extra-terrestrial entities would logically have forms and capacities shaped by the characteristics of the planets or vibrational frequencies they inhabit' (Gamble). Gamble offers numbered footnotes to support his claims that as many as fifty to sixty types of extraterrestrial entities have recently visited earth, and that 'the international elite bent on total domination' are likely being influenced by reptilian extra-terrestrials from a vibrational frequency that is beyond, but overlapping our own (ibid.). The first of these footnotes links to two web pages – one called *UFO Evidence*, the other entitled *Cosmic Conspiracies – Europe's Biggest and Most Popular UFO/Paranormal Website*. The second footnote links to the website of David Icke – a former professional footballer–turned–'Son of the Godhead' – who offers an information package on how the reptilian brain is vital 'to the manipulation of the world by the Illuminati-reptilian bloodlines' (2000). Icke, in turn, cites a Zulu shaman apparently able to see through people's bodies as if they are made of glass.

The conspiracist reliance on academic affectations to create an image of scholarship has a long history which predates the Internet. Exhibit A is Joseph McCarthy's 96-page pamphlet, *McCarthyism: The Fight for America; Documented Answers to Questions Asked by Friend and Foe*, which contains 313 footnote references (cited in Hofstadter 1964, 86). Exhibit B is the work of Robert W. Welch Jr – the American businessman, political activist, and author who accused President Dwight D. Eisenhower of being a 'conscious, dedicated agent of the Communist Conspiracy' based on 'an accumulation of detailed evidence so extensive and palpable that it seems to put this conviction beyond any reasonable doubt' (cited ibid., 82). Welch's anti-Eisenhower polemic *The Politician* includes no less than 100 pages of bibliography and notes (86). The fastidious pedantry of McCarthy and Welch leaves Hofstadter standing in wry admiration of the obsessive commitment to accumulating 'evidence' he sees as characteristic of the paranoid political style:

> One of the impressive things about paranoid literature is the contrast between its fantasied conclusions and the almost touching concern with factuality it invariably shows. It produces heroic strivings for evidence to prove that the unbelievable is the only thing that can be believed … The higher paranoid scholarship is nothing if not coherent – in fact the paranoid mind is far more coherent than the real world. (85–6)

Aaronovitch refers to the above phenomenon 'as death by footnote' (2009, 12), while Pipes makes his own, idiosyncratic protest against this potentially deadly state of affairs by using small capitals for conspiracists so as to clearly distinguish legitimate written work such as his own from those texts which are 'published by reputable publishers, have all the apparatus of a scholarly book, with footnotes and appendices and bibliographies and all the rest, and yet, are stark-raving mad' (1997).

In addition to murderous footnotes, a common conspiracist move when attempting to establish academic credibility involves the citing of ostensibly objective outside 'experts', many of whom turn out to have credentials or viewpoints which are dubious to say the least. A film made about the 2005 London bombings, for example, includes the testimony of Nick Kollerstrom, a scholar billed as a 'lecturer and researcher'. As it turns out, at least some of this lecturing was on the effect of planetary motions on alchemy, while a big chunk of the research was in aid of a book on crop circles (Aaronovitch 2009, 11–12). Further investigations revealed that Kollerstrom's work had been published on Holocaust denial websites and includes an essay in which he expresses his hope that schoolchildren will one day be taught about 'the elegant swimming-pool at Auschwitz, built by the inmates, who would sunbathe there on Saturday and Sunday afternoons while watching the water-polo matches' (cited in Cohen 2008). Kollerstrom's reimagining of life in the Nazi death camp as an idyllic leisure-fest led, in 2008, to the University College, London, terminating his position as an Honorary Research Fellow.

On other occasions, the role of expert witness or informed commentator in conspiracist narratives is filled by celebrities – another variation, perhaps, on the theme of validity by association. Actors Martin Sheen and Woody Harrelson have been aligned with the 9/11 'truther' movement (Carroll 2012), while writer Gore Vidal supports the conspiracy theory that the Roosevelt administration consciously provoked the Pearl Harbor attacks (Frum 2012). Similarly, Henry Ford's extraordinary endorsement of *The Protocols of the Elders of Zion* is likely to have leant weight to the anti-Semitic conspiracy theories contained within this infamous fiction. In fact, Ford's reading of the document is eerily similar to Hitler's. In February 1921, he told a newspaper, 'The only statement I care to make about the Protocols is that they fit in with what is going on' (cited in Warnock 2009, 82).

There is a constitutive paradox here, where the conspiracist partakes fully in a characteristic modern scene. The adoption of misanthropic – and highly questionable – sociopolitical viewpoints involve no uncertain refusal of 'authority', of *deference* to authority,[9] but only at a certain level. It does not imply, of course, no recourse to authority *per se*. Rather, authority

---

[9]Immanuel Kant, in 1784:

> Enlightenment is man's release from his self-incurred tutelage. Tutelage is man's inability to make use of his understanding without direction of another. Self-incurred is this tutelage when its cause lies not in lack of reason but in lack of resolution or courage to use it without direction from another. *Sapere Aude!* 'Dare to reason for yourself!' – that is the motto of enlightenment. (1963, 3)

is displaced to the self, as the individual subject as the arbiter and final court of all knowledge claims. But putting it in these terms is apt to mislead; this orientation is *itself* part of a *tradition* – one beginning with René Descartes, and continuing through Immanuel Kant through to the present day. At its least self-reflective, modern suspicions about authorities sometimes show a general unawareness of this attitude as itself part of a well-established philosophical and cultural tradition in the West. Without a hint of irony, the North Texas Skeptics website quotes approvingly from that great sceptical authority, Thomas Henry Huxley, who tells us that 'the improver of natural knowledge absolutely refuses to acknowledge authority' ('Skeptical Quotes'.) We are presumably required to assume that either the North Texas Skeptics or Huxley is momentarily exempt from the ambit of the assertion.

The balancing act of balance

Another way advocates of marginal or alternative forms of knowledge attempt to claim some space in the public sphere is through the ongoing demand to have 'balance' in any debate. This reflects the common journalistic convention of telling 'both sides' of a story to indicate an article is fair and balanced – although neither strident claims of impartiality nor the implication that this can be achieved via the presentation of two, polarized views guarantee such ideals will be realized.[10] Along with 'We Report, You Decide', we might recall that 'Fair and Balanced' is a much-used slogan of the Fox News Channel; indeed, the station takes these things so seriously it has gone to the lengths of attempting a monogamous relationship with the catchphrase via trademarking and litigation (Hirschkorn 2003).[11] Many viewers, however, seem to think that – again to reference *Hamlet* – this Lady Fox doth protest too much. A 2009 Pew Research poll shows that Americans view Fox as the 'most ideological' television network in the

---

[10]In *The Politics of Pictures*, Hartley problematizes the media convention of balance by noting that the 'two sides' to an Australian Aboriginal story is rarely – if ever – two *Aboriginal* sides, but 'only an Aboriginal side and a "balance" supplied by, for instance, police, welfare, legal or governmental authorities' (1992, 207, emphasis in original).

[11]The slogan 'we report, you decide' also involves the insertion of an implicit claim of journalistic objectivity by making an absolute distinction between reportage and commentary, a distinction that is very difficult (if not impossible) to uphold – not simply for Fox, but for journalistic and cultural theory equally. This is not equivalent to a radical subjectivism, but merely an acknowledgement that cultural bias inserts itself most surreptitiously when it goes unnoticed.

United States because it is regarded as having such a conservative bias ('Fox News Viewed as Most Ideological Network' 2009).

Fidelity to fairness and balance may also be problematic if it involves the idea that the credible presentation of viewpoints on an issue can be framed exclusively in terms of arithmetic parity, of 'equal time'. This risks legitimating views that would otherwise be consigned to the recycling bin in the history of ideas. An example is former Iranian president Mahmoud Ahmadinejad's conference on the Holocaust, held in Tehran in 2006, which was predicated precisely on the logic of giving equal time to historians who denied the Holocaust ever took place. There is also the 'he said/she said' style of media coverage of climate change which has been criticized on the basis that it allows 'a small group of global warming skeptics to have their views greatly amplified' (Boykoff & Boykoff 2007). The idea that counterviews *always* exist and are *always* legitimate is widespread and assists in advancing the plausibility of conspiracy. (After all, if Person A thinks we have not been visited by extraterrestrials, and Person B thinks we have, each person has a 50 per cent chance of being correct, no?) The Internet itself validates this idea in that there is virtually no view on any issue not represented by a website somewhere. This, of course, is one of the well-noted paradoxes of a globalized media – rather than a rubbing up together of various conflicting viewpoints, one can always select an opinion in advance and then Google to find a means of legitimating it. As such, the search engine may simply be one of the latest tools in what, in theological contexts, is known as 'apologetics'.

Apart from its susceptibility to lending credence to entirely unfounded views in the name of 'freedom of speech', (which Ahmadinejad – in his own idiosyncratic conception of 'freedom' – has advocated in this instance if not in most others (Harrison 2006)), the straightforward logic of 'for' and 'against' risks generating polarized views and rigidly binary framings. It also works against the possibility that those either 'for' something or 'against' it, might be sharing in some identical errors of framing. The very condition upon which oppositions can be played out requires a certain degree of shared conceptions and discursive modes. As Girard has pointed out, rivalry invariably involves a meticulous symmetry of antagonisms.[12] Further, philosophical history is littered with examples of debates where the points of agreement between opposing positions have themselves been shown to be erroneous. The millennia-long debate, for instance, between dualists and materialists in the philosophy of mind

---

[12]The place where this intuition is most rigorously pursued is in Girard's *Violence and the Sacred*, 1986, 42–7.

tended to reinforce – almost place beyond question – the view that the mind was itself a kind of substance (either natural *or* immaterial), which philosophers as varied as Ludwig Wittgenstein and Martin Heidegger thought to be fundamentally ill-conceived.

Conclusion

In this chapter we have examined those aspects of conspiracism which work to establish not only the plausibility, but also the out-and-out unfalsifiability of conspiracy theories. Often this occurs via a series of interlocking Catch 22s which typically make some combination of the following claims: all around us terrible things are happening. The authorities are guilty, so they must be called on to explain and confess. Because the authorities cannot be trusted, nothing they say can be believed. Conspiracists *can* explain and are righteous for wanting to do so. Conspiracists are laudably sceptical about consensus authority and have the courage and good sense to reject it. Conspiracist explanations are good explanations because they cite external sources and rely on ostensibly *credible* experts. Conspiracists are discredited by the authorities because the authorities know the conspiracists are right. If conspiracists look wrong, it is only because the authorities are so good at keeping their awful deeds secret. No one knows about these awful deeds and no one takes any notice of conspiracy theorists. When the silenced conspiracists speak of these invisible acts which cannot be made visible, they are persecuted by the authorities who have no authority, once more via clandestine evil that can never be known and must constantly be denied. All these things are terrible things and – what's more – they are happening all around us, all the time. And thus, via perpetually agitated cognitive motion, we are back more or less to where we started.

Having examined some of the inner workings of conspiracy *theories*, a number of questions arise about the inner worlds of conspiracy *theorists*. For example, if the information presented by conspiracists is false, do they *know* it is false? Further, if the information presented by conspiracists is false and they *know* it is false, what motivations might exist for spreading this false information? And finally, if the information presented by conspiracists is false but they *don't know* it is false, what explanations might explain this error? In *On Bullshit*, Frankfurt distinguishes between various forms of deceptive and deliberate misrepresentation and 'bullshit'. The essence of the latter, he decides, is a 'lack of connection to a concern with truth', an 'indifference to how things really are' which therefore makes the bullshitter a greater enemy of the truth than the liar, who at least has the decency to acknowledge the authority of the truth before desecrating it (2005, 33–4, 61). In popular media contexts, the term 'bullshit' is often used as a descriptor for conspiracy theories. 'It's about time somebody had the guts to call Bullshit on the great American craziness explosion', writes David Frum – another debunker contributor to Kay's book cover (cited in Kay 2011). Conspiracists even use the B-word against each other. Consider, as just one of many examples, the *Common Sense Conspiracy* website. With a motto of 'We filter through the bullshit so you don't have to!', it promises to help viewers separate the 'real information' on paranormal events and UFOs, from 'random musings with no factual evidence' and the 'latest tin-foil hat concoctions' (cscadm 2011).

Our conclusion, however, is that while many conspiracy theories do, indeed, exhibit the signal characteristics of bullshit, it would be a mistake to call conspiracy theorists bullshitters – at least according to Frankfurt's figuration of the term. By continuing to look backwards (through time) and inwards (into our individual and collective psyches), we will see that conspiracists do not lack 'a concern with the truth' or display reckless indifference to 'how things really are'. Instead, many are *fixated* on truth, reality, and knowledge to the point of arguably unhealthy obsession. This paradox is explained over the coming chapters, where we show that the very philosophical, social, and technological changes which have elevated the importance of knowledge-acquisition and truth-seeking have made these activities nigh-impossible – at least if attempted via the epistemological methods prescribed during the Enlightenment.

3 A SHORT HISTORY OF AN EPISTEMIC AMBIENCE

A human being should be able to change a diaper, plan an invasion, butcher a hog, conn a ship, design a building, write a sonnet, balance accounts, build a wall, set a bone, comfort the dying, take orders, give orders, cooperate, act alone, solve equations, analyze a new problem, pitch manure, program a computer, cook a tasty meal, fight efficiently, die gallantly. Specialization is for insects

ROBERT HEINLEIN, *TIME ENOUGH FOR LOVE*

Aussie kids think yogurt grows on trees

2012 NEWS HEADLINE

A recipe for reptiles: Truth, daring to reason, and a touch of laboratory-strength audacity

Having examined the 'whats' of conspiracy theories, we turn our attention now to the 'whys' – its historical 'conditions of possibility', to put matters in a Kantian idiom. This chapter explores the social psychology of conspiracism by examining the emergence of an epistemic ambience liable to produce paranoid thinking such as that associated with conspiracy theorizing. In a nutshell, our case is that we live in an age in which the vast bulk of knowledge can only be accessed in mediated forms which rely on the testimony of various specialists. Contemporary approaches to epistemology, however, remain anchored in the intellectual ideals of the Enlightenment.[1] These demand first-hand inquiry, independent thinking, and a scepticism about information passed down by authorities and experts. As such, we may find ourselves attempting to use an epistemological schema radically unsuited to a world whose staggering material complexity involves an unprecedented degree of specialization and knowledge mediation (*cf.*: Coady 2012, 28). Odd results – such as contemporary forms of conspiracy thinking – ensue.

This forms the basis of our claim that there is a counterintuitive reasonableness, even *rightness* to conspiracy thinking (in terms of etiology if not always with respect to outcome). It also paves the way for our proposal – outlined in more detail later – that the epistemological archetypes associated with the Enlightenment require re-thinking and recalibration given the challenges posed by the Internet-driven information age. We inhabit, after all, a world where the generalist is an endangered species, where our networked home computers contain a googol bytes of information, and where even that most basic of activities – the preparation of food – is no longer solely the domain of cooks and chefs, but is the rarefied realm of chemists and engineers, of bromatologists and trophologists, of microbiologists and molecular gastronomists. Put simply, this place we inhabit is far too complicated to be understood via a knowledge-seeking and sense-making program formulated nearly four centuries ago at a time when the sum total of all technical, scientific, and philosophical knowledge was at least thought amenable to fitting into a relatively slim *Encyclopédie*.[2]

---

[1]The issue of 'mediation' in analytic epistemology seems largely restricted to debates about the substance and validity of Kant's first critique and issues arising out of various so-called 'skeptical challenges': issues, for instance, of justification (such as what constitutes warrant, or cognitive 'proper function'), or solipsism (the notorious 'brain-in-a-vat' and related scenarios). To simplify greatly, what many of these debates tend towards are *formal* issues – that is, they attempt to address, given certain 'facts' (of an analytic or synthetic nature), how we might make statements resulting in ways that are 'truth-preserving'. Even philosophy that is historically nuanced tends to only take into consideration *philosophical* history.

[2]We refer, here, to the *Encyclopédie, ou Dictionnaire raisonné des sciences, des arts et des métiers* (Encyclopaedia, or a Systematic Dictionary of the Sciences, Arts and Crafts) edited by Denis Diderot and originally published in France between 1751 and 1772. The *Encyclopédie* comprises seventeen volumes of text and eleven volumes of illustrations (d'Alembert 1995, ix), and contains 71 818 articles totalling about twenty one million words. In comparison, the user-generated online encyclopaedia *Wikipedia*, currently contains nineteen million articles totalling about eight billion words in approximately 270 languages ('Wikipedia:Size comparisons'). While this is purely a quantitative – as opposed to qualitative – comparison, it does illustrate our point about the overwhelming mass of information confronting contemporary knowledge-seekers.

Contra the common wisdom of the debunkers, conspiracy theorists can therefore be seen as one of the symptoms – rather than the cause – of a problem with the Enlightenment's epistemological legacy.

First, however, a word on the whys of conspiracism offered by others writing on this topic. A common thesis is that the rise of conspiracy theories is a sociopsychological response to contemporary political episodes. Barkun, for instance, traces the contemporary 'mushrooming' of conspiracy theories to the traumatic effect of specific events such as the assassination of President John F. Kennedy in 1963 (2003, 2). Knight agrees, describing Kennedy's assassination as 'the mother-lode' of a new conspiracy style, 'an inevitably ambiguous point of origin for a loss of faith in authority and coherent causality – the primal scene, as it were, of a postmodern sense of paranoia' (2000, 4). The 9/11 terrorist attacks are seen as seminal, not only in terms of the increase in the popularity of conspiracy theories, but in the development of a new conspiratorial style as well. Kay's edge-of-your-seat cover blurb, for instance, claims that the 2001 al-Qaeda strikes not only annihilated New York's World Trade Center complex but also 'opened a rift in the collective national psyche' (2011). He blames this gaping wound for causing the shell-shocked citizens of America to retreat to Internet-enabled fantasy worlds, to a vast conspiracist subculture of birthers, truthers, radical alternative medicine advocates, financial neo-populists, obsessive Islamophobes, and fluoride phobics (not that a debunker would ever be guilty of collapsing disparate agents of evil into a single grand narrative the way conspiracists do, of course). To add insult to apocalypse, this 'countercultural rift in the fabric of consensual ... reality' is occurring in America, a nation 'founded by rational deists' and long considered 'the crown jewel of the Enlightenment' (xix, xiii). Arthur Goldwag is also on board with the conspiracism-as-post-traumatic-shock thesis – albeit somewhat less hysterically than some of his peers. His case is that crises can produce 'a certain paranoid, pattern-seeking frame of mind', partly because catastrophes seem to demand 'a significance that's proportionate to the gravity of the events' (2009, xxxii, xxxiii).

Like the mass communication media itself, these mass communicated political events do provide fertile ground for conspiracy theories to develop, but our case is that – unsupplemented – they do not furnish an adequate explanation for the conspiracist response. For this we need to return to certain episodes in cultural history in order to survey some of the epistemological conditions that together constitute a range of historical preconditions in which conspiracy theory locates both part of its appeal and intellectual lineage. The claim here is not that conspiracists self-consciously refer to Kant or Karl Marx and thereby establish their intellectual credentials, but rather that the philosophical ambience created by certain Enlightenment and post-Enlightenment thought has seeped into the groundwater of contemporary culture and informed – often without explicit awareness – a wide variety of discursive deployments. To understand conspiracy, therefore, we need to survey and render explicit some of its philosophical precursors in order to see it in its epistemological context – to survey the kinds of knowledge claims upon which it rests and some of the canonical texts upon which such claims are predicated.

Descartes' *Meditations on First Philosophy* – written in the mid-seventeenth century – represents a certain foundational moment in the development of modern thought. Descartes begins his *Meditations* with a statement of the distrust he now has for the authorities which taught him – both the broadly circulated pieties of his age, the 'common sense' of his era, as well as his Jesuit education. Descartes resolves, therefore, to begin the task of establishing knowledge on a sure footing by starting with doubting all that he could reasonably (and perhaps unreasonably) doubt and then re-building the edifice of knowledge from the ground up. At one level we can see the French philosopher as engaging in a critique of authority.[3] This, however, is only true if we conceive of authority in terms of sociopolitical institutions. At another level, Descartes is actually repositioning authority: it now resides in the subject, who will henceforth be the ground of knowledge. Within a century Kant had produced the following claim: ' "Dare to reason for yourself!" – that is the motto of enlightenment' (1963, 3).[4]

This is also a motto which has endured, and which goes part of the way to explaining the profound distrust of authority figures and institutions that exists now. In 2010, the University of Chicago's National Opinion Research Center measured public confidence in institutional leaders. The most trusted sector was the military, but even then, only half of respondents said they had a 'great deal of confidence' in those in charge of the armed forces.

---

[3] An interesting analysis of the place of authority in modernity – and Descartes as typifying this – has been done by Jeffrey Stout (1981).

[4] The choice of the Enlightenment as a starting point for this kind of thought is not arbitrary, even though we can see strains of the rejection of authority and the repositioning of knowledge into the hands of the individual, which precede it. Most notably, pre-Reformation thinkers such as John Wycliffe (1330–1384) and John Huss (1369–1415) paved the way for ideas such as *sola scriptura* and the so-called 'priesthood of all believers' which later took root in texts such as Calvin's *On the Babylonian Captivity of the Church* (1520) and then – in a profoundly more secular key – in the centuries that followed. One of the factors influencing our decision to stipulating the Enlightenment as the departure point is that conspiracy theory is regularly *contrasted* with the Enlightenment, against which it is seen as a departure.

The comparable figures were 41 per cent for medicine, 40 per cent for the scientific community, 30 per cent for the US Supreme Court, 26 per cent for education, 18 per cent for organized religion, 16 per cent for the executive branch of federal government, 12 per cent for major companies, and 10 per cent for Congress ('Science and Engineering Indicators 2012'). Similar trends are observable in relation to academics, with more than 58 per cent of Americans believing that political bias by professors is a serious problem (Jaschik 2007). In addition to distrusting the facts and views generated by these expert sources, the general public distrusts the agencies tasked with disseminating them: in 2012, Gallup revealed that Americans' distrust in the media had hit a new high (and metaphorical low), with 60 per cent of polled respondents saying they had little or no trust in the mass media to report the news fully, accurately, and fairly (Morales 2012).

Our primary aim here is not to attempt a comprehensive assessment of whether such scepticism is a proportionate response to the failings of these authorities, but merely to illustrate the extent to which such suspicion exists. That said, we note that, in at least some cases, these doubts are well-founded. Consider a recent run of stories in mainstream Australian media outlets about various high-tech (yet also 'magical') fat-fighting undergarments, billed as being scientifically proven to 'blast' excess weight and 'conquer' cellulite ('Fat Blasting Undies, Or Are They?' 2013). In 2011, the tabloid current affairs television program *Today Tonight* broadcast a story about a product called Peachy Pink leggings, which were apparently 'infused' with green tea, peaches and caffeine, and which were promising to micro-massage wearers' fat away: 'Not only does it instantly slim you but it does actually reduce your cellulite and your body measurements in 21 days and that's all been clinically proven', a Peachy Pink spokesperson gushed on the show (cited ibid.). The non-profit Australian consumer organization CHOICE decided to follow up on these claims of clinical proof, wondering which well-respected independent laboratory might have performed the tests:

> Turns out it was Spincontrol Laboratories ... which proudly proclaims: '2 doses of accuracy, 1 dose of creativity and a touch of audacity ... Since its creation our team of researchers works with the intention to offer you more and more creative techniques to prove your marketing claims' ... it seems that whatever you want to claim they'll prove it ... somehow. (Bray 2011)

The Spincontrol example illustrates the disintegration of the authority of the voice of science – as well revealing a conspiracy, of sorts, between players in business, in the media, and in the laboratory. As such, phrases such as 'studies show' and 'clinically proven' have become so meaningless, it seems only sane to doubt them. The problem, of course, is that the epistemological vacuum that remains may be filled by any number of DIY Knowledge Projects – including, of course, a large serving of suprarational conspiracy theory.

It also shows us that while it has become fashionable to use the term 'Cartesian' as a pejorative, to the extent that our own age has placed epistemic and moral authority in the hands of individuals, we are still very much Cartesian, despite our protests. Even so, between the *Meditations* and our own era, a more radical form of doubt emerged that could no longer find rest even in the individual subject. As Paul Ricoeur has pointed out, arguably the three major nineteenth-century figures in European intellectual life (and here we must except Charles Darwin, who would have to be figured somewhat differently) – Marx, Friedrich Nietzsche, and Sigmund Freud – all posit a kind of 'hermeneutics of suspicion' (1970, 33, 34). In different ways, all three argue that the supposed sovereignty of the rational ego is itself an illusion and that what the subject serves are far darker drives: the unconscious (Freud), the will to power (Nietzsche), and class consciousness (Marx). Even in those who profess otherwise no other kinship with Marx or Nietzsche have learnt from them that the lust for power and wealth lurk behind the ostensible social manifestations of beneficence and that powerful people will conspire with each other to serve these jealous gods.

To entertain suspicion of information derived from both external and internal sources could well lead to an immobilizing and absurdist state of uncertainty. The conspiracist conceit, however, is that she or he is able to stand apart from the masses of un-knowing, easily duped sheeple, immune to manipulative forces located both without and within. In this sense, conspiracists share a commonality with the all-seeing, all-knowing scholar whose theorems about the pervasiveness and insidiousness of false consciousness never extend to her or himself. Thus the conspiracist – apparently inhabiting a space outside the usual social order – is able to identify both the secret, nefarious motives in those who conspire, as well as the opium-like state of false consciousness in the masses being duped by the conspiracy theorists, without ever succumbing to such subterfuges themselves. We can also see that the trinary of participants identifiable in the conspiracist purview of events parallels the trinary of players involved in situations supposedly involving false consciousness. Both scenarios are constructed as involving: (1) the forces of self-interested manipulation; (2) the forces of courageous revelation; and (3) the masses. The first two groups in this formation are construed as elites (one evil, the other heroic), while members of the third are either implicitly or explicitly framed as victims, not only of the manipulative efforts of members of the evil geniuses involved in group one, but also of their own ignorance, unwillingness to question, and susceptibility to group-think.

In a communicational sense, conspiracy theories can therefore be seen as being both a result of as well as a reaction against mass consensus. It is tempting, here, to turn to the critique of Jean-François Lyotard who contends that consensus-breakdown leads to the onset of a 'postmodern condition', which consists in '*L'incrédulité à l'égard des métarécits*' (an incredulity towards metanarratives) (1979, 7).[5] But while conspiracists reject grand narratives produced by authorities and the agents of mass mediation, they replace these not with a plurality of micro-narratives but with new, alternative metanarratives which explain things outside and around those versions of reality produced by the supposedly untrustworthy institutions of government, science, the mass media, and so on. Thus we see that conspiracists are able to reconcile a modern/postmodern distrust of authorities with an apparently overpowering urge to embrace all-encompassing explanations.[6]

This resonates with Bernard Williams' claim that two currents of ideas are very prominent in modern thought and culture: an 'intense commitment to truthfulness – or, at any rate, a pervasive suspiciousness, a readiness against being fooled, an eagerness to see through appearances to the real structures and motives that lie behind them', together with 'an equally pervasive suspicion about truth itself: whether there is such a thing; if there is, whether it can be more than relative or subjective or something of that kind; altogether, whether we should bother about it' (2002, 1). Bringing together the ideas of Lyotard and Williams we can see that conspiracy thinking involves a different sort of postmodern condition, one which does consist of an incredulity towards metanarratives – but only authorized metanarratives. Outsider metanarratives, in contrast, are enjoying astounding popularity. Consider, as just one example, the plethora of 'outside physicists' so affectionately documented by Margaret Wertheim in *Physics on the Fringe: Smoke Rings, Circlons, and Alternative Theories of Everything* (2011). Wertheim's case is that the inaccessibility and complexity of contemporary physics are leading many non-scientists to propose odd,

---

[5]Chapter 6 of Lyotard's *La Condition Postmoderne* – 'Pragmatique du savoir narratif' (1979, 35–42) – treats this issue more generally.

[6]Contrary to the notion that the 'postmodern' represents a radical break from the modern, Lyotard holds – coherently, in our view – that postmodernism is not the end of modernism, but modernism in its nascent state: 'Postmodernity is not a new age, it is the rewriting of some features modernity had tried or pretended to gain…' (1987, 8).

alternative theses (such as the idea that the universe is a bouncing machine shaped like a giant twelve-lobed raspberry that spews particles from a Giant Virgin Black Hole): 'They feel that physics has been hijacked, and that nature must speak a language that ordinary people can grasp' (cited in Hoffman 2011, 40).[7]

If we look only at the *outré* end results of conspiracy thinking – at the claims that Fox News is controlling our sense of smell, that dentists are putting microwaves in our teeth, and that redheads are actually alien-human hybrids – it's little wonder that contemporary conspiracy theorizing is compared with the superstitious excesses we often associate with pre-Enlightenment thinking. This view of conspiracy portrays conspiracists and their mumbo jumbo-ing ilk as the intellectual equivalent of failed dieters: while the great thinkers of the Age of Reason whipped society's flawed and flabby thinking into shape, the masses have let themselves go, distracted by the colour and movement of mass communication and the spectacles of political catastrophe; they are caught in the thrall of 'anti-realist' doctrines[8] which insist that the real truth is that there is no such thing as reality or truth. Even worse, just as someone who has been overweight and has slimmed will always be more likely to become fat than someone who was never overweight in the first place,[9] critics of conspiracy

---

[7]Another element of conspiracy theory deserving mention here is the way in which its contemporary popularity comports more generally with a social trend towards the legitimation of non-expert knowledges that often have little or no institutional support: alternative medicine and a wide range of 'psychotherapies', recreational astronomy, and various types of revisionist history. The claim here is not that these approaches are *a priori* irrational. What sometimes begins as heterodox and amateur later becomes professionally underwritten dogma – this has been especially so in the case of amateur astronomy, where non-professional scientists have contributed significantly to our knowledge of the solar system – but merely to note a cultural trend in which conspiracy finds part of its context and intelligibility. We can see here a kind of antagonism of professional versus unprofessional rivalry with respect to conspiracy theory, which has played out in a number of other domains over history. For example, one context for understanding the 'science versus religion' conflict in the nineteenth century concerns less a contestation of incompatible beliefs than a struggle between two elites: the amateur (naturalist-parson) and the emerging professional (scientist). *cf.*: Turner 1974, 1978; and Welch 1996.

[8]Anti-realist doctrines' is the term Frankfurt uses to describe those 'various forms of skepticism which deny that we can have any reliable access to an objective reality' and which contribute to the contemporary proliferation of 'bullshit' by undermining confidence 'in the value of disinterested efforts to determine what is true and what is false, and even the intelligibility of the notion of objective inquiry' (2005).

[9]This view has become common wisdom in literature on weight loss. For one lay explanation of this phenomenon, see Professor Garry Egger cited in Dapin 2003.

thinking seem to be suggesting that our susceptibility to irrationality has never been greater – or more likely to result in catastrophic consequence.

Wheen, for example, argues that the glorious illumination of the Enlightenment has been all but snuffed, that we have entered an obfuscous epoch in which reason sleeps and neo-irrationalist monsters reign: 'Cumulatively … the proliferation of obscurantist bunkum and the assault on reason are a menace to civilisation', he concludes gloomily – and also rather smugly given that he clearly considers his own intellect safe from these monstrous assaults and menaces (2004, 7). As we shall soon see, however, many of the ideals which Wheen sees as paradigmatic of the age of Enlightenment – 'an insistence on intellectual autonomy, a rejection of tradition and authority as the infallible sources of truth … a commitment to free inquiry, a belief that … knowledge is indeed power' (2004, 5–6) – are far from missing in action in the contemporary popular public sphere. Instead they are being deployed in a way that is a recipe if not for the sort of disaster divined by Kay and Wheen, then most definitely for reptilian conspiracy theories. To illustrate this further, we look now to food, and to some of the curious ideas emerging from the epistemological alienation and anxiety surrounding what we eat.

The unnatural history of tree yoghurt

The year is 2012, the place is Australia, and the debate *du jour* concerns the jaw-dropping ignorance of The Youth (also known as The Yoof) of Today. The Australian Council for Educational Research has just identified an extraordinary new knowledge gap: according to a survey of 900 students, three-quarters of Australian children in their final year of primary school believe that cotton socks are derived from animals, while 27 per cent are convinced that yoghurt grows on trees (Howden 2012). Furthermore, many think pasta comes from animals, and scrambled eggs are harvested from plants. These revelations spark mocking headlines around the world, as well as soul searching among the international commentariat about the calibre of modern education, of modern parenting, and of modern young people themselves. Certainly the mind boggles when considering exactly what part of a cow, sheep, or hirsute boar a student thinks it might be possible to extract a pair of socks. Yet should children really be expected to know about the make-up and origins of modern food given that so few are qualified industrial chemists?

Cast an eye over the fine print of the average ingredients list on the average grocery item and, in many cases, the numerals outnumber the nouns. The wavy blue box design and drawing of an octopus on the exterior packaging of a carton of lightly crumbed calamari rings suggests the content's origins are predominantly oceanic. Inspect the fine print, however, and it emerges that a full 50 per cent of this product is not squid. These not-squid components include acidity regulators 450 and 451, flavour enhancers 627 and 631, and thickeners 1420, 1422, and – wait for it – 1414 (Jane 2012). School children from Australia – indeed grown adults from any nation – could be forgiven for thinking such calamari is harvested not from the sea but from battery farmed calculators. Equally mystifying are the origins of a packet of creamy ricotta cheese pastizzis whose enticing labelling claims they are proudly handmade according to an authentic recipe. Their constituent parts include acidity regulators, ascorbyl palmitate, and tocopherols concentrate from soy, raising the obvious question of exactly how many authentic Italian recipes call for a cup of di-glycerides of fatty esters. Consider, also, the ingredient list on a jar of yoghurt which boasts that it has 'no added artificial colours or flavours'. These ingredients include preservative 200, mineral salts 341 and 452, sweeteners 951 and 950, acidity regulators 330 and 331, natural colours numbers 160a and 120, and thickeners 1442, 440, 406, and 410 (ibid.). Well, what could be more natural than natural numbers?

These observations are offered not to critique contemporary cuisine (despite their delicious suitability for this purpose), but – once again – to illustrate the simple fact that contemporary life has become exceedingly complex. Indeed it has become so complex that even a question as basic as 'what am I eating?' has become too difficult to answer accurately without recourse to the testimony of expert authorities – expert authorities who may also be attempting to sell us their fatty ester pastizzis. We can see, therefore, that an insistence on intellectual autonomy and a commitment to free inquiry offers little insight into the history or constituent parts of modern comestibles. The first-hand data gleaned from an eating experience may certainly lead the average masticator to the provisional thesis that a McDonald's Big Mac burger probably contains more than its advertised claim of 'two all-beef patties, special sauce, lettuce, cheese, pickles, [and] onions on a sesame seed bun'.[10] It is difficult, however, to imagine an amateur taster being able to determine – without outsourced research assistance – that these seven recognizable burger elements are comprised of six, 28, one, 14, nine, one, and 36 individual components, respectively (Kennedy 2013, 5), and quite possibly include the 'dough conditioner' azodicarbonamide ('McDonald's USA Ingredients Listing for Popular Menu Items' 2013).

---

[10]This line was first used in McDonald's 'Big Mac' advertisements in the 1970s (VintageTVCommercials 2009).

An authorial confession: as the in-text references in the previous paragraph probably let slip, we did not conduct our own, first-hand Big Mac deformulation analysis in our very own, unaffiliated, reverse-engineering food lab. Instead, the only way we were able to assemble this information was by consulting a variety of outside authorities, including an essay written by the head of the US National Center for Food Protection and Defense and published in an academic monograph, as well as an official ingredient list published online by McDonald's. Any or all of these authorities could obviously be engaged in an act of diabolical deception. As for azodicarbonamide, we have since engaged in a further outsourcing of knowledge-provision by consulting a report prepared under the joint (and incredibly conspiratorial-sounding) sponsorship of the United Nations Environment Programme, the International Labour Organisation, and the World Health Organization, and produced within the framework of the Inter-Organization Programme for the Sound Management of Chemicals. This reveals that azodicarbonamide aka $C_2H_4O_2N_4$ aka the yoga-mat chemical is a yellow-orange crystalline solid whose principal end use is as a blowing agent in the rubber and plastic industry, but which moonlights as a flour improver in the bread-making industries ('Concise International Chemical Assessment Document 16 – AZODICARBONAMIDE'). Again, the knowledge claim we are attempting to stake is not that our sesame seed buns contain industrial foaming agents, but that most of us have no authority-free way of knowing that our sesame seed buns contain industrial foaming agents. This is a problem concerning not so much *what* we know, but *how* we know: we find ourselves entangled, in other words, in an epistemological imbroglio.

Food deserves further discussion because it is part of daily life about which we once possessed intimate knowledge but from which we have since become alienated. (Once more: to assert this should not be read as constituting a romantic paean to the simple pleasures of earlier times, but merely affirming the existence – and persistence – of a historical trend that is extraordinarily difficult to gainsay.) This disconnect manifests in an acute epistemological anxiety which, in turn, produces a smorgasbord of, in the least, highly imaginative ideas. Consider the large number of conspiracy theories circulating around the subjects of food and health. These include claims that global honeybee die-offs are due to a secret mega-cabal's attempt to control the food supply; that monosodium glutamate (MSG) has been engineered to cause brain death; that chocolate milk contains an excess (as opposed to a reasonable amount) of blood and pus; that genetically altered edibles are being used by Western elites to cause infertility and kill babies; and that the real reason KFC – formerly Kentucky Fried Chicken – removed 'chicken' from its name is because it uses genetically modified demi-birds which are bone-free and have six legs, no feet, and no beaks. (Why Colonel Sander's evil empire would go to such lengths to cover up such fowl crimes yet still adhere to the ethics of truth in advertising is anyone's guess.) Diseases are engineered; cures are suppressed; and water fluoridation continues calling forth schizophrenia, and transmogrifying the masses into subservient zombies. In response, many anxious eaters are utilizing Enlightenment-inspired methods of inquiry in an attempt to return to a secure, DIY knowledge about dietary matters. The inevitable failure of this enterprise is, in turn, resulting in all manner of strange regimes and back-to-basics prescriptions, many of which – like the style of thinking used to produce them – involve awkward attempts to graft ideas and logics from the past on to contemporary settings.

Michael Pollan is a journalist who has devoted no less than seven books to helping people not only prepare but *identify* food – a mission which sounds simple until you consider the extraordinary proliferation of non-foods, quasi-foods, and food-adjacent substances in grocery stores today. Pollan thinks it is ridiculous that humans require professional guidance about something as basic as eating, but concedes this is just how things are now that supermarket shelves are filled not with food, but with 'edible foodlike substances' – novel products grown not in gardens but in petri dishes (2008, 1, 2). A professor of science and environmental journalism at UC Berkeley's Graduate School of Journalism, Pollan is not the sort of commenter who would normally be labelled a conspiracist. Among many other markers of mainstream success, four of his books have been *New York Times* best-sellers, *TIME* magazine has named him one of the world's 100 most influential people, and his non-fiction writing has garnered multiple prestigious awards ('About Michael Pollan'). Nevertheless, his endorsement of independent inquiry and rejection of institutional expertise unfold alongside contentions and rhetorical moves that have conspiracist-like dimensions. They also comport with the common conspiracy theory that the government is corrupting our food supply 'to keep us sick and distracted' (Luedtke 2013) – although Pollan's implication is that this is mostly an accidental phenomenon.

Pollan's overall argument can be parsed into four basic steps. First, he identifies a knowledge-related problem: a populace which has become increasingly confused about how to eat well, partly because the more it worries about nutrition, the unhealthier it seems to get ('In Defense of Food – An Eater's Manifesto'). Second, he nominates an authority-related villain: the 'Nutritional Industrial Complex' – an *ad hoc*, government-sanctioned collective made up of scientists and food marketers 'only too eager to exploit every shift in the nutritional consensus' (2008, 8). Third, he warns of a dangerous collusion: a 'great Conspiracy of Scientific Complexity' which, he claims, is benefiting from the campaign to professionalize dietary advice at the expense of the health and happiness of ordinary eaters (6–7). Fourth, he reveals the terrible extent of the deception, urging citizens to avoid food packets 'elaborately festooned with health claims' because such claims are a strong indicator that the contents are not really food (2008, 2).

Pollan then steps in with a folksy intervention which rejects the knowledge-claims of authorities and experts in favour of individual intuition. One of his homey mantras for nutritional health is, 'Eat food. Not too much. Mostly plants' (1). There is also, 'Don't eat anything your great-great-grandmother wouldn't recognize as food', and 'avoid food products containing ingredients that are … unpronounceable' (2007). As with other professional sceptics, there is tension between what Pollan says and what he does. He rejects nutritional authorities while positioning himself as another one. (He is also, we should recall, a tenured professor at one of the top-ranked tertiary institutions in the world.) Pollan critiques self-interested members of the Nutritional Industrial Complex, yet – as the best-selling author of so many books on food – appears to be at least an adjunct member of this collective himself. As we have seen in the case of the North Texas Skeptics, absurdity is inevitable the moment anyone starts ordering others not to do what they're told. As per the liar's paradox, the only option for loyal followers is to rebel – by obeying orders. (Except then they would be doing what they are told. Unless, of course, they…) Tempting as it is to wallow indefinitely in this infinite regress, we reiterate our central point, which is that using Enlightenment-inspired 'reasoning' (with all its emphasis on first-hand inquiry and distrust of authorities) to try to make sense of contemporary existence (with all its staggering complexity and proliferation of mediated information) can often produce peculiar outcomes.

Another exemplar of this food-related phenomenon is Mark Sisson – an American exercise, nutrition, and lifestyle entrepreneur who advocates a 'primal' diet and exercise plan incorporating elements of what is also known as the Palaeolithic diet, the Stone Age diet, the hunter-gather diet, and the caveman diet. Sisson, a retired triathlete and Ironman, is vociferously opposed to 'the mass-marketing of deadly drugs, surgery, and lifestyles that do nothing more than destroy people's lives' (Sisson(b)). Instead, he is an advocate of tanning, saturated fats, wearing home-made turkey jerky on one's gym belt, and metaphorical time travel. Photographed sitting on what looks like a mammoth-sized animal pelt (2009b), he uses a conspicuously twenty-first-century laptop to broadcast his message that we should all return to Palaeolithic eating and living habits *tout de suite*. To make his case, the blogger-cum-'ancestral health guru' (Luedtke) then makes a quick pit stop in the cognitive stylings of the seventeenth and eighteenth centuries. He positions himself, for instance, as a renegade thinker who uses truth, logic, and reason to battle 'an entrenched, illogical enemy' (Sisson 2009b). This enemy, he says, relies on a 'Conventional Dietary Wisdom' that is as dogmatic and 'deep-seated as religion' (2009a). 'My mission', he writes, 'is to empower people to take full responsibility for their own health and enjoyment of life by investigating, discussing, and critically rethinking everything we've assumed to be true about health and wellness' (Sisson(b)).

As with Pollan, Sisson's rhetoric displays distinctly conspiracist inflections. His joking reference to 'a major media **vegetable conspiracy**' (2007a, emphasis in original) exists alongside the claim that the American government–recommended food pyramid will not, as it claims, cure diabetes but *cause* the disease. Condemning the 'current lemming fidelity' to grain-heavy diets, Sisson deplores what he sees as the hidden commercial bias of health news, claiming that profit-making diabetes companies are promoting the pyramid because they want 'to sell more glucose monitors and syringes' (2007b). Furthermore, he says, there is an 'insidious underbelly' to nutritional science and the advice given by conventional doctors and health experts more generally: 'They wield the power, and unseating them is going to be tough' (2009a). In place of the 'BS' of conventional wisdom (2009a), Sisson offers a 'health paradigm' which he calls 'The Primal Blueprint', and which relies on the claim that it is possible to 'reprogram your genes in the direction of weight loss, health, and longevity by following 10 immutable "Primal" laws validated by two million years of human evolution' ("The Primal Blueprint").

Sisson's fluency in conversational (and commercial) genetics may be linked to his enthusiasm for generalists – as opposed to specialists. Relating this topic to pre-agrarian living, he notes that the inherent risk of hunter-gatherer life meant no single primal could afford to put all their eggs in one basket:

> If a band had one person who made spearheads, they were pretty much screwed if that person up and left one day to marry the beauty in the next band over or if he got torn apart by a hungry predator. **It was crucial that each individual know the skills of survival – hunting strategies, terrain familiarity, plant cataloging, shelter construction, weather reading, cooking, child rearing, etc. They knew it as necessity and embraced it as cultural value**. (Sisson 2012, emphasis in original)

Articulated in a different key, in a different venue, Sisson's argument comes tantalizingly close to what Marx and Friedrich Engels in *The German Ideology* (2004) say about the alienating effects of modern capitalist labour as opposed to pre-modern – often guild – forms. But this, of course, is not where Sisson's argument takes him; and as a 'generalist', he certainly practises what he preaches. Beyond extolling the virtues of primeval age living, he is also a thriving e-capitalist who purveys goods and services which would no doubt seem alien to 'Grok' – the caveman mascot he uses to brand his product line. In Sisson's e-store, modern primitives can enrol in a $US2, 200 Primal Blueprint residential retreat, as well as stock up on primal fuel protein powder which contains ingredients such as whey protein isolate, maltodextrin, sodium caseinate, and prebiotic fibers (Sisson (d); Sisson (e)). Sounding slightly more like the sorts of food Pollan would recognize *as* food are the recipes in Sisson's Primal Blueprint cookbook: the tomatoes stuffed with ground bison, and the marrow and parsley spread as just two examples. Unfortunately for its author, however, this recipe collection was named one of the five worst cookbooks of 2010 by a vegan physicians group ('The Five Worst Cookbooks of 2010'). Apparently the Physicians Committee for Responsible Medicine was unconvinced by Sisson's message that we re-harmonize 'our diets with our abiding evolutionary genetic mandate' rather than remaining in 'an aberrant culinary universe' (Sisson 2010, 1–2). Again, our primary intention here is not to take a cheap shot at Sisson's primal beef enchiladas, but to illustrate the odd results which can ensue when seventeenth-century approaches to sense-making and knowledge-gathering are applied – uncooked – to twenty first-century contexts.

'What is electricity?'

A similar sense of epistemological alienation can be observed in the domain of employment which – like the domain of food and eating – has witnessed the terminal demise of the generalist, and the vertiginous rise of the specialist. In *The Pleasures and Sorrows of Work*, Alain de Botton muses on the 'deadening, uniquely modern sense of dislocation' between the things we consume and their unknown origins and creators (2009, 47). Of a British container terminal, he writes:

> So arcane are the operations around the port that no single person could ever hope to grasp more than a fragment of their totality. A ship's captain may enjoy superlative command over the contours of the lower Thames, but no sooner has his vessel docked than he will be relegated to

the status of an apprentice observer of the business of jetty engineering and the long-term refrigeration of citrus fruit – his jurisdiction ending as abruptly as the authority of his nautical chart. (21)

Fascinated with industrial minutia, de Botton marvels at the hidden lubricants that ensure the smooth functioning of a utilitarian civilization – the citric acids stabilizing laundry detergent, the glyceryl tristearate used to make soap, and the polyols added to toothpaste to safeguard its moist texture. He goes on to imagine – with what reads like equal parts fascination and horror – those workers who have spent decades specializing in the storage of flammable solvents or the reaction of wood pulp to water vapour. Botton's attention to industrial detail has not met with universal appreciation. In a scathing review of the book for the *Times*, the feminist writer Naomi Wolf condemns the millionaire pop philosopher for 'poking' at his topic 'with a gentlemanly stick', for 'peering at it under a bell jar' instead of seeing work as 'a source of ambition or dread or survival – or money' (2009). Yet, tempting as it may be to resort to class-based analyses of labour-related issues, an important point to be drawn from de Botton's book is that our alienation from the products of our labour is best assessed not in Marxist terms, but as simply an inevitable side effect of the discomfiting fact that the physical world has become far too complex for any single individual to comprehensively understand. Like de Botton's container terminals, the operations of just about everything have become so absurdly impenetrable, stick-poking and bell jar-peering may be the best we can do.

Consider the Douglas Adams' novel *Mostly Harmless* in which Arthur Dent, that well-known hitchhiker of the galaxy, is chastened to realize that although he originally came from a world which had 'cars and computers and ballet and Armagnac', he personally didn't know how any of it worked: 'Left to his own devices he couldn't build a toaster. He could just about make a sandwich and that was it' (1992, 88). This poignant admission of defeat prompted Thomas Thwaites – a non-fictional British conceptual designer – to dismantle a £3.94 toaster, study its 400-plus parts, and attempt to replicate an identical device via the dark arts of reverse engineering (2011, 13, 21). In addition to travelling a total of 1900 miles, Thwaites mined ore, smelted said ore in a microwave, called BP to see if he could visit an oil rig for a jug of petroleum, and had a shot at making plastic from potatoes (Kabat 2012). The end result was perhaps the world's most expensive toaster. It cost £1187.54 (not including labour), looked like a domestic prank perpetrated by Antonio Gaudi, and failed at the one task it could reasonably be expected to perform: it was unable to toast. The project did, however, succeed at showing that while the sum total of human knowledge is greater than ever before, the percentage of this knowledge aggregate able to be possessed by any single individual has never been lower. As David Crowley writes of the toaster project, 'Modern myths of omnipotence come to seem like hubris when Thwaites is defeated by the task of smelting metals, something first practiced eight thousand years ago ... Submerged in our toasters are layers of hard-won and deeply practical knowledge – if only we could tap it' (cited in Thwaites 2011, 11).

Similar themes of epistemological helplessness are explored in the domain of fiction in DeLillo's *White Noise* (1999), a novel populated by characters who respond to the suffocating weight of everything they do not know with a bewildered and deadpan numbness. Unsure of anything, *everything* becomes equally meaningful and meaningless: fragments of talk radio, calls from automated telemarketers, missing pets, the omni-threat of chemical apocalypse, skin chewed off the ends of New Yorkers' fingers, mushroom-shaped pancreatic tumours, conversations *about* mushroom-shaped pancreatic tumours, sexual conspiracy ... Knowledge circulates in such volume and in so many obscure specialty forms, it is entirely useless: there is no reliable mechanism by which anyone can obtain a reliable signal from the white noise of facts, factoids, and factiness. In one, telling scene, the protagonist – a college professor of Hitler Studies called Jack Gladney – struggles to engineer a reassuring parental moment with his 14-year-old son, Heinrich, in a Boy Scout barracks after the family take refuge from an 'airborne toxic event'. The boy, however, is not persuaded: not only are the family in the dark about the reasons for and ramifications of this particular emergency; an esoteric and unnerving new dark age has enveloped every aspect of their lives. 'It's like we've been flung back in time', Heinrich tells his father:

> Here we are in the Stone Age, knowing all these great things after centuries of progress but what can we do to make life easier for the Stone Agers? Can we make a refrigerator? Can we even explain how it works? What is electricity? What is light? ... Name one thing you could make. Could you make a simple wooden match that you could strike on a rock to make a flame? (147)

Jack attempts to reassure his son that at least whoever's in charge seems to have things under control, and that at least the Boy Scout centre has heat and light. Once again, however, Heinrich is unconvinced. 'These are Stone Age things', he replies:

> They rubbed flints together and made sparks. Could you rub flints together? Would you know a flint if you saw one? If a Stoner [*sic*] Ager

asked you what a nucleotide is, could you tell him? How do we make carbon paper? What is glass? ...What is a radio? What is the principle of a radio? Go ahead, explain. You're sitting in the middle of this circle of people. They use pebble tools. They eat grubs. Explain a radio ... What good is knowledge if it just floats in the air? It goes from computer to computer. It changes and grows every second of the day. But nobody actually knows anything. (148–9)

Conclusion

Food that is not food, unfathomable toasters, the relative knowledgeability of Stone Agers ... in this chapter we have shown that the increasing complexity of the material world – alongside rapid increases in human knowledge and specialization – has resulted in an ambience of acute epistemological alienation. We have *less* access to primary sources of information and facts, and are consequently *more* reliant on various agents of mediation such as political parties, the media, and scientific organizations – all of whom we have never trusted less. To further complicate matters, the number of potential facts available to us is rapidly increasing (azodicarbonamide, as just one multisyllabic example, has only been on the radars of bakers and cereal chemists since the 1960s (Joiner et al. 1963, 539)). To grasp the radical unknowability of the material reality of so much of modern life, we return to the ingredients of Big Macs and note that it was necessary for us to consult numerous authorities, experts, and mediated sources even to know we didn't know exactly what was in this fast-food staple. Yet the scepticism demanded when dealing with information gleaned from multinational fast-food companies, globalist bodies, and the Internet renders even this modest conclusion doubtful. We are left, in other words, unsure about whether we even know whether we do or do not know.

4 PLEASURES, SORROWS, AND DOUBLING

I know you are, but what am I?

PLAYGROUND TAUNT

While the epistemic dilemmas just discussed go part of the way to explaining the current proliferation of conspiracy theories, a more comprehensive understanding of the phenomenon requires examining the psychosocial dimensions of a cognitive style which is marked by doubt and scepticism, and which manifests in complex and often-paradoxical relationships with established institutions and the idea of the truth. In short, we ask, *what does the conspiracy theory offer the conspiracist? What's in it for her or him?* When we then extend these lines of inquiry to conspiracy theory debunkers, a fascinating picture emerges. Despite – and also *because of* – the ferocity of their attacks on conspiracism, the discourse produced by (and likely motivations of) debunkers often bears striking similarity to that of conspiracists. As we shall see, conspiracists and debunkers both rely on a sceptical and antagonistic explanatory style which offers consolation and ego boost, as well as reasserting a sense of individual agency and empowerment. Paradoxically, however, these pleasures and benefits sit alongside – indeed, to a certain extent, *are reliant on* – paranoia and the prediction of various catastrophes. While the nature of these prognoses of looming calamities varies, there are some striking symmetries in both the substance and the style of the rhetoric produced by debunkers and that deployed by their putative opposites in the conspiracy camp.

Doubling *has* been addressed in relation to conspiracy discourse, but mostly only in terms of the way conspiracists emulate aspects of the dastardly conspirators who feature in their theories. Hofstadter goes so far as to suggest that, for the paranoid thinker, the adversary is, on many counts, the projection of both the ideal and unacceptable aspects of the self, and requires outwitting on her or his own terms: 'The enemy may be the cosmopolitan intellectual, but the paranoid will outdo him in the apparatus of scholarship, even of pedantry. Secret organizations set up to combat secret organizations give the same flattery. The Ku Klux Klan imitated Catholicism to the point of donning priestly vestments, developing an elaborate ritual and an equally elaborate hierarchy' (1964, 85).[1] Hofstadter also sees psychosexual projection at work, suggesting that paranoid thinkers in political domains are able to express unacknowledgeable aspects of their own psychological concerns by attributing to their enemies sexual freedom, lack of moral inhibition, and possession of particularly effective techniques for fulfilling desire: 'Very often the fantasies of true believers reveal strong sadomasochistic outlets, vividly expressed, for example, in the delight of anti-Masons with the cruelty of Masonic punishments' (1964, 85). We can only assume he would see something similar in ufologist accounts of alien abduction, invasive experimentation, and intimate probing.

But obviously we should not get carried away. It is all too easy to play a Freudian game in which one projects on one's enemies a kind of perennial psychic immaturity from which all of their epistemological gambits spring. It's an old rhetorical technique, in which one accounts for disagreement by insisting *they* are afraid of the facts, while *we* – having reached intellectual maturity – can look reality squarely in the eye. Even cultural theorists, with their recent orientation towards analyses of 'panic' and 'anxiety', seem to cast themselves as perennial knowers, who not only adopt the position of understanding, but also claim a capacity to diagnose the ills of others. There are, of course, sociopsychological motivations for belief, but a too-quick readiness to explain – or rather, explain away – the ideas of others through an *ad hominem* pathologization of the believers might prevent us giving an account of what a disagreement might *mean* in terms that are irreducible to economies of desire and fear.

---

[1] The first thinker to theorize certain forms of paranoid thinking in term of 'projection' (*Vergegenstandigung*) was Freud (1958, 66 Orig. 1911.).

Know your enemy

While there exists some discussion about the similarities between conspiracist theorists and the primary objects of their concern (those agents allegedly engaged in conspiracy), there is, in contrast, virtually no recognition of the similarities between conspiracists and debunkers. This is despite an abundance of evidence that – if not quite separated at birth – these two key conspiracy-related players *do* share some striking family resemblances. Several debunkers, for instance, boast of engaging in strategic doubling of the sort Hofstadter observes in relation to conspiracists. In the opening pages of *The Hidden Hand*, Pipes writes that the 'effort to penetrate the conspiracy theorist's mind means replicating his processes of thought. Though never tempted by conspiracism, I tried to order the theorist's assumptions, partake of his obsessions, and draw conclusions as he might' (1998, xi). Lest anyone get the wrong idea, Pipes also notes that 'The conspiracy mentality … reaches even the world of scholarship, compelling me to state what I wish were obvious but fear is not: I have no covert purpose in writing on this topic' (7).

Pursuing a similar – if more radical – trajectory is Sunstein and Vermeule (2008; 2009), whose recommendation of a government program of anti-conspiracist 'cognitive infiltration' was discussed in the Introduction of this book. Sunstein and Vermeule's tactic of snooping to conquer – apart from *itself* seeming somewhat paranoid – obviously appears to confirm exactly what conspiracists might believe about the 'established order': that its political power involves underhanded techniques of ideological reinforcement; that its ersatz 'truths' can only be upheld through a surreptitious manipulation of perceptions; that its representatives – and actions – extend well beyond the standard arms of government; and that the power-that-be's shills walk among us, undetected. The theme, and tactic, isn't unique, although it has different registers and domains of application. Consider the cover blurb of *Among the Truthers*, which spells out the author's mission with hard-boiled aplomb: 'For two years journalist Jonathan Kay immersed himself in this dark subculture, attending conventions of conspiracist theorists, surfing their discussion boards, reading their websites, joining their Facebook groups, and interviewing them in their homes and offices …' (Kay 2011). The language here is revealing – and diagnostic. Apart from wild self-romanticization, one could be forgiven for thinking that the task Kay was charged with here was somehow equivalent to infiltrating the Stasi or the Red Brigades, with all the attendant dangers.

It would be unfair, however, to figure the whole field in this manner. A notable exception is Knight, who spots some striking resemblances in the discourse produced by conspiracists and debunkers. He identifies, for instance, a degree of 'academic alarmism' in the proliferation of scholarly tomes determined to condemn and disprove the cultural logic of paranoia:

> Together, these investigations uncover traces of conspiracism in almost every era and in every aspect of American culture, and they warn of the unparalleled power of popular paranoia to foment hatred. However, it might be argued that the tendency to find evidence of conspiracism behind every major event in world history is itself in danger of producing a conspiracy theory of conspiracy theories. The more we learn about its sinister ubiquity, the more conspiracism becomes not merely a powerful ideology but a mysterious force with a hidden agenda that takes over individual minds and even whole societies. (2000, 5, 7)

Knight – one of the few debunkers of debunking discourse – notes that, in their condemnations of the dangerous delusions of paranoid politicians and the zombie-making influence of mass culture, these commentators replicate the very mode of thinking they purportedly condemn: 'In listing the tell-tale traits of the paranoid style, they duplicate the tendency of paranoid political tracts to provide an indentikit picture of the demonized enemy (the "How-to-tell-if-your-neighbour-is-a-Communist" approach)' (7). Endearingly enough, he then admits his own research methods have much in common with the cognitive style of conspiracists in terms of obsession, the search for a unifying narrative, and paranoia: 'I first began thinking about conspiracy before *The X-Files* had aired. At first the television show seemed to have been deliberately planted for me as a clue that I had tapped into something significant (not, of course, that I would entertain such a suspicion)'. Knight acknowledges that this 'sensation of vertigo, of both fearing and desiring a sense of coherence beneath the incomplete fragments' is not so far from conspiracy culture itself (ix).

We concur with Knight's conclusions about the commonalities between conspiracists and debunkers (if not about his wry suggestion that paranormal cryptids might be using *The X-Files* to mess with the minds of cultural theorists). That said, the arguments we will make over the course of this chapter are *not* that conspiracists and debunkers are perfect mirror images of each other; that the ultimate conclusions reached by each side are equally valid; or that the social and cultural ramifications of conspiracy theorizing are identical to those associated with debunking. We agree that the proliferation of conspiracy discourse is problematic. Where we diverge from debunking orthodoxies, however, is in our claim that the – often adversarial – interventions offered by debunkers are *exacerbating* rather than *ameliorating* the situation. In other words, in many ways they are part of the problem rather than the solution.

Explanatory reaching

A common critique of conspiracy theorists is that their exegeses of events exploit several well-known epistemic virtues – such as the virtue of explanatory reach or explanatory scope – by deploying these virtues in an illegitimate manner. As Keeley notes, unified explanation is 'the *sine qua non* of conspiracy theories. Conspiracy theories *always* explain more than competing theories, because by invoking a conspiracy, they can explain *both* the data of the received account *and* the errant data that the received theory fails to explain' (1999, 119, emphases in original). This phenomenon has certainly been observed in the paranoid and universalizing accounts offered by some of history's most infamous conspiracy theorists. In his examination of the social psychology of the Holocaust, for example, David R. Mandel notes that Hitler's belief in a Jewish world conspiracy involved an intolerance of ambiguity and a strong need for 'cognitive closure' – habits of mind common to conspiracy theorists as well as to authoritarian personalities (2002, 275). Hitler's all-or-nothing thinking reduced everything to the two unambiguous possibilities of '*utopia* or *perdition*' (ibid., emphasis in original). For Hitler,

> belief in an international Jewish enemy provided a means to find the locus of all the numerous perceived threats to Germany and himself. Ironically, all the inconsistencies – the improbable twists and turns inherent in the 'conspiracy' – are willingly accepted by believers because the conspiracy provides the degrees of freedom necessary for many of their deeply held attitudes to cohere and to be consolidated in a single account that has storylike properties. (ibid., internal citations omitted)

Without wishing to stoop to a *reductio ad Hitlerum*,[2] our case is that many conspiracy theory debunkers share a similar interest in explanatory

---

[2]Leo Strauss coined the term *Reductio ad Hitlerum* to refer to a form of association fallacy in which an opinion is dismissed by comparing it to a view or policy of Hitler or the Nazi: 'A view is not refuted by the fact that it happens to have been shared by Hitler' (1965, 42–3).

scope, and may also use this particular explanatory virtue in a manner which undermines its strength. In Chapter 3, we witnessed Kay's imaginings of a vast conspiracist underground which not only contains – but *explains* – a very large number of social formations with which he takes issue – from prescribers of homeopathic medicine all the way through to those citizens who think the American president might (quite literally) be an illegal alien. While Kay concedes that different breeds of conspiracists come to their paranoias for different reasons, ultimately he figures them all as being bound together by a single 'increasingly common trait: They have spun out of rationality's ever-weakening gravitational pull, and into mutually impenetrable Manichean fantasy universes of their own construction' (2011, xx). Pipes indulges in a similarly ambitious explanatory narrative when he argues that conspiracism (with all its 'wrong-headed' and 'distorted' approach to explanation) explains much of what 'would otherwise seem illogical or implausible' about the political culture of the Middle East, including its history of political extremism and volatility, its 'culture of violence, and its poor record of modernization' (1998, 1, 2). Wheen, meanwhile, sneers at the human requirement for an 'illusion of order and narrative', in a book which does something strikingly similar in its colossal claim to have pinpointed 'a period in the world's history when everything began to stop making sense' (2004, 64–5, cover blurb).

Injury → agent → intention

In addition to unification narratives, another area of commonality between conspiracists and what we shall try to refrain from referring to as a vast debunking subculture is the tendency to conflate injury with willed agency. Once again, this is a phenomenon that has been frequently observed and analysed – but only when it occurs in the conspiracist scene. As Jeffrey M. Bale puts it, for conspiracists, giving misery and injustice an identity makes life more bearable: 'Conspiracy theories ... explain why bad things are happening to good people or vice versa' (cited in Parsons 2001). Similarly, Barkun notes the way conspiracy thinking offers a reassuring construction of a world that is meaningful rather than arbitrary (2003, 4). Hofstadter's observation is that conspiracists construct their enemy as 'a perfect model of malice, a kind of amoral superman – sinister, ubiquitous, powerful, cruel, sensual, luxury-loving'. As such, the paranoid's interpretation of history is 'distinctly personal: decisive events are not taken as part of the stream of history, but as the consequences of someone's will' (1964, 85). DeLillo writes of something similar in *Libra* when he observes that, for those on the outside, a conspiracy 'is the perfect working of a scheme … everything that ordinary life is not' (1991, 440).

The idea of conspiracy thinking as a type of God replacement is canvassed explicitly by Popper, who figures his conspiracy theory of society as a version of theism, as 'a belief in gods whose whims and wills rule everything. It comes from abandoning God and then asking: "Who is in his place?" His place is then filled by various powerful men and groups – sinister pressure groups, who are to be blamed for having planned the great depression and all the evils from which we suffer' (2006, 13). As such, conspiracy thinking figures world events as the work of an intelligent – albeit evil – designer. Perhaps, therefore, one of the great appeals of paranoia as it surfaces in conspiracy theory is that it is a reaction to a fear, not that big brother is watching us, but that big brother *doesn't really care that much about us at all*. A corollary anxiety here might be less that there is a small bunch of people who are in control of the world, but the fact that the driver's seat is empty: *no one* is in control. Such thoughts are – at least for some of us – as disconcerting as guilds of hooded men carrying out strange ceremonies in front of giant statues of owls. They also bring to mind the old cartoon in which a psychiatrist tells a patient, 'Everyone doesn't hate you – there are millions of people who don't care one way or the other.' This joke trades on the counterintuitive notion that hate can be far more affirming to an individual's ego than indifference.

For the socially or economically marginalized, conspiracy thinking may offer an odd inroad to dignity in that theorists figure themselves as victims of an evil plan orchestrated by perpetrators whose conniving malevolence matches the extent of the suffering of their victims. In the United States, for instance, Roy Baumeister notes that

> many African Americans have subscribed to the theory that crack cocaine and AIDS are part of a systematic plot by the government and white establishment to annihilate the black community, and some have even asserted that black-on-black violence is in fact a result of manipulation by the white-controlled government. In a similar vein [it has been] asserted that the acts of rape scattered all over the country (and probably the world) are linked as part of a conscious, deliberate conspiracy by all men to intimidate and subjugate all women. It may be easy to dismiss such theories as preposterous rantings or paranoid fantasies, but … they have a psychologically important foundation in the victims' wish for dignity. (2002, 247, internal citations omitted)

Baumeister's point here is that there is more self-esteem and importance in being the target of 'a huge, demonic conspiracy that will take a large, evil satisfaction in your death' than the lacklustre alternative: that powerful people are getting what they want and do not give a tinker's cuss what happens to you along the way (ibid.).

Once again, a similar phenomenon is observable – to a certain extent – in the way debunking discourse figures its enemies as powerful figures in possession of both the intention – and the agency – to do Very Bad Things. Following Scruton, Wheen identifies not only a counter-revolution to reason, but a counter-revolution with actual leaders who are 'aided and abetted by a latter-day *trahison des clercs*' (2004, 7). His partiality for grand narrative and causal linearity is also evident in his declaration that 1979 was the year of a 'voodoo revolution', and that two events from that year – the return of the Ayatollah Khomeini to Iran and the election of Margaret Thatcher's Tories in Britain – were harbingers of a new era 'whose "conflict" … found its most gruesome expression some twenty-two years later, when the twin towers of the World Trade Centre in New York were reduced to rubble' (9). Pipes' suspicion of the extent of and hazards posed by conspiracy, meanwhile, finds expression in anthropomorphic extremes:

> In the pages that follow, I have done my best to separate conspiracism from conspiracy, reality from fantasy. Yet no one can be sure in every case which is which, and I make no claim to certainty. Conspiracism manages to insinuate itself in the most alert and intelligent minds, so excluding it amounts to a perpetual struggle, one in which the reader is invited to join. (1999, 49)

Note, here, the *agency* apparently possessed by conspiracism, the way it is able to insinuate itself and infect even mental faculties as keen as Pipes' own. Yet while this cognitive infestation sounds undeniably unpleasant, it is difficult to ignore the fact that Pipes – by virtue of his supreme suspicion and grim, survivalist-style call to arms – has many parallels with the alarmist paranoiacs about whom he warns.

Noooooooooooooooooooo!

The conspiracist penchant for routinely predicting Armageddon has been widely reported and critiqued. Hofstadter, for instance, observes the way the paranoid spokesman sees the fate of conspiracy in apocalyptic terms, the way 'he traffics in the birth and death of whole worlds, whole political orders, whole systems of human values. He is always manning the barricades of civilization. He constantly lives at a turning point. Like religious millennialists he expresses the anxiety of those who are living through the last days' (1964, 82). Intriguingly enough, debunkers often evince similarly survivalist tendencies, although they are less likely to predict the world's material end, so much as to announce the end times for reason, rationality, and *en masse* social sanity. Kay's case is that just as the Great Lisbon Earthquake is said to have inaugurated the Age of Reason, the conspiracy thinking proliferating as a result of the 9/11 terrorist attacks may 'prove to mark its end'. He condemns the way truthers seem to need to 'reduce the world's complexity to good-versus-evil fables' while using a similar 'goodies versus baddies' logic to implore his readers to defend the rationalist tradition by defeating the 'enemies' of the Enlightenment (2011, xxiii). Likewise, Wheen ridicules 'catastrophists' as real-life Chicken Lickens in a book which not only diagnoses an invasion of neo-irrationalist monsters, but whose very title announces that mumbo jumbo isn't simply on the rise, but has *already* conquered the world (2004, 7, 117).

Pipes edges in on the performative contradiction act, too, writing that what began as 'a lighthearted collection of anecdotes' on conspiracism in the Middle East, 'quickly turned into something deeper and darker' (1998, xi). Leaning heavily on the imagery of science fiction and contagion, he figures the spread of paranoid thinking as an epidemic, a plague, an infiltrator of innocent minds. Conspiracism, Pipes claims, is not only 'immune to rational argument' but 'spawns its own discourse' and foments conspiracism in other parts of the world (1, 2). Hodapp and Kannon, meanwhile, warn of the dire consequences 'when the lit match of a fiery, professional conspiracist touches off the powder keg of a susceptible believer' (2008, 2) conjuring – in addition to metaphorical explosions – not just conspiracists, but *professional* conspiracists (undoubtedly a deeper and darker breed). Melley's thoughts about the paradoxes associated with conspiracy thinking might have traction here. He argues that conspiracy theory, paranoia, and anxiety about human agency 'are all part of the paradox in which a supposedly individualistic culture conserves its individualism by continually imagining it to be in imminent peril' (2000, 6). This could also be true of the defence of rationalism: that a supposedly rationalist culture conserves its rationalism by continually imagining it to be similarly imperiled.

Perhaps, also, both conspiracists and debunkers are the unlikely beneficiaries of an 'almost masochistic yearning for gloomy jeremiads' (as

Wheen puts it in relation to those writers in the 1980s and 1990s who announced 'the end' of art, nature, science, history, and so on (2004, 65).) When we talk of someone being 'horrified', we are usually referring to something deeply unpleasant. It is also true, however, that human beings have an ambiguous relationship to horror: being scared by stalk-and-stab cinema is both enjoyable pastime and lucrative industry. This dynamic will be explored at greater length in the next chapter. For the time being, we note only that it may go part of the way to explaining why sections of the conspiracy community are able to parlay such dire warnings of impending apocalypse into such tidy profits. University of Utah historian Robert A. Goldberg points out that various 'conspiracy entrepreneurs' have been in operation at least since the waves of 'red scares' in the early twentieth century (cited in Seitz-Wald 2013). A thriving example of this species is Alex Jones, the high-profile American conspiracist once described by *Rolling Stone* as the most paranoid man in America (Zaitchik 2011). In addition to running the extremely popular[3] – and heavily monetized – *Infowars. com* website, Jones produced *Loose Change,* the infamous 'documentary' claiming the 9/11 attacks were an inside job by the Bush administration. Jones believes – or at least *says* he believes – that the US government engages in staged mind-control operations and deliberately manipulates unstable people through the mass media. The endgame, he predicts, is 'a mass eugenics operation that will depopulate the planet by poisoning our food and water with fluoride, radioactive isotopes and various futuristic toxic soups being engineered in New World Order laboratories' (ibid.). (Perhaps realizing this sounds far-fetched, Jones acknowledges that his reasoning involves a degree of conjecture. That said, he boasts that his theories are based on about 95 per cent publically available facts and only about 5 per cent speculation: 'we're talking high 90s accuracy' (Jones 2013).) The important point here is that, in deep contrast to images of kitchen-based think tanks where scruffy people compile paranoia lists, Jones operates from a state-of-the-art 7,600-square-foot radio and TV studio which broadcasts around the clock. These broadcasts are only one part of his revenue stream. Discounting royalties from book and DVD sales, merchandise, paid appearances, and promotional tie-ins, his media income is estimated to be between $2.7 and $10 million per year (Seitz-Wald 2013). As we will discuss in greater detail in Chapter 5, the end of the world is not only nigh – it is highly profitable.

---

[3]*Infowars.com* was estimated to have received 2.14 million unique visitors and twenty million page views over the month of February in 2013 (Seitz-Wald 2013).

Psychological perks

It would be presumptuous to claim absolute knowledge of the innermost motivations of either conspiracists or debunkers. That said, it is still useful to consider the types of psychological perks available as a result of participating in conspiracy conversations (an area in which we currently have inside information). Conspiracy entails any number of pleasures, particularly in terms of the way it places both conspiracy theorists and conspiracy theory debunkers at the vanguard of knowledge – offering the gnostic pleasure of being 'the ones who know'. Secrets, of course, are a rich source of psychological attraction and revulsion depending on whether one feels positioned on the inner or the outer. Mark Fenster, for example, remembers his preoccupation with a conspiratorial children's book from his childhood. The 'infantile but resonant source of power' of the secret club in this book was not located in its mere existence, but additionally in 'its exclusivity of membership and language'. The latter caused Fenster grave envy, concern, and longing; he recalls wanting to both join *and* expose it (1999, vii). Unearthing – or thinking one has unearthed – evidence of a conspiracy is likely to stir similarly complex emotional reactions. The same goes for exposing evidence of a conspiracy *theory*. Thus, we can see that much of the discourse produced by debunkers is also anchored in the claim that what these perceptive sceptics are seeing is something other people are not. To a certain extent, all participants in the conspiracy game (including the authors of this book) are taunting other players with a version of the playground chant, 'I know something you don't know'.

We have examined, already, the way pattern-seeking, grand narration, and the imagining of wilfully evil enemies can help give meaning and order to chaos and trauma. The psychological attractions on offer here relate to consolation: they may ease the discomfort experienced in the face of ambiguity, uncertainty, and the apparent senselessness of misfortune. Ego bolstering is also available in the way both conspiracist and debunker discourse positions the speaker as being superior – in various ways – to their audience. For conspiracists, this sense of superiority may relate to their ability to 'join the dots', and resist the persuasion, coercion, and/or buttocks probings of an energetic enemy. Debunkers, in contrast, elevate themselves above the riff-raff in their claim to superior reason, intellect, and ability to resist the senseless yet seductive narratives of mass and popular culture. Aaronovitch's argument is that subscription to a conspiracy means that believers feel part of a 'heroic elite group who can see past the official version duplicated for the benefit of the lazy or inert mass of people by the powers that be' (2009, 10). There is a case, however, that debunkers also feel part of a heroic, elite group whose intellectual acumen and advanced bullshit detection permits them to see what the lazy, inert, and deluded masses cannot.

As such, we can see that both conspiracists and debunkers position themselves as independent thinkers and arbiters of the truth. Both frame their work as providing a critical corrective to a serious problem, and offer self-help-style manuals for motivated recruits. The activism section of *Infowars.com*, for example, urges urgent grassroots action to wake people 'from their corporate media induced slumber, so they can... resist the coming tyranny' – that is, the draconian power grab by Barack Obama and his New World Order minions designed to engineer 'an agenda of slavery', to turn America into a 'third world nightmare', and to establish a 'one-world dictatorship' ('Infowars Activism'). Over at *New Humanist* magazine, Gray engages in a debunker version of this gauntlet throwing by advocating a rationalist 'fightback' at the local level, and imploring rationalists to take 'a more assertive stand for evidence and reason' (2012). Ever helpful, Kay also offers 'concrete steps that intelligent, culturally engaged Americans can take to reject conspiracism and help regain control of the intellectual landscape' (2011, cover blurb). Among other proposals, he believes a certain 'very specific kind of education can be helpful for inoculating young minds against conspiracy theories' (312). (Given the costs associated with providing quality pedagogy, hopefully it is just a matter of time before such inoculants are discreetly introduced into the world's water supplies – thus putting an end to suspicions of government-high conspiracy once and for all.)

Another undeniable – yet mostly unacknowledged or disavowed – attraction of participating in conspiracy conversations is the not inconsiderable enjoyment to be gained from mocking and derision. A thriving economy of insults is identifiable in the back-and-forthing between conspiracists and debunkers, with both parties calling the other the same things (stupid, blind, dangerous, and so on) for different reasons. The standard conspiracist swipe is that those who do not accept their theories are not people but sheeple; either that or shills for the enemy. Jones typifies the conspiracist mode of attack. While he is quick to quote Nietzsche, Plato, Alexis de Tocqueville, Edward Gibbon, and Aldous Huxley, his standard modus operandi involves 'machine-gun bursts of rage that crescendo with an adolescent snarl' (Zaitchik 2011). These self-described 'mega-rants' involve hurling all manner of florid insults at multiple enemies. The forces of evil are control-freak sadists, demonic high-tech tyrannists, and whores for the 'global Stasi Borg state'; there is a 'kleptocracy working with psychopathic governments – clutches of evil that know the tricks of control'; oh, and as an added bonus, everything the globalists touch turns to 'mutated death' (ibid.). In short, you're either with him or you're a Prozac-addled automaton.

As we have seen, however, debunkers are entirely capable of hurling equally excitable abuse at conspiracists. Goldwag calls the conspiracy realm 'superlatively nutty' (2009, xxxviii), while Hodapp and Kannon claim that conspiracism is made to order for misanthropes suffering a deficiency of reality combined with a surfeit of paranoia (2008, 22). Away from individual insults, we have seen the way that casting a theory as a *conspiracy* theory brings instant de-legitimization. It's shorthand for an accusation of any combination of naivety, gullibility, madness, paranoia, irrationality, panic, stupidity, divorcement from reality, and so on. Hofstadter, in particular, goes to great lengths to ensure his use of the term 'paranoid style' is not misunderstood: 'Of course this term is pejorative, and it is meant to be; the paranoid style has a greater affinity for bad causes than good' (1964, 77). He goes on – with scathing understatement – to say that while he lacks the competence to classify political figures from the past or present as *certifiable* lunatics, he does believe conspiracists have developed a special resistance to learning the lessons of history and reaching enlightenment (77, 86).

For the most part, the only charitability extended by debunkers to conspiracists is the insult of exaggerated patience or excessive paternalism – both of which have a tendency to cast conspiracists as pitiable and infantile idiots. Pipes – employing a somewhat inexact ethnic typology – says it does no-one any favours to suppress the unsavoury topic of conspiracy theories in the Middle East because 'doing so not only constitutes an act of condescension' but 'reduces the chances that Arabs and Iranians will come to terms with their weaknesses' (1998, 8). (Given that he believes intellectual rehabilitation is only a slim possibility for these confused, wrong-headed, volatile, and largely irrational peoples (2), we can only imagine what he'd say about 'Arabs and Iranians' if he *did* decide to stoop to condescension.) Similarly, Kay's call for liberal journalists to avoid vilifying those with disquieting conspiracy theories seems at odds with his own characterization of conspiracists as paranoia-peddlers, fantasists, delusionists, obsessives, echo chamber inhabits, megalomaniacs, lunatic fringe dwellers, nuts, campus crackpots, dunces, and people who reject 'the basic tools of logic and rational discourse' (2011, xxiii). At the very least, he certainly seems equally guilty of the sort of 'smug' demeanour and 'us-versus-them' mentality he critiques (314, 315).

Resistance is fertile

Of all the psychological perks associated with conspiracy discourse, perhaps none are quite so potent as those associated with the feeling that one is not powerless in the face of an enemy, but is instead *fighting back*. As we have seen, conspiracy discourse trades in extremes: the colluding forces of conspiracy darkness are immense – therefore the fight back must also manifest in a maximal form. Resistance may be futile, but that doesn't mean it shouldn't also be flamboyant. What's more, big claims demand not only big counter *claims*, but big counter *claimsmakers*. Thus celebrity conspiracists such as Jones position themselves as information crusaders risking nothing less than their lives to do battle with the forces of evil:

> People ask why am I alive. Thirty years ago, if you talked about the New World Order, nine times out of 10, they did kill you. They'd come shoot you in the back of the head, they'd grab you and stick a needle in your arm, give you an overdose, they'd kill you … They don't now today because … back then they were trying to contain it … Now it does the opposite if they kill me or kill other people like me because then it makes us a martyr. (2011)

While it is less common for debunkers to claim they are in physical danger from their foes, there are some commentators in the popular media domain who do engage in what reads very much like *boasting* about having been threatened with death for their conspiracy-busting campaigns. Mark Roberts, for instance, is a New York tour guide who has devoted considerable effort and cyber real estate to disproving 9/11 conspiracy theories. His website includes a page called 'Paranoid Creeps Who, Either Because They Are Off Their Meds or Because They Are Incompetent Intellectual Cowards Who Cannot Defend Their Claims with the Slightest Shred of Evidence or Logic, Resort to Masturbatory Fantasies About the Execution of Mark Roberts' (Roberts). One comment – drawn from a UK truther site – claims Roberts deserves to be executed for being 'an inherently loathesome, bile-inducing, shill TWAT!'. This person goes on to say that all 'dirty' shills 'will be covered in piss and petrol and shot when the truth comes out' (Prole Art Threat cited ibid.). Another case of a debunker citing a death threat as a sort of badge of honour can be found on *Thrive Debunked* – a blog dedicated to investigating and exposing 'the errors of fact, distortions, and incorrect statements' in the conspiracist film *Thrive* ('About'). On a page called 'Who Wants Me Dead?' the website owner notes that criticizing 'a quasi-religious belief system as deeply held as conspiracy theories' will inevitably attract enemies, then draws attention to a reader's comment calling him a 'bastard whore' and expressing the wish – parsed in more colloquial terms – that he consume faeces, pass away, and putrefy in the underworld ('Who Wants Me Dead?'). This prompts another commentator to suggest that the author of this site isn't *worth* killing and probably manufactured the threat himself (Joe commenting on ibid.).

On the subject of fighting back, we note that some scholars lend considerable support to the notion that conspiracy theorists are indeed engaged in acts of laudable resistance – although in this context resistance is framed as pushing back against various hegemons and dominant discourses, rather than globalist cabals and undercover aliens. In *Aliens in America: Conspiracy Cultures from Outerspace to Cyberspace,* Jodi Dean claims that ufologists resist the view – established within scientific and governmental-juridical discourse – that the judgements of significant numbers of Americans are unreliable (1998, 39). Her case is that, far from being 'crazies', these canny insurgents are actually *rejecting* the presumption that they are mentally challenged and should be excluded from serious discussions about America's security, that they are, in fact, using 'outerspace and the possibility of extraterrestrial visitations to challenge military and scientific hegemony' (39, 42). Her contention is that ufology is located outside 'the constraining equation of truth with security and identifiability', which means it is free 'to focus on the unknown ... and to validate the experiences of witnesses without necessarily claiming that it [can] identify or establish the object of their experiences' (42). As she puts it,

> To claim to have seen a UFO, to have been abducted by aliens, or even to believe those who say they have is a political act ... it contests the status quo ... Insofar as its practitioners can link together varieties of disparate phenomena to find patterns of denial, occlusion, and manipulation, conspiracy theory, far from a label dismissively attached to the lunatic fringe, may well be an appropriate vehicle for political contestation. (6, 8)

Fenster figures conspiracy theories in similarly political terms. He sees them as constituting an 'Other to a "proper" democratic politics'; as a tactical response to the condition of political voicelessness; and as representing a resistance to power that imagines a better, collective future (1999, xii, xiii). Knight, however, responds with some counter-counter-resistance by questioning Fenster's implicit requirement that conspiracy theory fulfil an unfulfillable political function: 'The cultural studies wager is that there are hidden utopian yearnings buried deep within popular culture ... which can be rearticulated to more productive political projects ... [This] can end up insisting that other (usually less sophisticated) people's everyday cultural practices fulfill one's own political agenda – and then chastizing them for failing at what they never intended in the first place' (2000, 21). Knight's point is a good one, and more than a little reminiscent of some reactions to the Catholic theologian Karl Rahner's attempt to maintain the doctrinal primacy of Catholicism while, in the spirit of the 1960s – and Vatican II – being inclusive of all other faiths. Rahner's solution was the contention that, to the extent that the people of these faiths did what was good and believed what was true, they were 'anonymous Christians' (1976, 283). In a different key, some cultural studies theorists have figured conspiracy theorists as anonymous utopians, itinerant and tireless 'resisters' possessing valuable and politically subversive 'counterknowledge'. Yet neither the unwitting Buddhist nor the person who believes that AIDS is the result of a plot between the CIA and a cabal of extraterrestrial hygienists may appreciate being enlisted as advocates for belief complexes they neither care for nor possibly understand.

Our case is that one better way forward is not to figure conspiracy theories as constituting an *en masse*, sociopolitical struggle for equality, solidarity, and a transparent, participatory democracy (Fenster 1999, viii), but – in part – as one of many possible *sociopsychological* responses to a world which is as difficult to understand as it is to influence. To be clear, to call the phenomenon under consideration 'sociopsychological' is to neither *necessarily* pathologize it, nor to negate, in principle, its truth-value. (One may find the laws of gravity *profoundly* reassuring, but that makes them no less true.) Equally, though, given conspiracy theories' particular profiles – their self-gratifying gnostic overlay, their attribution of Pure Evil to a faceless horde of 'Them', their extreme causal linearity and simplifications, and so on – they offer something of a privileged path by which individuals can be made to feel better by being elevated to a position of special understanding and agency, and a position where a certain *esprit de corps* emerges by virtue of the identification of a common enemy.

Melley's case is that the proliferation and trans-ideological reach of contemporary conspiracy stem from profound anxiety about the viability of Enlightenment-era conceptions of individual autonomy and uniqueness. As he sees it, the antithesis of liberal individualism is the 'other-directed' individual, the person who is 'made' and 'possessed' by powerful people or structures, and who thus has little ownership of their own capacities (2000, 53). His argument is that the central role of conspiracy theory in American political discourse is symptomatic of a broader sense of anxiety about perceived rises in the 'autonomy' of social structures such as government and corporate bureaucracies, control technologies, and mass media. Despite the diverse contexts in which these anxieties appear, they have remarkable consistency in the form of what Melley calls 'agency panic' – an intense anxiety that one's actions are not autonomous but are being controlled by someone else or 'constructed' by powerful, external agents' (vii). His conclusion is that liberal humanism is giving way to newer models of subjectivity, but is unlikely to do so without a struggle:

> In postwar American culture, that struggle has been most conspicuous in the rhetoric of paranoia, conspiracy, and diminished human agency. At its best, this rhetoric offers a way of conceptualizing and resisting the controlling power of mass-communication systems, bureaucracies, and regulatory discourses. At its worst, it becomes coupled to an antisocial fantasy of autonomy, a vision that rejects the promise of collective resistance and sometimes even celebrates violent responses to 'oversocialization' … In postwar culture, however, an intending, monolithic agent still seems easier to comprehend and resist than a complex array of structures and communications, even if we know down deep that self-control is not an all-or-nothing proposition. (201–2, internal citations omitted)

Whether or not the rhetoric of conspiracy theory actually *does* offer a way of conceptualizing and resisting *any* sort of political power is an open question; a hyperbolic shrieking from the sidelines about faceless elite may end up amounting to an unwitting (and an admittedly *loud*) form of political quietism. One ramification of many sorts of millennial panic is that its political effects are almost identical. If we really are at the devil's doorstop, then there's little left to do except exercise our duty to be right; we are relieved of doing much except enjoying our superior cognitive status and the privileges of being one of the select. In *The Eustace Diamonds*, Anthony Trollope offers a suggestive aside concerning 'a fine old Tory of the ancient school, who thought that things were going from bad to worse, but was able to live happily in spite of his anticipations' (Trollope). It is difficult to avoid parallels to many forms of contemporary critique, a difficulty that becomes even harder to surmount when Trollope goes on to describe the pleasures involved: 'To have always been in the right, yet always on the losing side; always being ruined, always under persecution … – and yet never to lose anything, not even position, or public esteem, is pleasant enough. A huge, living, daily increasing grievance that does one no palpable harm, is the happiest possession that a man can have' (ibid.).

Conclusion

In this chapter we have attempted to assay the kind of mimetic stichomythia to which both conspiracy theorists and debunkers are prone. This aspect of the scene undoubtedly has a comic aspect to it, one which writers such as Molière (whose seventeenth-century play *Le Bourgeois Gentilhomme* we mentioned in the first chapter) continually exploited. Indeed, in Molière's play – to draw again on the resources of fiction – an increasingly heated debate ensues concerning the superiority of the disciplines of fencing, music, and dancing by their respective masters. Late to proceedings, the philosopher enters and attempts to instruct by the use of reason but soon ends up mirroring the others in their attitude and rhetoric:

> PHILOSOPHY MASTER: A wise man is above all the insults that can be leveled at him; and the grand reply one should make to such outrages is moderation and patience.
>
> FENCING MASTER: They both had the audacity of trying to compare their professions with mine.
>
> PHILOSOPHY MASTER: Should that unsettle you? Men should not dispute amongst themselves about vainglory and rank; that which perfectly distinguishes one from the other is wisdom and virtue.
>
> DANCING MASTER: I insist to him that dance is a science to which one cannot do sufficient honor.
>
> MUSIC MASTER: And I, that music is something that all ages have revered.
>
> FENCING MASTER: And I insist to them that the science of fencing is the finest and most necessary of all the sciences.
>
> PHILOSOPHY MASTER: And where does that leave philosophy? I find you all very impertinent to speak with such arrogance in front of me, and impudently to give the name of science to things that one shouldn't even honor with the name of art, and that cannot be classified except under the name of miserable fighter, singer, and fool!
>
> FENCING MASTER: Get out, you dog of a philosopher!
>
> MUSIC MASTER: Get out, you worthless pedant!
>
> DANCING MASTER: Get out, you insolent dog!
>
> PHILOSOPHY MASTER: What! Reprobates that you are…

It is part of the problem, surely, that the Philosophy Master considers himself above the fray and is blind to his own participation in the mirroring of antagonisms.

But to draw attention to this factor is not equivalent to the claim that 'all the participants are the same (except for the authors of the book you are holding, of course)'. Instead, our line of reasoning is that the more heated, heavy-handed, and hypercritical a debate becomes, the more it tends to reduce the antagonists to doubles of each other. Of course, this point itself is not one either side would be happy to hear; it is likely they only see enormous, unbridgeable gulfs – those that separate knowledge from ignorance, reason from superstition, people from sheeple, sanity from madness, naiveté from sophistication. There is a conviction operative here that if someone disagrees, the best method to gain more assent is to shake one's head despairingly, raise one's voice, and jab one's finger. It is an assumption surely worth questioning, and not simply with respect to how conspiracy theory is discussed. Even if we accept for the sake of argument the contention of those critics who see the unmistakable signs of sociopsychological adaptation in conspiracy theorizing as a phenomenon – that, say, part of the attraction of conspiracy thinking is to assuage feelings of powerlessness or 'agency panic' – then debunkers are likely to worsen this predicament (and thereby inadvertently increase the circulation of conspiracy theories) by telling conspiracists they are benighted, witless, dense, foolish, insane, and dangerous. To which a conspiracy theorist *might* respond with, 'I know you are, but what am I?' At which point, we might hope to realize that we have not gotten very far.

5 CULTURAL RAMIFICATIONS AND REFLECTIONS

For we are opposed around the world by a monolithic and ruthless conspiracy that relies primarily on covert means for expanding its sphere of influence – on infiltration instead of invasion, on subversion instead of elections, on intimidation instead of free choice, on guerrillas by night instead of armies by day. It is a system which has conscripted vast human and material resources into the building of a tightly knit, highly efficient machine that combines military, diplomatic, intelligence, economic, scientific and political operations. [I]ts preparations are concealed, not published. Its mistakes are buried, not headlined. Its dissenters are silenced, not praised. No expenditure is questioned, no rumor is printed, no secret is revealed.

JOHN F. KENNEDY, 35TH PRESIDENT OF THE UNITED STATES AND CONSPIRACY THEORIST

This place is an X-file, wrapped in a cover-up and deep-fried in a paranoid conspiracy.

GENERAL W. R. MONGER, *MONSTERS VS ALIENS*

Sunstein and Vermeule, whose anti-conspiracist cognitive infiltration campaign we have encountered in several chapters now, realize their proposed remedy has weaknesses. Initially the task of their Sub Rosa Reason Agents would involve 'countermisinformation'; however, the pair realize this dialectical game might soon imbricate them in unwitting legitimation of that which their agents came to discredit. After all, rebuttal is predicated on the fact that what is being rebutted is *worthy* of rebuttal – and that it makes enough sense such that we can adduce reasons 'for' and 'against' the belief. This is an obvious danger facing their undercover agents. Further, this unwanted 'legitimation effect' may be amplified in contexts of public reception, where the very act of rebuttal may cause otherwise sensible people to now believe the conspiracy theory to be worthy of serious consideration (2009, 221). Sunstein and Vermeule consider the circumstances of so-called 'pluralistic ignorance', where citizens don't know what other citizens believe, and then encounter a rebuttal of some improbable view:

> Citizens may take the fact of rebuttal itself as supplying information about the beliefs of other citizens, and may even use this information in forming their own beliefs. If the number who follow this cognitive strategy and thus adopt a belief in the conspiracy theory exceeds the number who are persuaded by the rebuttal, the perverse result of the rebuttal may then be to increase the number of believers. (221–2, *cf.*: Knight 2000, 27)

Consistent with their somewhat Zelig-like profile, it should be no surprise that Sunstein and Vermeule seem to have infiltrated their own remedy and neutralized it from within. Indeed, what they indicate here as a socio-psychological possibility is, as it turns out, a persistent historical actuality. Those behind the Warren Commission attempted to quell rumours about JFK's assassination with a 'definitive' report – a remedy which ended up doing precisely the opposite. Written by the most eminent of authorities, it was a hastily assembled document, riddled with errors. Offered in an attempt to diffuse speculation, it has become in the eyes of many a kind of bible of bad-faith denial – a political rune against which 'inquiring minds' can endlessly pit themselves, and into which they can read the most heinous of cover ups. The Warren Report might be seen as setting the template for being both a kind of sacred text *and* its very own heresy.

We live in a time where, as we have seen, a widespread suspicion of institutions shifts the burden of proof, where authorities are now expected to furnish evidence that claims of conspiracy and cover-up are implausible. The problem is that this represents a double-bind: there is no need to *provide* counter-evidence unless a conspiracy *is* plausible. In fact, with respect to people's belief, *denial* of a conspiracy is usually taken as evidence of precisely what that evidence is supposed to assert. But before we further contemplate Sunstein and Vermeule's proposed solution, or try to improve or modify it, surely we need to determine whether we should even be looking for remedies. The assumption here is that conspiracy theories are bad things that require radical solutions. But *are* they? And *do* they?

Dangerous nonsense

Aaronovitch certainly thinks so. His view of conspiracy theory is, put simply, that it is 'dangerous nonsense' (2009, 41) (contrasting it, perhaps, with Edward Lear's non-dangerous nonsense, or Thai boxing's dangerous non-nonsense). 'The belief in conspiracy theories is', Aaronovitch says, 'harmful in itself. It distorts our view of history and therefore of the present, and – if widespread enough – leads to disastrous decisions' (15). Part of the justification he supplies for this view includes interpretations of the devastating historical impact of *The Protocols of the Elders of Zion* and the fanciful narrative justifications which propped up Stalin's farcical Moscow Trials. At the level of these actual, historical examples, what Aaronovitch is asserting is not particularly controversial: that, for instance, belief in a Jewish world-conspiracy has had utterly devastating consequences.[1] The capacity for texts such as *The Protocols* for fuelling and justifying violence scarcely needs to be argued – although we will shortly have some things to say about this matter. We are certainly aware of the centrality of *The Protocols* on the book shelves of various influential anti-Semites, and the role of that fiction in justifying various kinds of anti-Semitic persecution. However, *The Protocols* represents only one kind of conspiracy literature, and Aaronovitch's binary construction of whether conspiracy theory is 'fun or frightening' (15) is too blunt a heuristic to be of service beyond highly historically specified domains. How would his argument fare if it used, rather, the theory that Elvis has been abducted by aliens and is currently a grossly obese interplanetary pop star? 'Fun'? Or 'frightening'?

More pointedly, what Aaronovitch neglects mentioning, of course, is that Stalin's trials didn't just involve conspiracy *theorizing* – they involved *conspiring*. It seems odd to have to point out that a text such as *The Protocols of the Elders of Zion* is not only a dangerous conspiracy theory text – and one that, worryingly, still sells very well in certain parts of the world – but that it has led to *actual conspiracies* against the Jews. Moreover, the production of *The Protocols* in the late nineteenth and early twentieth century was itself most likely the result of an actual conspiracy against the Jews, perpetrated by members of the Russian Secret Police and other, still unidentified,

---

[1]See, for instance, Cohn (1996, 32–6).

collaborators. In some ways closer to the truth, Pipes describes conspiracy theories as composed of 'a farrago of nonsense', before then linking their spread in the twentieth century to a 'plethora of actual conspiracies' (1998, 4–5). Given that Aaronovitch and Pipes are hardly alone in their view of the danger conspiracy theories represent,[2] we are obliged to address the issue they raise.

Conspiracy theory and its victims

Few thinkers in the last hundred years have done as much as the French anthropological philosopher René Girard to theorize the ways in which cultures attain sociopsychological stability through the selection and persecution of victims. Girard – as well as thinkers such as Eric Gans and Jean-Michel Oughourlian whose work grew out of the Girardian paradigm – have pointed out the ways in which positing a common enemy to loathe and struggle against offers psychological benefits for individuals (Fleming 2004, 41–69; *cf.*: Barkun 2003, 4.) Yet for all the payoffs of generating in-ground solidarity, the location of common enemies risks bypassing the demands of justice altogether and fuelling pre-existing prejudices which, in turn, can lead to the demonization – and unjustified targeting – of individuals and groups.

As complex as conspiracy theories may sometimes market themselves to be, they invariably furnish causal accounts that allow for simple, monocausal attributions of malevolent actions, carried out by a specific individual or groups of individuals. Conspiracies, in other words, look for *scapegoats* – allow their subscribers to attribute blame in such a way that it exculpates those who discover the 'hidden truth'. The imagined Jewish world conspiracy enabled Hitler to deflect blame from Germany and Germans, and redirect it towards Judaism and 'the Jew'. While the Holocaust stands as a singularly horrendous example, a survey of conspiracy theories through the ages shows the unfortunate frequency with which Jewish people are cast – along with secret societies such as the Illuminati and the Freemasons – in leading roles in what Girard calls 'texts of persecution' (Fleming 2004, 162–3). There is a disturbing, quasi-algebraic quality to conspiracy theories in that ostensible villains can be substituted without greatly affecting the

---

[2]Many others regard the circulation of conspiracy theories as constituting a grave threat to the body politic. Lee, for example, argues that conspiracy theories which challenge political legitimacy have 'a potentially serious impact on the health of democratic political regimes' and can be used to 'justify violence' (2011, xiii).

structure of any particular conspiracy narrative. Appositely, in *Ecstasies*, Carlo Ginzburg has analysed the ways in which certain stereotypes and motifs have been continually reworked through medieval and modern European history, attaching themselves to a variety of victims who these narratives discredit and at whose expense they furnish justifications for persecution (Ginzburg 1991).[3]

The elasticity of conspiracy theories – and fungibility of putative conspirators – allows groups of schemers to be interchanged with gay abandon and scant regard for their ostensible incompatibility as co-plotters. In America in the 1950s and 1960s, for example, there existed a protest movement known as The Ultra-Concerned, which maintained that the thought control brigade of the Communist Party was moving stealthily 'and almost unmolested' within the mental health and welfare programs of America (Boyvey 1964, 281, 286). 'FIGHT COMMUNISTIC WORLD GOVERNMENT by destroying THE UNHOLY THREE!!!', screamed a 1955 poster warning of the dangers of fluoridated water, polio serum, and 'mental hygiene'. The latter, better known today as 'mental health', was regarded as particularly insidious: part of a 'subtle and diabolical plan by the enemy to transform a free and intelligent people into a cringing horde of zombies' (281). America's anti-psychiatry crusaders feared that minor ailments, such as falling hair, ingrown toenails, and dandruff, could lead to incarceration in 'America's Siberia, a mental concentration camp in Alaska' where prisoners would become slave labourers subject to medical experimentation 'under the knives of butcherous doctors' (282). The blaggards behind these nefarious brainwashing schemes were variously named as Communists, Jews, Communist Jews, the Illuminati, and sometimes Sigmund Freud – alongside those misguided members of the 'booblic' the psychoanalyst had infected with 'Couchitis' (288). Brigadier General Herbert C. Holdridge, vice-presidential candidate on the Prohibition ticket, had other ideas. In 1956, he wrote to President Eisenhower explaining that this particular plot of wickedness fairly reeked 'of the evil odor of the forces of the Jesuits' (cited ibid., 283). Of the usual conspiracist suspects, only the lizards failed to get a look-in.

For many conspiracists, all that's required is knowing who the culprits are in advance; after that, the narrative can unfold with utter predictability. Consider the second chapter of *Mein Kampf*, in which – as Mandel points out – Hitler offers lengthy instruction on how one should read books 'in order to support the scaffolding of one's established beliefs' (2002, 275). There is a similar 'always-alreadyness' to much conspiracy thinking

---

[3]As such, Coady seems here quite off the mark when he sees more dangers in 'coincidence theory' than conspiracy theory (2008).

in that one cannot avoid the impression that the theories involved have been formulated well in advance of the assembling of evidence; these are conclusions lying in wait for friendly 'facts'. An illustrative example is the speed with which conspiracy theories began swirling after the bombing of New York's World Trade Center. Conspiracists, recalls Jeremy Stahl, began their theorizing within hours of the planes hitting the towers:

> Many used them to pin blame on their favorite pre-existing bogeyman. Days after 9/11, for example, a rumor spread that 4,000 Jews had been warned about the attacks and failed to show up for their jobs at the Twin Towers ... Career paranoiacs in America, meanwhile, were pointing the finger squarely at the U.S. government. People like libertarian radio host Alex Jones and alternative media reporter Michael Ruppert came from different ends of the political spectrum, but they both 'knew' instantly that powers more diabolical than al-Qaida were behind the attacks, specifically the all-pervasive New World Order and the oil-hungry, fascistic Bush administration. (2011)

Consistent with what Stahl says here, a number of scholars have pointed to the ways in which new media forms assist this kind of rapid dissemination of conspiracy theory; it is a communications environment where someone of the likes of Jones can snare over a million viewers for his documentary *The Obama Deception* within days of its release (Zaitchik 2011). Undoubtedly, the speed of dissemination has shifted. But this is only part of the story. The velocity here also relates to the speed at which the revised, conspiratorial accounts are formulated – what Bruno Latour has called 'instant revisionism' (2004b, 228). The rubble of a building – and the accompanying official explanation – has barely settled before an account *challenging* that version of events is put into circulation.[4]

---

[4]There are a range of further examples that could be cited here. Here is one: on 15 April 2013, two pressure cooker bombs exploded at the Boston Marathon, killing three people and injuring hundreds of others. In this case, journalists observed that it took only minutes before 'self-described "truthers" erupted worldwide across the Internet with conspiracy theories about the crime' (Hargrove 2013). These included the claim that various groups and institutions (including the media and US bomb squads) knew about the attacks before they took place, that the bombings were preceded by the creation of related Facebook pages, that the suspects – Chechen-born brothers Dzhokhar and Tamerlan Tsarnaev – were CIA doubles agents 'gone wrong', and that private security forces or Navy SEALS were behind the attacks (Sheets 2013). *Infowars.com,* meanwhile, reported that the cartoon *Family Guy* had 'eerily predicted' aspects of the bombing and that *YouTube* was censoring discussion of the issue (Watson 2013).

Yet if the speed at which 'official history' is challenged attains escape velocity, at least in part because ostensible culprits have already been lined up by conspiracy theorists before the fact, this apologetic pre-determined orientation is something conspiracy theorists neither invented nor monopolize. One of Aaronovitch's stated aims in writing *Voodoo Histories* was to provide a kind of apologetic text for 'the millions of men and women who have found themselves on the wrong side of a bar or dinner-party conversation that begins, "I'll tell you the real reason..." and have sat there, knowing that it was all likely to be nonsense, but rarely having the necessary arguments to hand' (2009, 15). This is an interesting admission for a defender of reason: to provide a text to help people who already know they're right but don't have any reasons to believe what they do – yet. Imagine for a moment, what this assertion would look like coming from the other side of the fence: a text made for people who simply know that 9/11 was an inside job – that the official account is 'nonsense' – but don't know why (yet) they're correct. (Actually, there's no need to imagine; all that's required is a viewing of *Loose Change*.)

It should come, therefore, as no surprise that contemporary debunkers can also be guilty of scapegoating and of directing blame at a line-up of putatively interchangeable social recidivists, including postmodernists; relativists; deconstructionists; religionists; mass culture-o-philes; DIY publishers; and pretty much any kind of sceptic who targets subjects which differ from theirs. As Knight observes, conspiracism itself can become 'a demonized and reified entity on which most of the ills of history can be blamed' (2000, 7). Coady – as discussed in Chapter 1 – goes so far as to claim that the contemporary fashion for castigating certain people as 'conspiracy theorists' and dismissing their beliefs as 'conspiracy theories' (a fashion he blames on Popper) amounts to no less than an intellectual witch hunt (Popper apparently at fault again) (2012, 111, 122). People, it's true, very rarely hunt witches these days. They do, however, still go hunting.

Politics and conspiracy: Business as usual

There has been a common perception in much of the mainstream media that conspiracy theory is generated almost exclusively by those on the Right. Part of this comes down to the fact that most of the critics of conspiracy theory are what – in the United States at least – are called 'liberals'. And while that which is often labelled 'conspiracy theory' has indeed been associated with those on the right of politics, it is not a cognitive or explanatory style which is owned by any political allegiance. Very few people who think about social issues self-identify *as* 'conspiracy theorists'. For most educated people, it is anathema – something they have transcended, even if many others haven't. That said, in *The Audacity of Hope*, Barack Obama concludes that the explanations of both the Right and the Left have become 'mirror images' of each other: 'They are stories of conspiracy, of America being hijacked by an evil cabal. Like all good conspiracy theories, both tales contain just enough truth to satisfy those predisposed to believe in them' (cited in Goldwag 2009, xxxviii).

Obama is correct, although – also like a good conspiracist – his statement neglects including the *centrists*. While there has been a common misperception that the Right somehow owns conspiracy theory, there has been another misconception that has run in parallel: that conspiracy theory is itself a marginal activity. Contrarily, in the history of US politics, conspiracy-minded policy and rhetoric has indeed been a mainstay since the nation's formation. Indeed, its very first president, keen to quash any speculation that Illuminati doctrines *hadn't* spread in the United States, wrote, in 1798:

It was not my intention to doubt that, the Doctrines of the Illuminati, and principles of Jacobinism had not spread in the United States. On the contrary, no one is more truly satisfied of this fact than I am. The idea that I meant to convey, was, that I did not believe that the *Lodges* of Free Masons in *this* Country had, as *Societies*, endeavoured to propagate the diabolical tenets of the first, or pernicious principles of the latter (if they are susceptible of seperation [*sic*]). That Individuals of them may have done it, or that the *founder*, or *instrument* employed to found, the Democratic Societies in the United States, may have had these objects; and actually had a seperation [*sic*] of the *People* from their *Government* in view, is too evident to be questioned. (Washington, emphases in original)

Washington was, of course, an 'independent' in today's parlance, but conspiracy rhetoric has been endemic in US public life since then, right into the contemporary era. Here we have the Republican, Theodore Roosevelt, and the Democrat, Woodrow Wilson, adopting homologous form of rhetoric:

Behind the ostensible government sits enthroned an invisible government owing no allegiance and acknowledging no responsibility to the people. To destroy this invisible government, to dissolve the unholy alliance between corrupt business and corrupt politics, is the first task of the statesmanship of the day. (Roosevelt 1912)

Since I entered politics, I have chiefly had men's views confided to me privately. Some of the biggest men in the United States, in the field of commerce and manufacture, are afraid of something. They know that there is a power somewhere so organized, so subtle, so watchful, so interlocked, so complete, so pervasive, that they had better not speak above their breath when they speak in condemnation of it. (Wilson 1913, 13)

Consider also, the conspiracism of one of Obama's heroes – the thirty-fifth president of the United States, whose address to the American Newspaper Publishers Association in April 1961 is this chapter's head quote. It is, however, important not to mash contexts. Certainly there is much in American politics that *isn't* conspiratorial. It's also imperative to know that Kennedy was talking about communism, rather than humanoid reptiles. This sort of delineation of context is, we feel, especially important in a book on conspiracy thinking given that conspiracy theorists have a seemingly unquenchable libido for historical time-space compression. The *Washington Post* recorded that, in his first 18 months on air, Glenn Beck – averaging around two million viewers nightly – managed (along with his guests) to mention Hitler 147 times, the Nazis 202 times, fascism 193 times, the Holocaust 76 times, and the proper-noun 'Goebbels' 24 times. The majority of these references were invoked to provide analogies of Hitler to Barack Obama and, somewhat less frequently, of Hitler or Goebbels to Woodrow Wilson (Milbank 2010).

The point is that what is often categorized 'conspiracy theory' – and figured as the marginal activity of young, hairy men running around playing soldiers in privately owned militia training camps in Oklahoma – is much closer to what, in other contexts, we might simply call 'political rhetoric'. Here we can witness the *mainstreaming* of conspiracy theory. It is highly culturally diagnostic that the debate about climate change has been, from all quarters, heavily shaped by claims of conspiracy. Almost from its inception, members of the Left have suggested that Big Business was engaging in secret strategies to deny climate change (Goldenberg 2013; Cohen 2013). At the same time we have had the Right claiming that trails of private e-mails lead inevitably to the conclusion that a private cabal of climate scientists are engaged in strategic deceptions, all the better to secure their precious research grants ('Global warming labeled a "scam"' 2007; Hickman & Randerson 2009). Stuart Varney, the host of Fox Business'

Varney & Co. – capturing the sentiments of many – has called the idea of climate change, simply, 'a scientific conspiracy' (cited in Fitzsimmons 2012).

Republican senator James Inhofe concurs – via an elaborate macramé of historical mismatch, wild paranoia, bible citation, and claims concerning plans by global networks to create a total world government. In a 2003 speech, the then chairman of the Senate Committee on Environment and Public Works announced, among much else, that parts of the Intergovernmental Panel on Climate Change (IPCC) process resembled 'a Soviet-style trial', and that the *real* objective for the Kyoto protocol had 'nothing to do with saving the globe. In fact it is purely political. A case in point: French President Jacques Chirac said during a speech at The Hague in November of 2000 that Kyoto represents "the first component of an authentic global governance"' (Inhofe 2003). (Climate change just an elaborate ruse to cover yet another One World Government plot? But of *course*!) Inhofe concluded this address with a question – and an answer: 'With all of the hysteria, all of the fear, all of the phony science, could it be that man-made global warming is the greatest hoax ever perpetrated on the American people? It sure sounds like it' (Inhofe 2003). On the off chance anyone missed the subtext, he went on to publish a book entitled *The Greatest Hoax: How the Global Warming Conspiracy Threatens Your Future* (Inhofe 2012), adding, during media interviews, that human-influenced climate was an impossible conceit because 'God's still up there. The arrogance of people to think that we, human beings, would be able to change what He is doing in the climate is to me outrageous' (cited in Tashman 2012).

Despite its potential to prove our point about conspiracy discourse and mimetic antagonism, we will refrain from entering the slanging match and speculating on the outrageousness quotient of Inhofe's voice. Instead, we will simply point out – as Melley does – that conspiracy narratives draw numerous advocates from both the Left and Right and cannot be explained with reference to any particular issue, event, or social organization. Of course this does not mean that conspiracy thinking is somehow free from political ramifications. The rhetoric of conspiracy can be utilized to effect by anyone who intuits a sense of their own victimization or manipulation (Melley 2000, 11). But despite the availability of conspiracy discourse, deploying it is not always a wise strategy. Conspiracy genies are highly resistant to being returned to their bottles and can behave both dangerously and unpredictably. Given the threat the 'birther' campaign has posed to the American Democrats, it is interesting to note that the original allegations about Obama's citizenship were raised by anonymous Hillary Clinton supporters during the presidential primaries in the spring of 2008 (Smith & Tau 2011).

Having said that conspiracy theory is not simply a party-political belief, it is important to acknowledge that meaningful empirical social scientific work has been done relating political affiliation to belief in conspiracy theory. The Public Policy Polling survey outlined in Chapter 1, for example, found that 34 per cent of Republicans polled believe a New World Order controls the world, compared with only 15 per cent of Democrats. While a total of 44 per cent of Americans think the Bush administration deliberately misled the public over weapons of mass destruction in an effort to start the Iraq war, this breaks down to 72 per cent of Democrats and only 27 per cent of Republicans. Republicans, meanwhile, are twice as likely as Democrats to think global warming is a hoax (Hall 2013). The lesson here is not so much that belonging to a particular voting public makes one susceptible to conspiracy theory, but that it tends to predict *which* conspiracies will be endorsed. Also interesting is the way that Conservative pundits tend to combine a highly simplistic biblical literalism with an occult hermeneutic sophistication when it comes to statements from a Democrat leader; the bible's declarations about most things are considered 'clear and distinct', while information provided by the government is taken as oracular and requiring serious decoding to get the references to the Illuminati. Here we see hermeneutic approaches dictated by political ideology.

The results of polls such as the one detailed above may prompt the reader to encourage scientists to design an effective medicine to cleanse the society of both conspiracy theories and those that devise them. The problem with that 'solution' (quite apart from being sociopathological and medically implausible) is that – as discussed earlier – there is ample evidence that there are people and organizations with both sufficient motive and capacity to carry out effective disinformation campaigns. As such, there is a danger in rejecting the conspiracy theory view of politics *in toto* because we would then be obliged to believe everything we're told – even if what we're told is at complete odds with what we are experiencing. At the risk of singling Sunstein and Vermeule out – once more – for special attention, it is difficult to ignore the absurdity of their purview of a cured populace: that is, a citizenship prepared to accept a secret government conspirator's case that there are no secret government conspirators. (In such circumstances, the powers-that-be are reminiscent of Marilyn Monroe's character Lorelei Lee in *Gentlemen Prefer Blondes* (1953); she wants a man who trusts her no matter how untrustworthily she behaves.) While it may be comforting for debunkers to conclude *a priori* that the kinds of suspicion exercised in conspiracy theory are, at base and in principle, misguided, we should perhaps look to the idea that there has arisen some very serious and widespread cultural concerns about public access to information and knowledge. By the same token, modern society seems more and more comfortable with the dearth of – at least institutional – privacy: anything withheld is *de facto* 'secret'.

Melley also reminds us that Noam Chomsky has pointed out that what he calls 'institutional analysis' is often dismissed as simply conspiracy theory by those who figure social institutions as unimpeachably fair (2000, 16. *cf.: Manufacturing Consent: Noam Chomsky and the Media*). Indeed, Chomsky has expressed his frustration both with those who indulge in conspiracy theories and those who confuse his work with it:

> [P]eople always ask, 'What can I do?' And then they say, here's something I can do. I can become a qualified civil engineer in an hour, and prove that Bush blew up the World Trade Center. I'm pretty sure that in Washington they must be clapping. A couple of years ago, I came across a Pentagon document that was about declassification procedures. Among other things, it proposed that the government should periodically declassify information about the Kennedy assassination. Let people trace whether Kennedy was killed by the mafia, so activists will go off on a wild goose chase instead of pursuing real problems or getting organized. It wouldn't shock me if thirty years from now we discover in the declassified record that the 9/11 industry was also being fed by the administration. (2007, 39–40 internal citations omitted)

So, Chomsky's repudiation of conspiracy theory involves the contention that the ultimate conspiracy may, in fact, be that the US government is conspiring to mislead people into thinking that the US government is conspiring to mislead people. His critique of conspiracy theory is, at least, ingenious. But what we see here is precisely that kind of cognitive style that people have called 'paranoid'. Chomsky has endless energy for reducing almost all political phenomena to a very small selection of causes, which he invokes repeatedly in order to explain almost all political phenomena. Furthermore, for Chomsky, there are *only* facts; in his own purview, he doesn't really 'theorise' at all. The world Chomsky talks about isn't one that there could be disagreements about – only lies, errors, or ignorance. Talking of the rhetoric of persuasion, he remarks, 'I would not feel comfortable thinking that I was able to change people's minds on a matter of human significance … Who am I to change their minds? If I can give them facts, fine. But nobody should want to have that kind of authority, and if you have it you shouldn't use it' (cited in MacFarquhar 2003, 76). Just the facts, then. It is precisely on these grounds that Slavoj Žižek critiques Chomsky: for his belief that there is no ideological component to his work (2013).

What conspiracy theories *do* tend to confirm is the increasing burden on public agencies charged with the task of providing reliable information. By throwing into doubt not just particular sets of data, but the institutions charged with generating them, it reveals the extent to which trust plays a huge role in the justification of our beliefs. Surely, however, it also highlights the importance of the proper functioning of institutions. Part of the political task is, therefore, to be able to engage in an ongoing critique of institutions, to be able to reform them – and to have institutions are capable *of* reform.[5]

To summarize this section, we've seen the way that there has, arguably, been a reflexive dismissal of conspiracy theories, by grouping all possible explanations involving conspiracy as by definition fabulous and fanciful. The problem with this kind of approach (apart, of course, from seizing evidence in advance, like conspiracists themselves) is that it too readily assimilates hyperbolic accounts of abductions by White House reptiles with the activities of secret and sometimes illegal political collectives, which are commonplace in contemporary society and politics. Bale points out that in refusing to theorize conspiracies, by stigmatizing an approach that would allow this as an explanatory possibility, a key element of modern political life has been systematically ignored (1995, 3). As such, despite the wildness of many of the claims made by conspiracy theorists, claims of conspiracy may be too important to be left solely to conspiracy theorists to make.

Surely, it cannot be an adequate 'corrective' to counter the idea of all political events being the result of covert action to argue that *none* of them are. To simply invert a distortion is to retain that distortion in an alternate form. By the same token, to argue that conspiracies exist need not preclude one from pointing out the kinds of excesses, errors, and dangers inherent in always attempting to theorize social events in terms of secret intents and covert actors. Coady points out that someone like him, who might well be seen as an apologist for conspiracy theory, isn't obliged to deny that there are those who have a lamentable tendency to see conspiracy *everywhere*. Equally, he says, we should be mindful that another, equivalent form of irrationality is made from the denial of conspiracy in the face – even in the teeth – of strong evidence. If the term 'conspiracy theorist' is automatically applied to those who see conspiracy all around them all the time, then

---

[5]One model here is *The Truth About the Drug Companies* by Marcia Angell – a medical doctor and former editor-in-chief of the *New England Journal of Medicine*. Her book exposes a 'conspiracy' of sorts: the increasing corruption of the pharmaceutical industry, which functions very often as a mere marketing machine with overwhelming influence over research, and medical education and practice – and an astonishing ability to generate profits for its members (2005).

Coady suggests 'coincidence theorist' for those who simply do not 'connect the dots' (2008). In the next chapter we will have reason to contest Coady's epistemology – and his opposition between 'conspiracy' and 'coincidence'; but, for now, his general point is well-taken.

The banality of conspiracy

One of the problems with locating conspiracies mightn't be that they are hidden, but that they are so banal that we believe it's hardly worth theorizing them. Indeed, we may even be so jaded by conspiracy that we'd prefer to look somewhere else, more interesting, for our theoretical enjoyment. Conspiracy fatigue? *Really*? Yes. At one level we've become so accustomed to companies and political parties spinning information, disguising their real agendas, protecting their commercial interests, and so on, that we can't be *bothered* rousing ourselves to think any more about, given its obviousness. Do we really *need* to *theorize* e-mails from Nigerian princes promising us unwarranted and unexpected inheritances? And how about all those junk-food multinationals 'optimising' their salad dressings and sodas in an attempt to override the triggers that tell our mouths to stop eating (Moss 2013)? Does this count as a conspiracy when surely we all *know* that junk food is addictive?

The endorsement, in principle, of the fact of conspiracies (and therefore, conspiracy theories that furnish theories about them), should not mislead us into assuming that they have the kind of profile that conspiracy theorists often suggest. Just as debunkers have often construed conspiracy theories in wildly simplistic terms, conspiracy theorists themselves have given the debunkers more than enough material to work with. Few theorists have pointed out as well as Bale (1995) the profoundly unglamorous and banal profile of conspiracies and conspirers. Even though covert politics and economics may have genuinely deleterious effects, we should not, therefore, conclude that we are dealing with a grand bunch of super-villains that appear to have walked off the page of one of Stan Lee's sketchbooks. Conspirers, Bale argues, are profoundly human, imperfect beings; they engage in a variety of schemes which often share little with other conspirers; they operate at very small scales, with stratagems that are often targeted against other small scale conspirers.

Although we shouldn't exclude the obvious fact that secret service agencies gather intelligence, we should be equally able to countenance the fact that a local bread shop is quietly developing a new kind of sourdough to gain competitive advantage against the bread shop down the road. (Further, there may be some internal conflicts in the bread shop – generating new, sub-layers of intra-bakery conniving – over the issue of whether or not this new loaf should involve sesame seeds.) As far as we are aware, we do not live in a world with one or two powerful conspiracies in operation – but one in which millions of minor ones – and perhaps a few medium-sized ones – are grinding away all the time. We are forced, therefore, to draw the contrast between conspiracy as social fact and the *representation* of conspiracies as these appear in the typical 'conspiracy theory'. The account that usually appears under that name tends less towards the specific and local, and more towards the general and the global; its protagonists are not petty and opportunistic, but demonic, exceedingly organized, and entirely irresistible. Apposite here, is Melley's point about the crude theories of ideology associated with conspiracy: 'crude not because they are wholly mistaken (advertisers *do* try to manipulate us and communists *do* train new recruits), but because they view social control as a mysterious and magical process, activated instantaneously and capable of utterly disabling rational self-control' (2000, 5, emphases in original).

We can also surmise that as a conspiracy theory persists, it tends to become progressively less accurate. Keeley points out that as a conspiracy theory 'matures' (for want of a better term), attempts at falsification tend not to infirm it, but merely increase its provenance and explanatory scope; as more and more people come to criticize the theory, this criticism comes to represent – in the eyes of the theorists – an ever-wider cohort of conspirators. Where at first a small group was conspiring, now – as the criticisms pile up – it seems that increasing numbers of participants are involved in an ever-bigger conspiracy, the protagonists of which are attempting to quash speculation about it (1999, 122).[6] Keeley's point is interesting, indicating as it does, one of the paths by which a conspiracy theory is elaborated in relation to its circumstances. A parallel point about the explanatorily expansive nature of conspiracy theory has been made by political theorist Martha F. Lee, who discusses how conspiracy discourse

---

[6]Another example of a kind of putative 'expansion' of conspiracies is evident in the way that people who believe in one conspiracy theory are more likely to believe in others which may not be thematically or logically related (Lee 2011, 4–5). This may be true, but again is not a phenomenon unique to conspiracy theory. One of the most tired popular critiques of green or leftist activism is precisely that people 'bandwagon'; the obvious response is that surely we should properly expect that a person who believes that one area of social transformation is necessary will have reason to believe that other, parallel changes are also required. Equally, if a particular epistemology or ontology of the social is assumed, we could expect that other hypotheses predicated on the same theoretical structure would also be more likely to be assented to.

has altered in the last 100 years. Where once conspiracists would be happy to focus on single events – like the assassination of JFK – we now see the emergence of 'superconspiracies', where the focus is not on a particular cultural event, but the totality of human existence: nefarious agents are not merely behind the abduction of Elvis or Harold Holt, but are responsible for a coming New World Order. Previous enemies such as the Freemason and the Knights Templar are now teaming up with the Illuminati to wreak havoc (2011 xi, 3; *cf.*: Knight 2000, 4).[7] That's right, you read it here, first: conspiracies are occurring all the time – and not *just* in reality.

Conspiracy culture: Anxious pleasures

Few cultural commentators have analysed what Peter Knight calls 'conspiracy culture' as well as... Peter Knight. He argues that, since the assassination of JFK in 1963, conspiracy has increasingly entered mainstream culture (2000, 1–2). No longer the private fetish of paranoid scaremongers (although, of course, it does not exclude them), conspiracy has become the *lingua franca* of everyday political discourse, as well as the cultural ground in which that discourse finds its principle of intelligibility. It has become both the way entertainment works *and* the way the world is seen to work. Knight makes the further, stronger, claim that this involves not merely a culture about conspiracy, but a culture *of* conspiracy. Conspiracy 'has become an implicit mode of operation in American politics, with the rise of the national security state over the last half-century... A presumption towards conspiracy as both a mode of explanation and a mode of political operation have together formed what might be termed "conspiracy culture"' (3).

Knight is pointing to what seems to be a mutual – and mutually reinforcing – expansion of both the map and the territory. Conspiracy has emerged as less an epidemic than endemic phenomenon; it denotes not merely an irruption in the social fabric but a kind of wearied 'business as unusual' mode of cultural operation, a symbolic witness to the ubiquity,

---

[7]Barkun also notes a hybridization of conspiracy theories which have resulted in strange and unpredictable combinations – where we combine the prophecies of Nostradamus, UFO phenomena, and the shady activities of the Illuminati, although he seems to tie this to the aftershock of September 11 (2003, ix). Another of Barkun's arguments is that there is no safe conspiracy theory because contemporary conspiracy theories evince a 'dynamics of expansion' relating to both the tendency for conspiracy theories to grow and involve an ever-expanding cast of malevolent agents (37).

even necessity, of clandestine forces operating in the world. And even if we can't see Them on the news each night, we can certainly keep the TV on and see Them in the program *after* the news. Inspecting the taglines of some high-grossing films from a single decade reads like a conspiracist's book of motivational quotes:

'Lie. Cheat. Steal. All in a Day's Work' – *Glengarry Glen Ross* (1992)

'Fifty million people watched, but no one saw a thing' – *Quiz Show* (1994)

'Everything is suspect … everyone is for sale … and nothing is what it seems' – *LA Confidential* (1997)

'What you know could kill you' *and* 'What if your most paranoid nightmares had just come true?' – *Conspiracy Theory* (1997)

'Believe Everything Except Your Eyes' – *Snake Eyes* (1998)

'Reality Is a Thing of the Past' – *The Matrix* (1999)

This is more than a case of merely asserting, like a marketing executive, 'conspiracy fiction is trending right now'. Rather, what is at stake is a generalized predicament where fiction and non-fiction trade metaphors and scenarios, where history, possible history, and non-history play 'swapsies' indefinitely. In one way, this isn't terribly surprising. The theoretical and the fictional have always been mutually reinforcing: both the hypothesis and the hypothetical expertly inhabit the domain of not what is, but what *might* be.

Yet there may well be risks associated with the fluidity between those kinds of social explanation that accommodate talk of hidden agents and agencies, and fiction that also works with this premise (that is, almost all fiction). Aaronovitch notes that one 'indefatigable activist' in the 9/11 'truth' movement explained that her 'political activism' had only begun in 1992 when a disturbing film spurred her to begin her own research on the government and media: 'The film was Oliver Stone's *JFK*' (2009, 10). What Aaronovitch neglects to mention, however, is that Stone's movie was *itself* based on the monomaniacal 'research' of New Orleans District Attorney Jim Garrison, one of the original JFK conspiracists.[8] And so things come full circle.

It is not simply Stone who has made use of the cultural aftershocks following JFK's assassination. DeLillo – dubbed 'the chief shaman of the paranoid school of fiction' (Robert Towers cited in Knight 2000, 226) – has

---

[8]Calvin Trillin's whimsical piece in *The New Yorker* provides one of the first profiles of a league of conspiracy 'buffs', including then New Orleans DA, Garrison (1967).

repeatedly referred to Kennedy's death in his work. Three of DeLillo's best-known novels – *Libra*, *Americana,* and *Underworld* – all deal with it in one way or another; in fact, the distinguished American author admits, 'it's possible I wouldn't have become the kind of writer I am if it weren't for the assassination' (cited in Knight 2000, 106). In *Libra*, for example, the character Branch is 'stuck' because he 'has abandoned his life to understanding that moment in Dallas, the seven seconds that broke the back of the American century' (DeLillo 1991, 181). Conspiracy here becomes one means by which the American public can preserve their self-regard; rather than think the citizenry is inherently murderous, the culpability is shifted towards secret government agencies.

Another exemplar of literature in the paranoid style (though one which is rarely cited as such) is the novel *If on a Winter's Night a Traveller* by the Italian author Italo Calvino (1998). In one chapter, a university professor – oppressed by an excessive girth and nerves – becomes increasingly anxious as he hears telephones ring in houses he passes while jogging. The weighty intellectual realizes these telephones are perhaps not calling him, have no relation to him at all, but the mere fact that he can be called to a telephone suffices to make it possible or at least conceivable that he may be called by *all* telephones. Convinced, one morning, that these ringing phones are chasing him, that there is somebody looking up all the numbers on the street he is jogging along in the directory, and calling one house after the other in an attempt to overtake him, the panting scholar eventually answers a call in what we are to believe is a stranger's house. Not only is this call indeed for him, but it is one of his students, a girl with whom he recently became entangled in an embarrassing situation and unpleasant misunderstanding. Apparently she has been kidnapped and is about to be burned alive (133–7). The problem, as it turns out, is not that the academic was paranoid, but that *he was not paranoid enough*. As Salman Rushdie puts it, 'Reading Calvino, you're constantly assailed by the notion that he is writing down what you have always known, except that you've never thought of it before. This is highly unnerving: fortunately you're usually too busy laughing to go mad ... I can think of no finer writer to have beside me while Italy explodes, Britain burns, while the world ends' (1981).

Rushdie, like many other consumers of popular culture, clearly enjoys the sense of agitated exhilaration offered by conspiracy-themed entertainment, especially one which cheerily predicts – or even back-announces – the end of the world. In this sense, he and his ilk constitute a sort of real-life version of the fictitious patrons in Douglas Adams' *Restaurant at the End of the Universe*, who watch the known universe end in a gnab gib (the opposite of a big bang) while fine dining on *filet* from the Ameglian Major Cow and sipping an assortment of Aldebaran liqueurs (2005, 129). The organizers of New York's Doomsday Film Festival also seem cognizant of the appeal of artistically exploring all possible permutations of society's demise. They breathlessly promise an apocalyptic package deal of 'Deserted streets!', 'Blood red skies!' *and* 'Total Social Breakdown!' (Doomsday Film Festival & Symposium). Then there is the dating site OkCupid which invites modern romantics to publically answer the question, 'In a certain light, wouldn't nuclear war be exciting?' to help determine their compatibility with other users. As one e-dater declares on an OkCupid forum, 'Really, how jaded do you have to be to NOT be excited by nuclear war? Who's going to hear air raid sirens and say, "Ho hum … another day. Wonder if I have time to take a shower before I go to work?"' (vampirepoet 2011). (As further testimony to the ability of apocalypses to pique the passions, consider the fact that OkCupid's number crunchers have determined that men who answer 'yes' to the nuclear war question have an 83 per cent implied odds of engaging in intimate relations on the first date (Rudder 2011).)

It is important to note, however, that not all commentators approve of such arousing frivolity in popular culture. Richard Dawkins, for instance, rails against the notion that the 'cult' of *The X-Files* is harmless because it is only fiction:

> The problem with *The X-Files* is that routinely, relentlessly, the supernatural explanation, or at least the Mulder end of the spectrum, usually turns out to be the answer … But isn't it just harmless fiction, then? No … Imagine a television series in which two police officers solve a crime each week. Every week there is one black suspect and one white suspect … And, week after week, the black suspect turns out to have done it … *The X-Files* systematically purveys an anti-rational view of the world which, by virtue of its recurrent persistence, is insidious. (2000, 28)

As we saw in the previous chapter, it is not just Dawkins doing the equivalent of making like Munch's screaming bridge man and howling 'Noooooooooooooooooooo!' In addition to Pipes' spawning contagions, Wheen's neo-irrationalist hell-beasts, and Hodapp and Kannon's fears of imminent conspiracist-kindled combustions, there is Kay's only slightly more sober conclusion that the proliferation of conspiracy theories in the contemporary era is both a cause and a symptom of an 'intellectual and civic crisis' (2011, xix). Our response is a resounding 'perhaps'. Intellectuals *do* love calling things 'crises', especially if they're *intellectual* ones (even the idea that there can be something called an 'intellectual crisis' is presumably wildly appealing to an intellectual, as a society going through a 'poetic crisis' might be to a poet). Whether or not it *is* a crisis might come down to a choice of labelling. There are, however, 'intellectual' – that is, *theoretical* – issues at stake. It is to these we shall now turn our attention.

6 CONSPIRACY AND THEORY

In a life we are surrounded by death, so too in the health of our intellect we are surrounded by madness.

LUDWIG WITTGENSTEIN, *CULTURE AND VALUE*

Watson: God! You're just like Don Quixote. You think everything's always something else.

Playfair/Holmes: Well he had a point. Of course, he carried it a bit too far. He thought that every windmill was a giant. That's insane. But, thinking that they might *be ... well....*

JAMES GOLDMAN, *THEY MIGHT BE GIANTS*

As we have seen, there exists an academic orthodoxy casting conspiracism as a debased form of thinking – if, indeed, it is even considered *thinking* at all. As such, at least in part, what we call 'conspiracy theory' derives not merely from the desire to identify a particular form of thought or cognitive style, but to *discredit* it. (By the same token, the term 'positivist' now not only serves to identify a particular form of epistemology, but moreover a *wrong* one. People tend not to line up these days proclaiming themselves to be 'positivists'.) Obviously, we have employed the expression 'conspiracy theory'; we could hardly do otherwise – but it would be a pity to end the discussion without settling on a slightly different sense of the term. Over the course of this book we have examined various dimensions of conspiracy discourse via a series of analytical rubrics and theoretical perspectives. Having pursued this analysis, we will now endeavour – through a kind of epistemological inversion – to use the original object under investigation as a lens through which to look more closely at, among other things, theory itself. Here, we will examine contentions that conspiracy theorizing is wrong, ill-conceived, or incomplete – not to unearth yet more revelations about what conspiracists are up to, but in search of insights into what it is that *theorists* think they are doing. As such, looking at conspiracy theory as 'folk sociology' might shed some light on what we think we're doing when we're explaining things (or 'understanding' them) in the academy. This exercise also hopes to offer some interesting insights into the eschewing of personal causation in social theory, as well as showing that conspiracy theorists are hardly alone in suffering painful epistemology-related maladies such as proof paranoia, mediation misery, and (ouch!) agency-itis.

From Socrates to haunted vaginas

One point that debunkers regularly make is that conspiracy theories of society *sell*. The implication is that, just as McDonalds, André Rieu, and neo-Furbys are all popular, so is conspiracy theory. This trades on the tired, elitist assumption that popular entertainments are crass and appeal only – or mostly – to the lowest common denominator. The parallel point, usually unstated, is that *other* theories of society *don't* sell. This serves to underplay the influence and popularity of the debunkers – and create for them a sense of being culturally superior but numerically outnumbered.[1] That said, it is, to a large extent, true. In 2012, the UK conspiracist David Icke sold out Wembley Arena for a talk about 'interbreeding reptiles, shape-shifters, invisible light, mind parasites and heartless bankers' that went for 11 hours (Mesure 2012). It is difficult to imagine 6,000 (or even considerably fewer) people turning out to see Anthony Giddens give a talk on society and structuration theory for more than, say, 11 minutes. After all, not only is Giddens' institutionally approved 'official knowledge' boring, it is – according to the conspiracist purview – automatically corrupt (because of the whole, origins-in-officialdom thing). As discussed in Chapter 3, however, in this rejection of the official knowledge of the day, the contemporary conspiracy theorist has some distinguished allies.

In an address delivered at the South Kensington Museum in 1860, Thomas Henry Huxley provided intellectual guidance to his audience by

---

[1]Similarly, we can see that the paranoid style involves a kind of self-inflation combined with ideas of persecution: the paranoid intellectual overstates her or his own significance; she or he is the last of the vanguard standing against the ignorant masses.

first posing an oft-repeated query and then answering it: '"What books shall I read?" is a question constantly put by the student to the teacher. My reply usually is, "None"' (1911, 366). Huxley's recommendation was part of a characteristic polemic that finds currency not only in the Victorian era, but our own. His view was that so much of what passed for knowledge had simply been gossip – officially sanctioned prejudice that enjoyed status only because of a tradition of dubious endorsements. If anything has changed since Huxley's time, it may be that the irony of his advice is now more obvious than it was at the time he made it. How else could we source this recommendation of his except through the printed word he so distrusted?

Deep suspicion concerning the mediation of knowledge goes back at least to Plato's *Phaedrus*, written late in the fourth century BCE. In what is ostensibly Plato's key dialogue on the topic of love, we are also treated to a series of reflections on everything from madness, the soul, and pederasty. In the final section of the dialogue (1973, 257c–279c), the reader comes across a consideration of knowledge and its relation to writing. Socrates tells of an Egyptian myth in which Theuth, the god of thunder, presents King Thamus with the gift of writing. While the god's perspective is that writing is a remedy for forgetfulness, the King's perspective is the opposite: that it is a *conduit* for forgetfulness – and, moreover, a channel for the simulation of knowledge, rather than the thing itself. In the future, Thamus prophesies, people will hear much and learn little (274e–275b). Socrates, concurring with the Egyptian king, argues that written instruction can offer little except to those who already know, and here only for the sake of revision (275d–e). Writing, he argues, is mute; it cannot answer questions, cross-examine its readers, or defend itself (275e). Writing misses dialectic – the immediacy of the known through the one who knows. The dialectician, Socrates says,

> chooses a proper soul and plants and sows within it discourse accompanied by knowledge – discourse capable of helping itself as well as the man who planted it, which is not barren but produces a seed from which more discourse grows in the character of others. Such discourse makes the seed forever immortal and renders the man who has it happy as any human being can be. (276e–277a)

Although the kinds of immediacy Huxley and Socrates have in mind are different – the 'bare fact' versus the dialectician – their suspicions regarding mediation are of a piece. The problem, once again, is that the very conditions of possibility of these cautions against the alienating effects of mediation on knowledge are those which the cautions are supposed to steer us away from: media. Between Socrates and Huxley we have a wide variety of advocates for parallel views. Descartes, for instance, casts suspicion on mediation (particularly the mediation represented by his Jesuit education), which he then personifies with the image not simply of ignorance or error, but deceptions wrought by an evil demon.

Suspicions of agents of mediation – especially those associated with *The* Media – continue to run deeply in contemporary society (although these suspicions are less likely to be expressed in philosophical treatises, so much as around dinner party tables where the guiding principle among sophisticates is not 'I think therefore I am', so much as 'I drink therefore I claim the global politariat is a hapless ventriloquist dummy of those gastromancing Murdochs'). One of the radical developments of this trend, however, has not been suspicion concerning merely the means by which knowledge is arrived at, but belief *simpliciter*. Gerry Spence, the American trial lawyer who became famous during the Karen Silkwood case, has now become a successful self-help author. The epistemology he offers targets not simply untested or mediated beliefs, but belief *itself*:

> The most formidable chains are forged from beliefs. Ah, beliefs! Beliefs tear out the eyes and leave us blind and groping in the dark. If I believe in one proposition, I have become locked behind the door of that belief, and all other doors to learning and freedom, although standing open and waiting for me to enter, are now closed to me. If I believe in one God, one religion, yes, if I believe in God at all, if I have closed my mind to magic, to spirit, to salvation, to the unknown dimension that exist in the firmament, I have plunged my mind into slavery. Test all beliefs. Distrust all beliefs. (2002, 37)

'A belief is an idea going bald', as Francis Picabia is reputed to have said … or André Breton, or Lautréamont (nobody quite remembers). Behind Spence's Oedipal hysteria of poked-out eyes, there is a kind of existential anxiety at work – that cohabiting with some belief kicks all others out of bed, and why not *have it all*? Spence articulates a species of reverse existentialism – a sort of existential Sizzler, where one needn't choose *anything* from the menu. (Of course that this conception of belief is *also* a belief is exempted from Spence's attention.) Is it any coincidence that Spence is also the lawyer who – in a televised mock trial in 1986, involving an actual judge, a jury of citizens, and witnesses – defended Lee Harvey Oswald against the charge of assassination? (Zoglin 1986)

But notice what we just wrote: *Is it any coincidence …* (and so on). Presented in this form, our implication is clear; we needn't spell it out, we're not asking the reader to believe anything, we're *just throwing it out there*. This, of course, is a trick. As we've seen, the 'I don't necessarily believe it, I'm just offering it for consideration' is a pose which exempts claimants from furnishing evidence or being accountable for a claim. In fact it relieves the claimsmaker of even being cornered about actually having *made* a claim. And, as outlined in Chapter 2, it is a technique used by conspiracy theorists with risible regularity. One might wonder whether there is a difference between 'sayin' it' and '*just* sayin' it'. Our case is that, in the context of conspiracism, sometimes there *is* a difference between genuine hypothesizing and the rhetorical ass-save. Not all conspiracy theory is glib or offered in such bad faith, as a kind of vulgar writing *sous rature*.[2] It also has its epistemologically aware defenders whose approach to making connections are quite some distance from the reasoning which leads celebrity conspiracists such as Icke to conclude that 'slutty sellouts' like Lady Gaga and Ke$ha are 'poisoning the youth of the world with traumatic mind-control performances and "haunted vaginas"'[3] (2013).

Two games for epistemologists: Connect the dots or kill the subject

Coady is one of the few analytic philosophers – or indeed, philosophers of *any* kind – to discuss in detail conspiracy theory in its epistemological dimensions. As previously discussed, his advocacy of the epistemic cogence of conspiracy theorizing leads him to advocate a kind of linguistic proscription; he dreams of a world in which expressions such as 'conspiracy theory' and 'conspiracy theorist' would be relegated to the historical dustbin – 'recognised as products of an irrational and bigoted outlook' (2012, 126). This world would be one in which people would be ashamed to dismiss a view simply on the basis that it involved recourse to a conspiracy. Admitting the historical improbability of unilaterally editing the English language, Coady suggests an alternate strategy: to preserve the loaded

---

[2]'Sous rature' – usually translated as 'under erasure' – originated in the work of Martin Heidegger and was subsequently used by Jacques Derrida. To put a term *sous rature* means to write a word, cross it out, and leave it visibly crossed out to acknowledge 'both the inadequacy of the terms employed – their highly provisional status – and the fact that thought simply cannot manage without them' (Sarup 1993, 33, 39).

[3]This is a reference to the American rapper Ke$ha who, in various media interviews, has claimed that her vagina required exorcism after she had sex with a ghost (cited in Spitznagel 2013).

terms but alter their valence or connotation. His models here are those words that have shifted from being pejoratives to being more ambiguous in meaning – like 'queer' or 'witch' (126; 2007, 196–7). In pursuit of this goal, we're already acquainted with Coady's suggestion that we use the term 'coincidence theorist'

> to denote those who, like Hume, are skeptical about inferences 'beyond the present testimony of our senses or the records of our memory' (Hume, 1966/1748, p. 26), but who, unlike Hume, do not confine their skepticism to theoretical philosophy. Coincidence theorists are people who fail, as it were, to connect the dots; who fail to see any significance in even the most striking correlations. To give you a sense of the influence of coincidence theory on our political culture, consider the theory that terror alerts in the United States were manipulated for domestic political advantage by the Bush administration. (2012, 127; *cf*.: 2007, 196–7)

Even bracketing, for a moment, his figuring of Hume, Coady sets out the issue in a way that stacks the decks somewhat. It is, of course, true that conspiracy theory attempts to 'connect the dots'. In Icke's *The David Icke Guide to the Global Conspiracy (and how to end it)* (2007) the word 'connect' and its correlates ('connected', 'connecting', 'connections', and so on) are found on 229 of the 625 pages – and on many of those pages, numerous times. 'Only when the dots are connected can the picture be seen', Icke tells us at the beginning, letting us know what to expect (xi). Icke is equally interested in coincidence: 'not coincidentally' (63); 'Can it really be a coincidence?' (75); 'This is no coincidence' (128); 'I cannot believe this was a fortuitous coincidence' (276); 'Coincidence?' (279); 'no coincidence' (291), and on … and on … and on. The head quote for a chapter entitled '9/11: The Big Lie' is from John Judge, co-founder of '9/11 Citizens Watch': 'I'll call myself a conspiracy theorist if you call yourself a coincidence theorist' (280). Perhaps Judge and Icke have been reading Coady – or Coady, them. Could it *really* be a coincidence? Just throwing it out there…

Of course, 'tracing connections' isn't unique to conspiracy theorists. In *Cults, Conspiracies, and Secret Societies*, Goldwag, for instance, claims the 'presiding spirit' of his book 'is exploratory rather than encyclopedic; I am more interested in finding underlying commonalities and connections between groups and theories' (2009, xxxix). The cogent point about most alternative explanations for sociocultural or political events is not that they are 'coincidences', but that recourse to words such as 'intent', 'subterfuge', or 'evil ambition' won't give us as much explanatory scope as we require. Foucault's influential *History of Madness* (2006), for instance, doesn't present an account of devious people plotting to incarcerate others for their miscellaneous abnormalities. Yet this does not mean the French historian and philosopher therefore sees all judicial and medical decisions as strings of mere 'coincidences', as events with no relation to each other. If that *were* the case, Coady's point would be well taken; but it's not. 'Conspiracy' and 'coincidence' simply do not exhaust all explanatory possibilities. Arguably, traditional social theory 'connects dots' as well as anything; the issue is not a Humean one (which Coady seems to think it as), but one about what we think we're doing when we explain things, and especially the relationship of explanation to *teleology* – of saying what is happening (or has happened) in culture and society, and its relation to human intents and purposes.

As we saw in Chapter 4, Melley's case is that the spread and wide appeal of conspiracy theory relate to anxieties about individual agency – a condition he dubs 'agency panic' (2000, vii). In this light, then, perhaps one of the features that conspiracy theory offers those who wish to think about society is an account of social and political life precisely in terms of human agency; that is, conspiracy theory operates with the assumption that things happen in society because people *cause* them to happen. Put like that, it doesn't seem like a horribly outrageous idea. Yet it is a notion that is monumentally out of step with what usually constitutes 'explanation' in the humanities and social sciences. At least since Émile Durkheim, the social sciences have foregrounded ideas of society, which have figured a world where the ability of individuals to exercise their agency is radically constrained. When, as a discipline, sociology talks about 'agents', it refers not to people, but 'agents of socialisation' – the family, peer relationships, schools, the mass media, the workplace, and so on. In the social sciences, society invariably has a temporal, epistemological, and ontological priority over the individual. 'Society', in other words, is not simply an arithmetic term expressing an aggregation of individual acts and actors, but a force external to the individual, which not only constrains his or her actions, but gives the actor precisely the sense that their actions are *not* so constrained. Here is Durkheim, from *Les régles de la méthode sociologique*:

> When I perform my duties as a brother, a husband, or a citizen – when I execute the commitments I have entered into – I fulfill obligations that are defined in law and custom and which are external to myself and my actions. Even when they comport with my own feelings and when I feel their reality inside me, that reality does not cease to be objective, because it is not I who have prescribed these duties to myself; I have received them through education … The system of signs that I use to express my

thoughts, the currency I use to pay my debts, the credit instruments I use in my commercial relationships, the practices I follow in accord with my profession, etc., all operate independently of the uses I make of them. Considering one after the other, each member of society, we can say the same of every one of them. Therefore, there are ways of acting, thinking, and feeling which have the remarkable property of existing outside the consciousness of the individual. Not only are these types of conduct and thinking external to the individual, but they are imbued with a compelling and coercive power by virtue of which, whether he likes it or not, they impose themselves upon him. (1919, 6)[4]

Durkheim may be simply one example among many – but his is, at least with respect to the autonomy of the social sphere, highly typical. Foucault could never be accused of being a follower of Durkheim, but he is still a thinker for whom individual human subjects are in no sense the *causes* of social or cultural change. He challenges the idea that any inquiry can begin with the human as its basis; indeed, he finds such an idea to be so hopelessly *naïve* that the only appropriate response to such a proposal, were it to be offered, would be to *laugh* at it:

To all those who still wish to talk about man, his reign or his liberation, to all those who still have questions about what man is in his essence, to all those who wish to use him as their starting-point in their attempts to access the truth, to all those who, contrastingly, refer all knowledge back to the truths of man himself, to all those who refuse to formalize without anthropologizing, who refuse to think without immediately thinking that it is man who is thinking, to all these twisted and warped forms of thinking, we can answer only with a philosophical laugh – that is to say, to a certain extent, a silent one. (1966, 353–4; *cf*.: 398)

(One gathers that Foucault here is claiming – or assuming – that we possess no capacity adequate to transcribe guffaws; there's little reason to gainsay him on at least this point). Foucault's account of modern subject-formation provides a history (alternatively, an 'archaeology' and, later, a 'genealogy') of the ways in which persons are constituted *as* persons; the subject is an historical artefact, a residue of a conglomeration of discursive constructions or regimes of statements (1972, 94). Foucault's musings here, as dramatically couched as they are – and, admittedly, omitting reference to his later, somewhat different, work – are not unique. One gets pretty much the same

---

[4]Translations, unless otherwise stated, are the authors'.

message from Foucault's numerous disciplinary targets: phenomenology, structuralism, Marxism, and psychoanalysis. In his later works, Heidegger, for instance, engages repeatedly in a characteristic conceptual inversion: humans do not speak language; rather, language speaks us.[5]

It is important to note that this is not a matter simply of high theory, but what also regularly gets *taught* as theory. In the entry on 'subjectivity' in *Communication, Cultural and Media Studies: the key concepts,* Hartley refers readers to Stuart Hall's argument that there have been five 'decentring shifts' in the concept of identity since the Enlightenment that have informed our contemporary understanding of 'the subject' (2002, 222). One of these, he writes, is that Marxist theory undermines the notion that there is 'a universal essence to mankind' by arguing instead that individuals are 'products of social relations'; another is the idea that Saussurian semiotics and structuralism shows that 'we cannot know ourselves outside of language, that it *constitutes* our reality – in a sense, language speaks us' (ibid., emphasis in original). Along a similar line – and also in a textbook – Chris Barker argues that his earlier metaphor of 'language as a tool' should 'not be read as implying the rational intentionality of a pre-existent subject'. Why not? 'Language speaks us as much as we speak language… [D]iscussion of agency is consistently marred by the assumption that it consists in the premeditated acts of rational beings…' (2002, 94).[6]

---

[5]For instance, in a series of lectures he gave in the 1950s, Heidegger says, 'We do not just speak language, we speak *out of it.* We can do this only by having always-already listened to language. What do we hear there? We hear the speaking of language [*das Sprechen der Sprache*]' (1990, 254. *cf.*: Heidegger 1971, 193; 1982, 124). To this – in his magnum opus – Hans-Georg Gadamer adds very little: 'It would be more accurate to say that a language speaks (*die Sprache spricht*) us than to say that we speak a language' (1986, 467). In political theory, we could mention Louis Althusser's concept of ideology as being made by discursively 'constituting' or 'interpellating' (*interpelle*) individuals as subjects (1971) – or Ernesto Laclau and Chantelle Mouffe's reconceptualization of hegemony as entailing a sidelining of the power of economic and social factors, in the sense that ideology has no home in a particular class. History, therefore, has no principal agents of social change; rather hegemonic and counter-hegemonic blocs arise and pass away through the temporary alignment of discursively constituted subjects (1985).

[6]Obviously, there are other, alternate, accounts. Sociologist Anthony Giddens has produced a theory of agency in the form of what he calls 'structuration theory' (1984). He contends that social systems shape individuals that are external to those individuals, although these structures also admit degrees of freedom within which actions can eventuate and partially re-shape and partially reproduce the social systems within which they initially occur. (He is still unlikely, however, to ever sell out Wembley.) Another, alternate tradition here is that developed out of the work of Talcott Parsons, an admittedly marginal school of thought often called 'action theory' (1968).

Language speaking us is an exciting proposition because of the inversion of agency involved. Interestingly enough, a parallel tendency has also been operative in the sciences as well as in the scientifically servile branches of modern analytic philosophy.[7] In philosophy of mind, for instance, eliminative materialists have done their best to attack 'folk psychology', a mildly condescending name for the supposedly radical idea that people act with beliefs and intentions, and that those beliefs and intentions are integral to explaining those actions.[8] Paul Churchland sees that folk psychology constitutes a provisional *theory* for the explanation of behaviour, and – as a theory – is therefore replaceable. Although we might think we're explaining our getting up and getting more pepper because we really like pepper and desire more of it, the theoretical term employed ('want') has no real basis, and the ontology on which it is predicated is roughly in the same category as phlogiston, caloric fluid, ether, or 'vital spirit'. Churchland argues that folk psychology employs these mentalistic terms to explain human behaviour by recourse to an 'attitude' about mental states that will undoubtedly be eliminated in any mature science (1989, 1–22). He puts the matter this way: 'Eliminative materialism is the thesis that our commonsense conception of psychological phenomena constitutes a radically false theory, a theory so fundamentally defective that both the principles and the ontology of that theory will eventually be displaced, rather than smoothly reduced, by completed neuroscience' (1).

The interesting point is that modern theory in both the natural and human sciences does not, at this point, suddenly *drop* the language of agency. Rather, the tendency here is for non-intentional agents to become anthropomorphized; they receive intentional properties. So, 'literary culture asks us to disjoin political deliberation from...' (Rorty 2007, 102); 'History wants us to believe...' (Zinn & Arnove 2004, 463); 'civil society forces us...' (Cashmore 2010, 9); 'market society makes us...' (Spies-Butcher et al. 2012, 32), 'Culture forces us to...' (Hegeman 2012, 17). That erstwhile Oxford

---

[7]It is often with the work of John Locke that philosophy turns towards becoming, in Locke's words, a 'handmaiden to science' (Richardson 2007, vii).

[8]Philosophy of mind is that area of philosophy that deals with the metaphysical status and function of the mind, and – very often – the relation between mind and body (that is, the so-called 'mind-body problem'). Eliminative materialism is a thesis about the mind-body problem. It combines a metaphysical thesis (materialism: the assertion that mind and body are entirely material) with one concerning meaning: that the sense of terms like 'pain' or 'desire' are not derived from *experiences* but rather their place in a common sense (i.e. 'folk') *theory* used to explain what we see in others' behaviour.

zoologist and professional debunker Richard Dawkins explains that behind human life is DNA. And what is DNA with respect to human life? 'DNA neither cares nor knows. DNA just is. And we dance to its music' (Dawkins 2000, 133). Perhaps; but it pays to recall that this same public intellectual burst on to the scene with a book entitled *The Selfish Gene* (2006). Are genes both radically non-partisan and unknowing, *as well as* selfish? It is difficult to reconcile ourselves to a theory when it seems that the theory is finding it difficult to reconcile itself with itself.

If it *is* the case, pace Melley, that conspiracy theory is in some ways a response to 'agency panic' – originating in 'a sense of *diminished human agency*, a feeling that individuals cannot effect meaningful social action and, in extreme cases, may not be able to control their own behavior' (2000, 11, emphasis in original) – then we might want to entertain two further possibilities: that the theory which we (theorists) usually employ to explain the world of the conspiracy theorist may *also* induce agency panic; or, that those self-same theories are themselves further symptoms of it. As enjoyable as it may be to sit at our desks and contemplate the extent to which we are merely DNA dancing and language speaking itself, it is worth noting that denying our agency while attributing it to the world outside us has also gone under other names through history. One of these is 'paranoia'.

The paranoid style in contemporary theory

At least since Hofstadter's widely cited essay on American politics (1964), it has been common to read conspiracy in terms of the 'paranoid style'. As an analytic trope, characterizations of the 'paranoid style' vary from the specification of an epistemic or cognitive orientation all the way to a thinly veiled (yet outright) pathologization of people holding particular ideas. Let us backtrack somewhat. According to the DSM-IV, paranoia and paranoid delusions characterize a wide range of psychiatric conditions, including certain kinds of personality disorder and schizophrenia. But, as Freud was at pains to point out, there is also a certain *psychopathology of everyday life*. What separates the normal and the pathological is often a matter of degree or intensity rather than type. The DSM-IV itself includes in its ambit a startling array of maladies and symptoms of everyday psychopathology, ranging from coffee-induced anxiety (305.90 and 292.89) to shyness (299.80), jet lag (307.45), and – perhaps worst of all – *bad writing* (315.2).[9] One way of interpreting the DSM-IV's hodgepodge of behaviours (and misbehaviours) is that it stands as perhaps the ultimate *reductio ad absurdum* of the medicalization of all human oddities, a kind of radical democratization of insanity where everyone could potentially locate and even name their own affliction. (Which, of course, also entails that we might all one day be *cured*, given the limitless ingenuity of applied chemistry.) Or perhaps, more charitably – to construe this as a zero-sum game – we could see in this encyclopaedic survey of psychic pain some indication that much of what we call mental illness is simply quotidian suffering *in extremis*.

In a late work, Freud himself offers an indication of this in a surprising summation of the types of psychopathology: 'It might be maintained that a case of hysteria is a caricature of a work of art, that an obsessional neurosis is a caricature of a religion and that a paranoid delusion is a caricature of a philosophical system' (1985, 130). We needn't become sidetracked by the bloated theoretical framework Freud enlists in the service of his explanatory ambition. Regardless of the cogency of his general account of the origin of psychopathology – and we have decent reasons to doubt it – there is a plausible and suggestive indication here (and elsewhere) in his work of paranoia as not simply an 'illness', but a *cognitive style*. As such, Freud characterizes paranoia as a *functional* psychosis, one typified by delusions, but without the kind of intellectual deterioration evident in other psychoses like schizophrenia.[10] Paranoia, like obsessional behaviour, exists as both a symptom and a solution to that symptom. In *Totem and Taboo*, he writes,

> There is an intellectual function in us which demands unity, connection and intelligibility from any material, whether of perception or thought, that comes within its grasp; and if, as a result of special circumstances, it

---

[9]References here are to the *Diagnostic and Statistical Manual of Mental Disorders, Fourth Edition*.

[10]Freud's charitability with respect to intellectually functional paranoia might well relate to the fact that he displays symptoms of this condition himself. In a strange series of observations at the conclusion of his study of the German judge Daniel Schreber, Freud notes that, since he neither fears the criticism of others nor shrinks from criticizing himself, he possesses no motive for avoiding mentioning something which may work to damage the perception of his theory in the eyes of readers: the ostensible similarities between the 'details of Schreber's delusional structure' and *Freud's own theory of paranoia* (1958, 78). Freud is even worried people might think that his theory was actually *taken* from Schreber's in a way closer to plagiarism than case study. His defence to such an odd accusation? 'I can ... call a friend and fellow-specialist to witness that I had developed my theory of paranoia before I became acquainted with contents of Schreber's book' (79).

is unable to establish a true connection, it does not hesitate to fabricate a false one. Systems constructed in this way are known to us not only from dreams, but also from phobias, from obsessive thinking and from delusions. The construction of systems is seen most strikingly in delusional disorders (in paranoia), where it dominates the symptomatic picture. (1985, 154)

Paranoia imposes a harsh hermeneutic, a monomaniacal regime of situating all events – however seemingly disparate – into an intricate speculative system which is at once hyperbolically sceptical and (because of the rigors and ambit of the theory) surpassingly credulous. Here we can see why people have made use of the typology of paranoia to interpret conspiracy theory: the conspiratorial mindset is beholden to the idea that all facts are meaningful, that nothing cannot be incorporated into the interpretative scheme. But this is also, of course, one of the principal commitments of certain kinds of *philosophizing*. Georg W. F. Hegel perhaps captured this spirit best: 'The only thought which philosophy brings with it, in regard to history, is the simple thought of Reason – the thought that Reason rules the world, and that world history has therefore been rational in its course' (1988, 12). (In case it wasn't obvious, there's not much room in Hegel's scheme for 'shit happens'.) The habits of mind which allow for us to countenance the facticity of conspiracies also present snares for thought; like all else in human cognition, theoretical detachment is perpetually susceptible to the affective pulses of fear and fantasy. In some senses – as Jacques Lacan long ago pointed out – the theoretical ego itself is always engaged in a knowing which is structurally or formally equivalent to what he calls *la connaissance paranoïaque*: paranoid knowledge.[11] The mind surveys the seemingly incidental and tries to tie it all together; the theoretical task involves a variation on what surrealist Salvador Dali called 'the paranoiac-critical method' – an attempt to unite the unrelated, to entertain connections between phenomena that, as first inspection, have *nothing* in common.[12]

In the previous chapter we noted Keeley's contention that, as a conspiracy matures, criticisms of it – far from destabilizing it – tend towards increasing its explanatory ambit, evidence that the theory

---

[11]Lacan doesn't provide any particular analysis of this idea in a single essay, although the conception itself appears repeatedly in his writings. See, for instance, Lacan (1948, 17; 1981, 232–3; 1988, 163; and 1993, 39).

[12]Steve Fuller makes a similar argument about the intellectual task: that paranoia is simply the intellectual mind *in extremis* – a pathological form of abstraction. See Fuller (2005, 18–37, esp. 18–20).

has now even more theoretical traction, given, in part, the resistance it provokes (1999, 122). One might justifiably dub this reaction as 'paranoid' – yet, if it is, this paranoia is not merely a feature of conspiracy theory. Thinkers in the humanities and the sciences have often tied the truth of a theory to the psychic resistance it ostensibly invokes (Fleming & Goodall 2002, 260). Carl Jung famously questioned some of Freud's contentions about Oedipal dynamics being at the heart of psychological investments. Freud's response? That Jung's criticism not only was unjustified, but actually functioned to strengthen Freud's hypotheses: Jung *himself*, as an intellectual son, had a 'negative father complex', and was thus driven to question the master (Mattoon 2005, 103). How could there be a better proof of Freud's theory?

Theory and paranoia both require transcending the obvious and the concrete; they require transcending the obvious insofar as they demand that interpretation move beyond the merely present and they require moving beyond the concrete insofar as they demand an integration of facts into an explanatory scheme. That a rose isn't a rose – or a windmill isn't a windmill – isn't, of course, merely a habit of mind of Don Quixote. It's also a key tenet of what we call 'theory'. If Don Quixote has a theoretical home, it's 'semiotics'. Melley also points to the way in which psychoanalysis and paranoia depend upon an appeal to the category of the real, the ' "really operative factor," foundation, or causal agent for certain events' (2000, 17). It is this aspect, he contends, that has given rise to the fictional representation of paranoia and conspiracy during a period which is

> marked by skepticism about unmediated access to reality. Because diagnoses of paranoia depend upon a strong concept of reality – a conviction that the patient's claims do not correspond to events transpiring in a measurable reality – the postmodern tendency to put 'the real' in quotation marks has undermined the pathologization of paranoia. As a result, if what is real seems more and more to be a construct, and if the procedures for pathologizing insane interpretations seem increasingly indistinguishable from the procedures of the insane, then paranoia (or 'paranoia') becomes an obvious vehicle for writers to use in illustrating the politics of interpretation, normalization, and knowledge production. (17–18)

But it needs to be pointed out that paranoia in contemporary theory isn't restricted merely simply to explanatory ambition or indicative of a particular mood. In *Simulacra and Simulation*, perhaps his most influential work, Baudrillard's thesis is that what we think of as the 'Watergate scandal' is a site of 'simulation' (the 'third order of simulacra'), where people mistakenly read in a false distinction between truth and falsehood (2006). The error, for Baudrillard, is to believe that Watergate stands as a revelation of a cover-up, of evil uncovered and justice exacted. It is therefore, in this respect at least, an illusion. For Baudrillard, it doesn't *reveal* a conspiracy, but through the mask of revelation, hides conspiracy's relentlessness: '*Watergate is not a scandal*: this is what must be said at all cost, for this is what everyone is concerned to conceal' (2006, 15, emphasis in original). So how do we deal with the conspiracy that was Watergate? By assuming that it wasn't some fundamental rupture, but simply a case of 'business as usual'. To be scandalized by it is *naïve*, as it assumes that conspiratorial corruption is the exception rather than the rule.

Reading Baudrillard's essays on simulation, one is reminded of Eve Kosofsky Sedgwick's point that paranoia is an attempt to avoid 'bad surprises'. This, for Sedgwick, is what links what she calls 'epistemophilia' and scepticism. As an illustration, she supplies a brief and suggestive reading of Judith Butler's *Gender Trouble*, and Butler's 'scouringly thorough' demonstrations that there could be no possible prior moment to gender difference – that the bad news comes before any nostalgia for it having been different could arrive (2003, 130–1). We can see the same logic in operation in Baudrillard, a vigilance with respect to bad news, that we know that the conspiracies are happening in advance, that no revelation need be entertained, that the uncovering has always already arrived – that any remaining feeling of being scandalized functions simply to mislead us that this isn't the normal working of things. This is not to say that a paranoid position, as an epistemic stance, cannot be a fruitful means by which inquiry can proceed; there are elements of paranoid thinking and investigation which are certainly conducive to academic inquiry. Even so, Sedgwick wonders how it came to be that paranoia – once a focus of critique, a phenomenon that was seen to lie behind things such as homophobia – has now become a method *of* critique (126), always perched somewhere between a form of knowledge/method of inquiry, and a something already known ('bad times are here, and always were, so don't be shocked'). Paralleling what Sedgwick sees in the humanities has undoubtedly been a valorization of paranoia in many post-war writers as representing a form of intelligence, a productive kind of suspicion, rather than a pathological mental state. Pynchon's characters in *Gravity's Rainbow*, for example, often opt for forms of 'operational' or 'creative' paranoia as a means by which social or political control can be resisted (Melley 2000, 18). But is it really about resistance or – as we've argued elsewhere – more to do with comprehension?

Conclusion

Perhaps one of the things conspiracy theories might tend to point to is that we – as a society, including the 'writing classes' (that is, academics, journalists, and so on) – have become disoriented about just what is happening in the world, what is causing it, and who – if anyone – is to *blame*. This is not a matter of the particulars of any situation – about our capacity to assign the right proper names to the right documents in respect of the correct place names, and using the most accurate dates. It concerns, rather, our whole sense of what it means to say that *something* brings *something else* about, that society is in state *x*, because of cause *y*. Stating the matter simply like this, however, is likely to confuse. One of the intellectual legacies of the Enlightenment – although its basis stretches much further back than the seventeenth and eighteenth centuries – was a slow displacement of a certain idea of causation. An ostensibly 'scientific' model of causation – as opposed to a 'magical' one – is one that prefers, by and large, a conception of material over personal causation. For instance, the modern mind works towards believing that the causes of a plague or a famine are natural, rather than being the products of the malevolent intentions of witches or Jews.

The Enlightenment mentality sought to limit the idea of personal causation – that is, the idea that to explain an event we need recourse to ideas like 'belief' and 'intention' – to the realm of the social. This is not simply an epistemological issue of a division of labour; it has deep sociopolitical implications. That natural events are not subject to corrective intervention at the level of social relations means that people are no longer so easily thrown upon pyres for causing tornados. It took many generations for us to change long-held beliefs about these matters; however, this model has mutated in the last fifty years or so (a mutation that is rarely commented upon). Here we see a radical transformation in our ideas of causation that tend to overthrow the above Enlightenment ideal without reverting to a pre-modern conception.

We have seen, on the one hand, that the idea of personal causation – once the domain of the social – has now deserted this domain. Explaining social change in such terms is now commonly thought to be the heights of *naiveté* – either the expression of a regressive kind of Thatcherism or some other kind of individualism that fails to see that 'the subject' is not the *basis* of social change but the *consequence* of it. As discussed previously in this chapter, if we have learned nothing else from contemporary social theorists, it is this. (Let us return to Durkheim's thoughts on 'social facts': 'Here, then, is a category of facts which have very special characteristics: they consist of manners of acting, thinking and feeling – external to the individual – which are imbued with a coercive power by virtue of which they exercise control over him' (1919, 8).[13])

On the other hand, the idea of material causation – the domain of 'nature' – seems to be coming *back* into human hands. The very idea of the adjective in the phrase 'natural disasters' is under question; nature appears to be returning to the remit of human control. As Pascal Bruckner has put it, somewhat more radically, there *are* no longer any natural disasters (2013, 77). Humans, it seems, are the creators and not the mere victims of 'extreme weather': floods, droughts, heat waves, and epidemics. We are, in language taken from books by two influential Australian environmentalists, 'earthmasters' and 'weather makers'.[14] In *The Observer*, James Hansen – director of NASA's Goddard Institute for Space Studies – writes that the 'trains carrying coal to power plants are death trains. Coal-fired power plants are factories of death' (2009). The appropriation of the language of the Holocaust here may be hyperbolic, but it captures a more general point – and mood. The displacement of the language of genocide on to climatology is oddly symmetrical to an opposite trend that has become an orthodoxy in the social sciences. What seems apparent is that the social sciences have abandoned personal causation in favour of a species of efficient causation (the label 'cultural materialism' makes explicit the general ontology here), while – at the same time –segments of the natural sciences have progressively reframed domains once considered exclusively in terms of material (or 'event-event') causation, so that certain phenomena can now be explained in terms of human intervention. Is it any wonder, as

---

[13]If the sciences were going to account for 'nature', then the social sciences were going to account for 'nurture'. More greedily, they might even argue that the very idea of nature was itself the product of nurture, in a way that sociobiologists such as Edward O. Wilson have argued that nurture can still be incorporated within a naturalistic explanation. But what nature and nurture as explanations both have in common is the elimination of the first-person standpoint; social and natural sciences have thought themselves to be adequate to the extent to which they've been able to eliminate subjectivity through eliminating the subject. The stronger one makes the epistemological status of social theory, the weaker the agent becomes in the shadow of that explanatory model. Much the same can be said of neurology and evolutionary psychology. These explanatory models not only pit themselves against certain disciplines and social institutions – like law, for instance, which relies on ideas of culpability – but vast numbers of people in society, for whom ideas of individual responsibility still play an enormous role.

[14]We refer here to *Earthmasters – Playing God with the Climate* by Clive Hamilton (2013), and *The Weather Makers: How Man Is Changing the Climate and What It Means for Life on Earth* by Tim Flannery (2005).

we discussed in the previous chapter, that conspiracy rhetoric has become central to environmental debate – that area where our conceptions of agency are most in doubt?

Our intention, in all this, is not to try to resolve the so-called 'structure versus agency' debate in the social sciences but to point to the ways in which conspiracy theory, as well as its most strident opponents, might be considered to reflect different epistemological commitments, and the confusions which grow out of the explanatory disorientations unique to the era in which we live. Conspiracy theorists are indeed standing up for a tradition now somewhat fallow in current trends in social and cultural analysis: the idea that behind events are people.

CONCLUSION: WHERE TO NOW?

The reader will likely have noticed that there are relatively few words left in this book. We don't have much space to sort out a panoply of key issues: What is the moral of the story? Whose side are we on? Is there a winner? A prescription? A preventative? And who will be staying late after school? While we may struggle to provide definitive answers to all (or even *any*) of the above, hopefully we *have* established that conspiracy theory – and the shapes it takes – can be seen, ultimately, as offering valuable insights into the dynamics of contemporary culture, as well as our struggles to comprehend it. What's more, the way we talk about these subjects is equally diagnostic. While we are not presumptuous enough to think the current contribution to the discussion represents anything like a new high watermark for the debate – or the debate about culture generally – we hope, at least, that the manifold errors and short-sightedness contained herein are at least worth correcting. Not that we want to seem falsely modest, or pathologically pessimistic, or *paranoid* or anything … (please tell us that isn't what you're all whispering about).

Anyway. Over the course of this book we have attempted to make a number of modest, interrelated points about conspiracy that, to the best of our knowledge, have not previously been made – or at least have not previously been made at volumes loud enough to be heard above the tinnitus-inducing din of those cases being prosecuted by the conspiracy theorists and the conspiracy theory debunkers. (While the etymology of the word 'conspire' might involve quiet, communal breathing, we have seen that contemporary conversations about the topic are often marked by deafening shouts and bitter dissent.) In short, our contentions are: that the role and influence of debunkers has been under-discussed and under-theorized in considerations of conspiracy discourse; that conspiracism did not emerge fully formed and without precedent in the twentieth century but has epistemological antecedents dating back at least to the Enlightenment; that – despite the outlandishness of much of the propositional content of conspiracy theories – there exists a reasonableness, even a *rightness* to some aspects of conspiracists' modes of reasoning; and that paranoia, suspicion of mediated information, agency panic, and so on, are evident in the cognitive styles of not only those lower case conspiracists but also some capital 'T' theorists.

We will now recap the story so far on the off-chance readers have had their memories reduced to synapse-less porridge because of either: (a) Illuminati brain suckers from outer space; or (b) irrational, reason-crushing conspiracy theories *about* Illuminati brain suckers from outer space. After that, we will move on to the obvious question of What (If Anything) Should We Do Next? – unless, of course, the alarmist conspiracists and the doom prophet debunkers are right and it's all too, too late (in which case, perhaps the last conscious and fully volitional subject in possession of a modicum of alien- and structuralism-proof agency could turn off the lights).

Conspiracies, as we have seen, are very different from conspiracy *theories* in that the former are often the result of relatively banal decisions enacted at the local level – albeit within ethically questionable political cultures – rather than the result of grand schemes and plotting. Thus while conspiracies can be defined as powerful secrets, conspiracy theories require Powerful Secrets Forte involving multiple alleged conspiracies, ever grander accusations of intra- and interplanetary domination, and the sorts of visionary, all-encompassing expressions of organized evil that leave the political corruption of Watergate looking like careless playground fibbing. Tempting as it is to engage in an extended debunking of conspiracy theories, all we will say on this point is that there may well be a positive correlation between the truth of any given conspiracy theory and the banality of its alleged dimensions. This is because – time and again – we humans reveal ourselves to be vastly superior at *finding things out* than *keeping things secret*. The critical issues here, however, do not merely concern the correction of errors so citizens' truth ledgers could somehow be balanced. If that were the case, none of this would matter nearly so much.

In much popular and scholarly literature, the aforementioned dimensions of the field – conspiracies and conspiracy theories – are routinely framed as its *only* two dimensions. The former are customarily characterized as actual events which exist and which should, at least in the first instance, be taken seriously in terms of their sociopolitical ramifications. The latter, meanwhile, are mostly presented as irrational and dangerous ideas about phenomena which do *not* exist and which should therefore be treated and/or eradicated, perhaps via some form of Sunstein and Vermeule-style infiltration and/or Kay and Pipes-inspired intellectual purification.

A complicating problem is that much of the aforementioned literature implies that debunkers – especially scholarly debunkers – are not located *within* the field of conspiracy discourse but are instead positioned outside and perhaps just a little bit *above* it, safely ensconced in the intellective equivalent of a National Football League luxury box (or, perhaps more fittingly, a hovering Martian spy mothership). Our case, in contrast, is that debunking *is* an integral part of conspiracy discourse, and that acknowledging and analysing its influence is essential if we are to adequately assay the nature and force of contemporary conspiracy discourse *in toto*. Broader issues relating to scholarship's positioning of itself (and lack of positioning of itself) in relation to its objects of analyses are also at stake. Given that academics are customarily part of the debunking crowd, the risk here is that we are failing to recognize – and subsequently conceptualize our conspiracy discourse *as* discourse. This is not the only context in which we, as cultural inquisitors, may be tempted to consider ourselves above the fray, as external observers rather than participants in the processes about which we theorize (see Jane 2014, esp. 97). Yet conspiracy culture arguably demands a particularly high degree of reflexivity from scholarly analysts given the role of debunking discourse in the dynamics of mimetic antagonism discussed in Chapter 4. Like Moliere's Philosophy Master, our claims to impartial observation status are unlikely to wash if we make them between punches swung at conspiracist running dogs and reprobates.

We have also witnessed the way that much commentary tends to suggest – explicitly or implicitly – that what we have come to call conspiracy theories are new. To this contention we have offered an undramatic hedge: 'in some ways.' If they are new, conspiracy theories as we've come to know them are only new in the way the new model Toyota sedan is 'new': it is new by recent assemblage and certain kinds of refinement. Parts of the car aren't new whatsoever: the car company did not just invent the wheel; neither did it just devise automatic gears nor a combustion engine. The advertising shouldn't blind us to the fact that certain continuities abide, and that certain quite ancient phases of human technological development push up against more contemporary innovations. The parallels with conspiracy theory are apposite. Seeing conspiracy theory as irreducibly contemporary will oblige us to miss the signal conspiratorial moments in modern thought. To comprehend the object under analysis, therefore, not only necessitates a consideration of its contemporary varieties, but the way in which its key features carry signal moments, feelings, and aspirations of modern thought.

(This, of course, is not to deny that many aspects of conspiracy theories and thinking *are* novel in their historical particulars. To state the obvious, claims of a moon landing hoax, for instance, would undoubtedly have had far less traction if they had been made prior to the development of the science that made a real moon landing possible.)

Conspiracists are not Toyota sedans, but – like new car models – their approach to knowledge-seeking and knowledge-formation often evinces odd combinations of the old and the new. We have seen, for instance, the way that modern conspiracy theorizing gets part of its energy from anxiety relating to humanity's increasing technological prowess; this occurring at the same time that specialist knowledge is expanding at increasing rates and so further alienating individuals from a comprehension of that world over which human beings paradoxically exert ever more power. In her preface to *The Origins of Totalitarianism*, Hannah Arendt pinpoints this key modern predicament when she writes of the 'irritating incompatibility between the actual power of modern man (greater than ever before, great to the point where he might challenge the very existence of his own universe) and the impotence of modern men to live in, and understand the sense of, a world which their own strength has established' (1968, viii).

In short, contemporary life is technologically esoteric and maddeningly complex – and is getting more so. Many important things happen beyond the immediacy of our personal experience and/or comprehension, and therefore require explanation by powerful third parties. Yet the intellectual legacy of Enlightenment – the scepticism, subjectivism, and autocritique that continue to exert such a strong influence on contemporary sense-making – tells us that information mediated by authority figures cannot be trusted and that we must therefore explain the world via other means. Enter the alien Elvises, the imposter Obamas, the Roswell posterior probes, and all those other impossible things.

Far from representing a rupture from rationalism, therefore, we can see that conspiracy thinking is actually embarrassingly consistent with many ideals of the intellectual tradition that supposedly requires *saving* from conspiracy thinking. This problematizes the common tendency to dismiss conspiracists as stupid, irresponsible, insane, and so on, and forms the basis of our claim that there exists a certain *reasonableness* to conspiracy thinking which is commonly overlooked in the literature. Again, this reasonableness does not refer to the type of arguments made or conclusions drawn by conspiracists. Instead it relates to the understandable human appeal of conspiracies given the irreconcilable tensions between the material realities of twenty-first-century existence, and the intellectual tradition shaping our attempts to make sense of it.

Moreover, we can see that conspiracy theory *always potentially* serves a productive truth-seeking role in both epistemological and sociocultural senses. It is also true that much of what appears in and alongside conspiracy theory is perceptive cultural and social critique. What conspiracy theory offers is not so much – as some cultural studies theorists might suggest – new possibilities for resistance; but new capacities to understand and act at all. It is an attempt at social theorizing, sophisticated in its own way, which not only employs the techniques of the Enlightenment, but offers one solution to the problem of agency. Conspiracy theories are, to twist the words of the eliminative materialist, 'folk sociology'. Contrarily, the basis of explanation of much social theory and science would have us to accept not so much that 'there is no conspiracy', but 'there are no conspirators'.

This goes some way for accounting for the resistance – and the shrieking prophesy – that conspiracism encounters in scholarship. After all, the academy is one of the main sites that 'official' and 'authorised' knowledge is produced, even if those of us in it are loathe to think of ourselves as part of a hegemonic establishment. As discussed in Chapter 4, it is common for debunkers to construct the contemporary glut of conspiracy theories in apocalyptic terms, via warnings that the situation is bad, is getting much worse, and will soon reach a point of no return. While we do not endorse the alarmism that so often accompanies denunciations of conspiracism, neither do we think the excesses of conspiracy theorizing are socially, politically, or intellectually innocuous.

As reasonable as it may be to entertain doubts about powerful people and institutions, the epistemological promise of the conspiracist cognitive style is rarely realized. Instead, one unhelpful extreme is exchanged for another; supposedly simple-minded acceptance of *all* official stories is rejected in favour of the conspiracists' one-eyed belief in *none* of them. Thus, despite strongly avowed distinctions, the cognitive style of 'sheeple' and the cognitive style of conspiracists are similarly rigid in their *a priori* orientation and rubric-approach to reasoning. (If the only option is to believe either *all* of what we're told, or *nothing* of what we're told, our only act of intellectual independence lies in choosing either the former mode or the latter; after that, there can be no further deliberation, as our 'for' or 'against' alignment determines all conclusions in advance.)

Enter the debunkers, those rational, clear-thinking arbiters of all things truthful; whose diagnoses of conspiracism as the most malignant of intellectual ailments has the added advantage of framing their ability to concoct cures as nothing short of society-saving. Yet – while the contours of their prognoses of looming catastrophes vary, we have witnessed marked parallels between the alarmist – at times hysterical – rhetoric of conspiracists and that deployed by debunkers. Conspiracy theorists and their antagonists share a range of features, but few as starkly recognizable as their capacity to trade apocalypses – visions of a bad world gone mad and sliding irrevocably towards Armageddon. As such, what we can see here is a conspiracy version of what is known as 'the horseshoe theory' in political science, in that conspiracists and debunkers are best figured as lying not at opposing ends of a linear continuum, but at each end of a horseshoe. Like the far political Left and the far political Right, conspiracists and debunkers more closely resemble each other than those groups and ideas positioned in the lumpy centre.

This also helps explain why much of the conspiracy 'debate' works contrary to its ostensible aims. As temperatures rise around a particular issue, antagonists are not only prone to become more and more insulated from each other, only peeping over the barricades to take a quick look at the enemy – but this isolation tends to hide another crucial fact: that warring parties begin more and more to resemble each other. It has become a somewhat tired point, but no less true for being so, that current media forms allow adherents to particular ideologies to spend their whole intellectual lives encountering only versions of themselves or caricatures of their enemies. It isn't for nothing that critics have called Dawkins the high priest of atheism. One would say that this feature tends to make intellectual exchange into a kind of mimetic sport – except at least in sport, rivals actually encounter each other.

At this juncture, it is tempting to admit defeat. Conspiracists are not just immune to – but *thrive* on – counterargument, while any attempt to *debunk the debunkers* risks a conflagration of yet more mimetic fury (not to mention charges of hypocrisy). Furthermore, casting conspiracy discourse as a 'problem' which requires 'solving' risks precisely the sort of simplistic and un-reflexive thinking under critique. We will, however, press on and offer the following three 'remedies' for consideration. This is partly in acknowledgement that passing judgement is often far easier than the heavy lifting involved in proposing new and potentially improved ways of doing business. But it is also in reflection of our belief that *how* we think is more important than *what* we think, and that thinking about thinking is a worthy exercise for wider audiences (at the very least, it is far too pressing a project to be left to academics).

Remedy I: Applied epistemology

This book – helped out by all of recorded history – has shown us that, at various times, 'official' agents have failed us miserably and do not deserve our unreserved trust. We can all supply our own list of examples, from grand, transnational examples of military scheming recounted in the standard textbooks, through to the most banal kinds of embezzlements and travel rorts carried out by local politicians. The conspiracist intervention acknowledges this, begins with this as a given, and offers a form of DIY inquiry and discovery in which knowledge returns to – or at least *feels* as if it has returned to – the individual subject: what they themselves see, believe, and conclude based on their own approach to reasoning. This potentially empowering autodidacticism, however, carries risks. Like the members of a subculture who profess individualism while all dressing alike, the conspiracist may see themselves as a maverick truth-seeker but actually be engaged in an *en masse* trend. To be part of an *ad hoc* movement opposed to all variety of 'official accounts' is still to be part of a movement, however construed. Further, what this movement tends to ignore is the fact that the self-conception of 'direct' inquiry is *still* predicated on various forms of mediation – but mediation that is not acknowledged. Coady, for instance, argues that

> much of the epistemology we inherited from both the empiricist and rationalist traditions was overly individualistic. The paradigm of knowledge and justification in the empiricist tradition is an individual's perceptual encounter with an object of enquiry; in the rationalist tradition it is an individual's own powers of reasoning. Both traditions downplay the extent to which we are dependent on others, especially experts or those we judge to be experts, for many of the things we believe and many of the things we claim to know. (2012, 27–28)

He argues, therefore, for the development of a turn in 'applied epistemology' as per the 'applied turn in ethics'; this is in recognition of the way the 'information revolution and the knowledge economy have radically changed the way that we acquire knowledge and justify our beliefs' (2012, 2).

What conspiracists believe to be 'research' – indeed what *most* of us believe constitutes research – does need to be rethought given the contemporary media environment. As Boaz Miller and Isaac Record argue, given that we increasingly form beliefs on the basis of the results of Internet search engines, we need to reconceive what constitutes warrant in the formation of our beliefs. Search engines are automatically filtered, and their modes of operation concealed from users. Standard theories of justification simply don't deal with this. Miller and Record argue – persuasively – for a different kind of epistemic responsibility that obliges researchers to become knowledgeable about how filtering works. They also recommend triangulating Internet findings with other sources (2013). We agree that we need an epistemology suited for an age of (too much) information – to mediate mediation in a way. Regardless of what you think of it in principle, doubting and/or shunning all mediated knowledge is an impractical way to live. After all, if we commit ourselves to only accepting facts ascertained by first-hand inquiry, we could well devote the rest of our lives to trying to determine what time it is (or, by then, *was*).

Remedy II: Anti-dialectics (horsing around)

Rather than dignifying conspiracy theories with the response of rational argumentation, a more common – and sometimes more effective – rebuttal may involve humour. Jon Stewart of *The Daily Show* and Stephen Colbert of *The Colbert Report* devote considerable airtime to ridiculing conspiracy theories. In 2012, for example, Colbert lampooned conspiracy theories swirling around the Fast and Furious operation – a botched US government sting run from 2006 in which weapons sold to Mexican drug cartels did not lead to high-level arrests, but were found at violent crime scenes on both sides of the US-Mexican border. After a number of right-wing media commentators suggested the operation was an elaborate liberal ploy to flood Mexico with guns so the ensuing carnage could be used as an excuse for gun control in the United States (Limbaugh 2012), Colbert demonstrated his tireless commitment to what he calls 'truthiness' by replying,

> Yes, very clearly, Obama started this gun-tracking program in 2006, when he hypnotised George Bush. Then he secretly ordered Attorney General [Eric] Holder to order the Justice Department, to order the [Bureau of Alcohol, Tobacco, Firearms and Explosives] to order gun shops to sell guns to Mexican drug cartels, and then lose track of them, thereby panicking Americans to gin up support for the draconian gun control measures that Obama has never introduced. Complicated? Yes. The fevered ramblings of a syphilitic brain? Perhaps. But Occam's Razor says 'my answer is right, or I will cut you with a razor'. (2012)

Another example of the use of ironic humour to counter conspiracism is the Glenn Beck Conspiracy Theory Generator which, as previously mentioned, promises 'Fair and Balanced Paranoia, Delivered on Demand'. Two recently generated examples are: 'Liberal jihadists throughout the Democrat party are attempting to stifle all dissent so that they can kill and eat children using a recipe copied straight out of *An Inconvenient Truth*' and 'Climate Nazis are building a secret army to enforce their plan to give federal bailout money to radical Islamic groups, which, as you know, are plotting to blow up megachurches' ('The Glenn Beck Conspiracy Theory Generator').

This use of humour is not simply effective; it is perceptive. The many similar conspiracy generators found on the net are, in essence, structuralist devices: they offer key components of conspiracy theories and make the substitutions undecided but finite. These are either assembled randomly, using natural language generators (*Verified Facts*) or present drop-down menus where one can customize one's conspiracy, specifying domains of operation ('the world today', 'world history', 'American politics'), identifying nouns ('Jewish Illuminati bankers in London', 'really old Nazis', 'space alien lizard people'), adjectives ('crafty', 'sinister', 'evil'), apocalyptic scenarios ('the reign of the antichrist', 'a one world government', 'a corporate state'), and so on ('Conspiracy Theory Generator'). A great deal of intelligence goes into these systems; they are not 'gags' in the simple sense of the term.

Our conclusions are that the dialectical dangers mentioned earlier *may* render humour a better method of 'talking back' to conspiracists. But while the ready mockability of conspiracy theories make rising up in mirth an easy move, further research is required to investigate whether jeers and parodies join rational argument, the presentation of overwhelming counterevidence, and most other responses, in spurring the conspiracist to even greater conviction. We *can* contend, even with some reservations about its ultimate efficacy, however, that one of the advantages of humour is that it avoids the dialectical bind in which engaging with a rival's argument inadvertently legitimates it. Also, it is *not* doubling in that conspiracists rarely if ever use humour.

Remedy III: Praising naiveté

Debunking in various guises – and involving various degrees of intellectual hostility – has been in currency ever since Voltaire's *Candide*. Charles Taylor, for instance, has pointed out the way in which many defenders of the Enlightenment have only denunciation left. To be modern is always to be against something:

> What are the words of power they can pronounce? Plainly these are the passages in which the goods are invoked without being

recognized ... they mainly consist of the polemical passages in which error, superstition, fraud, and religion are denounced. What they are denounced for lacking, or for suppressing, or for destroying expresses what we who attack them are moved by and cherish. This becomes a recognizable feature of the whole class of modern positions which descends from the radical Enlightenment. Because their moral sources are unavowable, they are mainly invoked in polemic. Their principal words of power are denunciatory. (1992, 339)

Commenting on mainline intellectuals in particular, Jean Bethke Elshtain has remarked that 'to be an intellectual, you have to be against it, whatever it is. The intellectual is a negator. Affirmation is not in his or her vocabulary' (2003, 6). There is, behind denunciation, a desire to avoid *naiveté* – a determination to find a prophylactic against being duped. *Naiveté*, though, is perhaps a *good* thing. Perhaps now is a good time – and perhaps it may always be a good time – to inscribe *naiveté* as an epistemological ideal, to admit that we know less than what we think we do, and that we may be more in the dark tomorrow than we were today. Perhaps we should occasionally stop and say to ourselves, 'You know, maybe I have absolutely *no* idea what I'm talking about.' This is a practice likely to benefit both conspiracy theorists – confounded by life's relentless insistence on delivering bad surprises – and scholarly debunkers – confounded by conspiracy theorists' confoundedness and confoundingness.

Thinking it anew(ish)

'Maybe we have absolutely *no* idea what we're talking about', was certainly our view of ourselves when we first started writing this book. In fact it is a self-assessment that has returned – with uncomfortable frequency – at various points throughout the project. We will, however, press on with our concluding thoughts, which include the fact that there is a pedestrian messiness to daily life that is not adequately captured or accounted for in the grand, 'end-of-days' narratives of either conspiracists *or* conspiracy theory debunkers. The bad news flowing from this representational disjunct is that instead of nefarious schemes cooked up by CIA crypto-bombers in cahoots with Zionist space gods, we are left much of the time with the bumper sticker banality of 'shit happens'. But, of course, this is the good news, too – along with the fact that reason, rationality, and many other Enlightenment ideals are not dead but living among us like so many conspiracy Elvises. Like the King in his fried peanut butter sandwich period, however, some of them need work.

One can't 'repudiate' the Enlightenment without utilizing it. As we have seen, the luminaries of the Enlightenment era are responsible for producing more than just a manner of thinking. Thanks to their enormous intellectual labours, they have produced many more things requiring precise *thinking about*. That the Enlightenment emerges as much *a cause of* as *a solution to* the epistemological alienation which is so conducive to the contemporary proliferation of conspiracy theories contains no simplistic lessons. We cannot, for instance, repudiate or repeal the Enlightenment, as though this would be a salve to the paranoid tenor of contemporary culture. As far as philosophical thought goes, the Enlightenment is not so easily banished. We think as much *from* the Enlightenment as *about* it. But this does not relieve us of the burden of thinking it anew. In fact, the necessity of doing so reveals that there is much more than a few epistemological correctives at stake here; it is, ultimately, a question of the demand that the Enlightenment makes on us – and by 'us', it's not a question of 'versus them'. We are, for better or worse, all in this together.

REFERENCES

Aaronovitch, David. 2009. *Voodoo Histories: The Role of the Conspiracy Theory in Shaping Modern History*. London: Jonathan Cape.

"About Michael Pollan." Michael Pollan. "In Defense of Food: An Eater's Manifesto." *Michael Pollan*, http://michaelpollan.com/books/in-defense-of-food/.

———. *Michael Pollan*. http://michaelpollan.com/press-kit/

"'About'. Thrive Debunked." *Thrive Debunked*, http://thrivedebunked. wordpress.com/about/.

Adams, Douglas. 1992. *Mostly Harmless: Volume Five in the Trilogy of Five*. New York: Ballantine Books.

———. 2005. (orig. 1980). *The Restaurant at the End of the Universe*. New York: Ballantine Books.

Althusser, Louis. 1971. *Lenin and Philosophy and Other Essays*. London: New Left Books.

Andress, David. 2006 (orig. 2005). *The Terror: The Merciless War for Freedom in Revolutionary France*. New York: Farrar, Straus and Giroux.

Angell, Marcia. 2005. *The Truth About the Drug Companies*. New York: Random House.

"Apollo 11 Hoax: One in Four People Do Not Believe in Moon Landing". 2009. *The Telegraph*. July 17, http://www.telegraph.co.uk/science/space/5851435/ Apollo-11-hoax-one-in-four-people-do-not-believe-in-moon-landing. html.

Arendt, Hannah. 1968. *The Origins of Totalitarianism*. New York: Harcourt.

Assange, Julian. 2006. *Conspiracy as Governance*. December 3, http://web. archive.org/web/20070129125831/http://iq.org/conspiracies.pdf.

"Atheism and Obesity." *Conservapedia*, http://conservapedia.com/Atheism_ and_obesity.

Bailyn, Bernard. 1992 (orig. 1967). *The Ideological Origins of the American Revolution*. Enlarged Edition. Massachusetts: Harvard University Press.

Bale, Jeffrey M. 1995. "'Conspiracy Theories' and Clandestine Politics" *Lobster: The Journal of Parapolitics* June, http://www.lobster-magazine.co.uk/ articles/l29consp.htm.

Barker, Chris. 2002. *Making Sense of Cultural Studies: Central Problems and Critical Debates*. London: Sage.

Barkun, Michael. 2003. *A Culture of Conspiracy: Apocalyptic Visions in Contemporary America*. Berkeley, Los Angeles, London: University of California Press.

Baudrillard, Jean. 2006 (orig. 1981). *Simulacra and Simulations*, Trans. Sheila Faria Glaser. Michigan: The University of Michigan Press.

Baumeister, Roy F. 2002. "The Holocaust and the Four Roots of Evil". In Leonard S. Newman and Ralph Erber (eds.). *Understanding Genocide: The Social Psychology of the Holocaust*. New York: Oxford University Press. 241–58.

Beckhusen, Robert. 2013. "White House Can't Afford Its Shapeshifting Alien Reptile Guards." *Wired* March 26, http://www.wired.com/dangerroom/2013/03/secret-service-reptile-aliens/.

Berger, Peter. 1967. *The Sacred Canopy: Elements of a Sociological Theory of Religion*. New York: Anchor.

———. 1969. *A Rumor of Angels: Modern Society and the Rediscovery of the Supernatural*. New York: Anchor.

Birchall, Clare. 2006. *Knowledge Goes Pop: From Conspiracy Theory to Gossip*. Oxford and New York: Berg.

Borges, Jorge Luis. 1998. "On Exactitude in Science". In Andrew Hurley (ed.) *Collected Fictions*, Trans. Andrew Hurley. New York: Penguin, 325.

Boykoff, Jules and Maxwell Boykoff 2007. "Journalistic Balance as Global Warming Bias" *Global Envision* February 9, http://www.globalenvision.org/library/1/1458.

Boyvey, Roger. 1964 (September). "Mental Health and the Ultra-Concerned." *Social Service Review* 38 (3): 281–93.

Bray, Karina. 2011. "Peachy Pink." *CHOICE Online* October 24, http://www.abc.net.au/mediawatch/transcripts/1329_choice.png.

Bruckner, Pascal. 2013. *The Fanaticism of the Apocalypse*, Trans. Steven Rendall. Cambridge: Polity.

Bucci, Amy. 2012. "Obama vs. Romney: Who Would Handle an Alien Invasion Better?" *National Geographic NewsWatch* June 28, http://newswatch.nationalgeographic.com/2012/06/28/obama-vs-romney-who-would-handle-an-alien-invasion-better/.

Burroughs, William S. 1993. *The Letters of William S. Burroughs: 1945–1959*, Oliver Harris (ed.). New York: Penguin.

Calvino, Italo. 1998 (orig. 1980). *If on a Winter's Night a Traveller*. London: Vintage.

Campbell, Colin. 2002. "The Cult, the Cultic Milieu and Secularization". In Jeffrey Kaplan and Hélene Lööw (eds.) *The Cultic Milieu: Oppositional Subcultures in an Age of Globalization*. Oxford: AltaMira Press. 12–25.

Carroll, Rory. 2012. "Martin Sheen and Woody Harrelson Set for 9/11 'truther' Film September Morn" *The Guardian* October 18, http://www.guardian.co.uk/film/2012/oct/17/martin-sheen-woody-harrelson-9-11-truther.

Cashmore, Ellis. 2010. *Making Sense of Sports*. 5th ed. New York: Routledge.

Chomsky, Noam. 2007. *What We Say Goes: Conversations on U.S. Power in a Changing World. Interviews with David Barsamian*. New York: Metropolitan Books.

Churchland, Paul. 1989. *A Neurocomputational Perspective: The Nature of Mind and the Structure of Science*. Cambridge: MIT Press.

Coady, David. 2003. "Conspiracy Theories and Official Stories" *International Journal of Applied Philosophy* 17 (2), Spring: 197–209.

———. 2006. "An Introduction to the Philosophical Debate about Conspiracy Theories". In D. Coady (ed.) *Conspiracy Theories: The Philosophical Debate*. Aldershot: Ashgate. 1–12.

———. 2007. "Are Conspiracy Theorists Irrational?" *Episteme* 4(2), June: 193–204.

———. 2008. "The Philosophy of Conspiracy" *The Drum* May 22, http://www.abc.net.au/unleashed/31642.html.

———. 2012. *What To Believe Now:Applying Epistemology to Contemporary Issues*. Malden: Wiley-Blackwell.

Cohen, Andrew. 2013. "What the Scopes Trial Teaches Us About Climate-Change Denial" *The Atlantic* October 1, http://www.theatlantic.com/national/archive/2013/10/what-the-scopes-trial-teaches-us-about-climate-change-denial/280098/.

Cohen, Nick. 2008. "When Academics Lose Their Power of Reason" *Observer* May 4, http://www.guardian.co.uk/theobserver/2008/may/04/highereducation.

Cohen, Stanley. 2002. *Folk Devils and Moral Panics*. 3rd ed. New York: Routledge.

Cohn, Norman. 1996. *Warrant for Genocide: The Myth of the Jewish World Conspiracy and the Protocols of the Elders Of Zion*. London: Serif.

Colbert, Stephen. 2012. *The Colbert Report*. Broadcast in Australia on *The Comedy Channel*, Foxtel, June 21.

"Concise International Chemical Assessment Document 16 – AZODICARBONAMIDE." *IPCS INCHEM Home*, http://www.inchem.org/documents/cicads/cicads/cicad16.htm#PartNumber:2.

"Conspiracy Theory Generator." *Political Research Associates*, http://www.publiceye.org/conspire/generator.html.

"Conspiracy Theory Poll Results." *Public Policy Polling*. April 2, http://www.publicpolicypolling.com/main/2013/04/conspiracy-theory-poll-results-.html.

"Contact Us/We Need Your Help." *The Majestic Documents:Evidence That We Are Not Alone*, http://www.majesticdocuments.com/help.php.

Coward, Barry and Julian Swann (eds). 2004. *Conspiracies and Conspiracy Theory in Early Modern Europe: From the Waldensians to the French Revolution*. Hampshire: Ashgate.

cscadm. 2011. "Common Sense Conspiracy's Inaugural 'Top Five Conspiracy Sites for Bullshit' ". *Common Sense Conspiracy* November 4, http://commonsenseconspiracy.com/2011/11/common-sense-conspiracys-inaugural-top-five-conspiracy-sites-for-bullshit/.

d' Alembert, Jean Le Rond. 1995 (orig. 1751). *Preliminary Discourse to the Encyclopedia of Diderot*, Trans. Richard N. Schwab. London, Chicago: University of Chicago Press.

Dapin, Mark. 2013. "Fighting Fat One Waist at a Time" *The Sydney Morning Herald* June 1, http://www.smh.com.au/national/health/fighting-fat-one-waist-at-a-time-20130531-2nh5m.html.

Dart, Gregory. 2003 (orig. 1999). *Rousseau, Robespierre and English Romanticism*. Cambridge: Cambridge University Press.

Davis, David Brion. (ed.) 1972. *The Fear of Conspiracy: Images of Un-American Subversion from the Revolution to the Present*. Ithaca: Cornell University Press.

Dawkins, Richard. 1995. *River Out of Eden: A Darwinian View of Life*. New York: Basic Books.

———. 2000 (orig. 1998). *Unweaving the Rainbow: Science, Delusion and the Appetite for Wonder*. New York: Mariner Books.

———. 2006 (orig. 1976). *The Selfish Gene*. Oxford: Oxford University Press.

de Botton, Alian. 2009. *The Pleasures and Sorrows of Work*. London: Hamish Hamilton.

Dean, Jodi. 1998. *Aliens in America: Conspiracy Cultures from Outerspace to Cyberspace*. New York: Cornell University Press.

———. 2000. "Theorizing Conspiracy Theory" *Theory & Event* 4 (3) http://muse.jhu.edu/login?auth=0&type=summary&url=/journals/theory_and_event/v004/4.3r_dean.html.

DeLillo, Don. 1989 (orig. 1978). *Running Dog*. New York: Vintage Contemporaries.

———. 1991 (orig. 1998). *Libra*. New York: Penguin.

———. 1999 (orig. 1884). *White Noise*. London: Picador.

Diagnostic and Statistical Manual of Mental Disorders, Fourth Edition. 2000. Washington, DC: American Psychiatric Association.

Dimiero, Ben. 2011. "Beck: 'I'm Not Not Saying' God Is Causing Earthquakes" *Media Matters for America* March 14, http://mediamatters.org/blog/2011/03/14/beck-im-not-not-saying-god-is-causing-earthquak/177530.

"Doomsday Film Festival & Symposium." *doomsdayfilmfest.com*, http://www.doomsdayfilmfest.com.

Doyle, Sir Arthur Conan. 2003 (orig. 1890). "The Sign of the Four". In Kyle Freeman (ed.) *The Complete Sherlock Holmes: Volume 1*. New York: Barnes & Noble Classics.

Durkheim, Émile. 1919. *Les régles de la méthode sociologique*. 2nd ed. Paris: Félix Alcan.

Ellis, John M., Charles L. Geshekter, Peter W. Wood and Stephen H. Balch 2012. "A Crisis of Competence. The Corrupting Effect of Political Activism in the University of California" *National Association of Scholars* April, http://www.nas.org/images/documents/a_crisis_of_competence.pdf.

Elshtain, Jean-Bethke. 2003. "The Dissenters Club" *Books & Culture* 9 (4), July–August: 6.

Epstein, Richard A. 1973/74. "Pleadings and Presumptions" *The University of Chicago Law Review* 40: 556–82.

Farrell, John. 2006. *Paranoia and Modernity: Cervantes to Rousseau*. Ithaca: Cornell University Press.

"Fat Blasting Undies, Or Are They?" 2013. *Media Watch*. August 19, Episode 29, http://www.abc.net.au/mediawatch/transcripts/s3829077.htm.

Fenster, Mark. 1999. *Conspiracy Theories: Secrecy and Power in American Culture*. Minneapolis: University of Minnesota Press.

Feyerabend Paul. 1975. *Against Method: Outline of an Anarchistic Theory of Knowledge*. London: New Left Books.

Finocchiaro, Peter. 2012. "Rush Limbaugh Suggests 'Dark Knight Rises' Villain 'Bane' A Deliberate Romney Reference" *Huffington Post* July 18, http://www.huffingtonpost.com/2012/07/18/limbaugh-bane-dark-knight-rises_n_1681716.html?utm_hp_ref=media.

Fitzsimmons, Jill. 2012. "'Hard' 'Authoritative' Evidence Of Climate Change Begins To Overwhelm Even Fox" *Media Matters for America* November 30, http://mediamatters.org/blog/2012/11/30/hard-authoritative-evidence-of-climate-change-b/191610.

Flannery, Tim. 2005. *The Weather Makers: How Man Is Changing the Climate and What It Means for Life on Earth*. Melbourne: Text Publishing Company.

Fleming, Chris. 2004. *René Girard: Violence and Mimesis*. Cambridge: Polity.

——— and Jane Goodall 2002. "Dangerous Darwinism" *Public Understanding of Science* 11: 259–71.

Ford, Henry 2011 (orig. 1920, 1921). *The International Jew: The World's Foremost Problem: Volumes I and II*. East Sussex: The Historical Review Press.

Foucault, Michel. 1966. *Les mots et les choses. Une archéologie des sciences humaines*. Paris: Gallimard.

———. 1972. *The Archaeology of Knowledge*, Trans. A.M. Sheridan-Smith. New York: Pantheon.

———. 2006 (orig. 1972). *History of Madness*. Oxon: Routledge.

"Fox News Viewed as Most Ideological Network." 2009. *Pew Research Center*. October 29, http://www.people-press.org/2009/10/29/fox-news-viewed-as-most-ideological-network/.

Frankfurt, Harry G. 2005. *On Bullshit*. Princeton: Princeton University Press.

"French Official Suggested Bush was Behind September 11." 2007. *Reuters.* July 7, http://www.reuters.com/article/2007/07/07/us-france-sept-idUSL0735514520070707.

Freud, Sigmund. 1958. "Psycho-Analytic Notes on an Autobiographical Account of a Case of Paranoia (Dementia Paranoides)". In James Strachey (ed.). *Standard Edition of the Complete Psychological Works of Sigmund Freud (24 volumes),* New York: Norton 1953–74. Volume 12, (orig. 1911), Translated and edited by James Strachey in collaboration with Anna Freud, assisted by Alix Strachey and Alan Tyson. London: Hogarth Press and the Institute of Psychoanalysis, 3–84.

———. 1985 (orig. 1913). "Totem and Taboo". *The Origins of Religion. The Penguin Freud Library. Volume 13,* Trans. James Strachey. Ed. Albert Dickson. London: Penguin.

Frum, David. 2012. "Gore Vidal, 1925–2012" *Daily Beast* August 1, http://www.thedailybeast.com/articles/2012/08/01/gore-vidal.html.

Fuller, Steve. 2005. *The Intellectual.* London: Icon.

Gadamer, Hans Georg. 1986. *Gesammelte Werke. Hermeneutik I. Wahrheit und Methode: Grundzüge einer philosophischen Hermeneutik.* Tübingen: Mohr.

Gamble, Foster. "Diversity in the World of Extra-Terrestrials" *Thrive* http://www.thrivemovement.com/diversity-world-extra-terrestrials#ftn1.

Gans, Eric. 1997. *Signs of Paradox: Irony, Resentment, and Other Mimetic Structures.* Stanford, California: Stanford University Press.

———. 2011. *A New Way of Thinking: Generative Anthropology in Religion, Philosophy, Art.* Aurora, Colorado: Davies Group Publishers.

Gentlemen Prefer Blondes. 1953. Film. Dir. Howard Hawks.

Genovese, Michael A. 1999. *The Watergate Crisis.* Connecticut: Greenwood Press.

Giddens, Anthony. 1984. *The Constitution of Society.* Cambridge: Polity.

Ginzburg, Carlo. 1991. *Ecstasies: Deciphering the Witches' Sabbath,* Trans. Raymond Rosenthal. London: Penguin.

Girard, René. 1961. *Mensonge romantique et vérité romanesque.* Paris: Grasset.

———. 1986. *Violence and the Sacred,* Trans. Patrick Gregory. Baltimore: Johns Hopkins University Press.

———. 1987. *Things Hidden Since the Foundation of the World,* Trans. Stephen Bann and Michael Metteer. Stanford, California: Stanford University Press.

"Global Warming Labeled a 'scam'". 2007. *The Washington Times* March 6, http://www.washingtontimes.com/news/2007/mar/06/20070306-122226-6282r/?page=all#pagebreak.

Goldenberg, Suzanne. 2013. "Secret Funding Helped Build Vast Network of Climate Denial Think Tanks" *The Guardian* February 15, http://www.theguardian.com/environment/2013/feb/14/funding-climate-change-denial-thinktanks-network.

Goldman, James. 1970 (orig. 1961). *They Might Be Giants*. New York: Lancer Books.

Goldwag, Arthur. 2009. *Cults, Conspiracies, & Secret Societies: The Straight Scoop on Freemasons, the Illuminati, Skull & Bones, Black Helicopters, the New World Order, and Many, Many More*. New York and Canada: Random House.

Gray, James. 2012. "The Town that's Twinned with Narnia" *New Humanist* 127 (5) September/October, http://newhumanist.org.uk/2862/the-town-thats-twinned-with-narnia.

Greenberg, David. 2003. *Nixon's Shadow: The History of the Image*. New York: W. W. Norton & Company.

Hall, John. 2013. "Obama the Antichrist? Global Warming a Myth? Lizard People Controlling the World? Conspiracy Theory Research Reveals Bizarre Beliefs Prevalent in US" *The Independent* April 4, http://www.independent.co.uk/news/world/americas/obama-the-antichrist-global-warming-a-myth-lizard-people-controlling-the-world-conspiracy-theory-research-reveals-bizarre-beliefs-prevalent-in-us-8558384.html.

Hamilton, Clive. 2013. *Earthmasters: Playing God with the Climate*. Crows Nest: Allen & Unwin.

Hanson, James. 2009. "Coal-Fired Power Plants Are Death Factories. Close Them." *The Observer* February 15, http://www.theguardian.com/commentisfree/2009/feb/15/james-hansen-power-plants-coal.

Hargrove, Thomas. 2013. "Boston Marathon Bombings Fuel Conspiracy Theories" *NorthJersey.com* April 16, http://www.northjersey.com/news/Boston_Marathon_bombings_fuel_conspiracy_theories.html#sthash.8mLXhHGN.dpuf.

Harrison, Frances. 2006. "Iran to Host Meeting on Holocaust" *BBC News* December 5, http://news.bbc.co.uk/2/hi/middle_east/6209628.stm.

Hartley, John. 1992. *The Politics of Pictures:the Creation of the Public in the Age of Popular Media*. London, New York: Routledge.

———. 2002. *Communication, Cultural and Media Studies: The Key Concepts*. 3rd ed. London and New York: Routledge.

———. 2009. *//the_uses_of_digital_literacy//*. St Lucia: University of Queensland Press.

Hegel, Georg W. F. 1988 (orig. 1832). *Introduction to the Philosophy of History: With Selections from The Philosophy of Right*, Trans. Leo Rauch. New York: Hackett.

Hegeman, Susan. 2012. *The Cultural Return*. Berkeley and Los Angeles: University of California Press.

Heidegger, Martin. 1971. *Poetry, Language, Thought*, Trans. Albert Hofstadter. New York: Harper & Row.

———. 1982. *On the Way to Language*, Trans. P.D. Hertz. New York: Harper & Row.

———. 1990. *Die Sprache spricht, Unterwegs zur Sprache*. 9th ed. Pfullingen: Neske.

Herf, Jeffrey. 2006. *The Jewish Enemy: Nazi Propaganda during World War II and the Holocaust*. Cambridge, MA: Belknap Press of Harvard University Press.

Hickman, Leo and James. Randerson 2009. "Climate Sceptics Claim Leaked Emails Are Evidence of Collusion among Scientists" *The Guardian* November 21, http://www.theguardian.com/environment/2009/nov/20/climate-sceptics-hackers-leaked-emails.

Hirschkorn, Phil. 2003. "Fox News Loses Attempt to Block Satirist's Book" *CNN* August 22, http://edition.cnn.com/2003/LAW/08/22/fox.franken/.

Hitler, Adolf. 2002 (orig. 1925). *Mein Kampf*. Trans. James Murphy. Project Gutenberg Australia, http://gutenberg.net.au/ebooks02/0200601.txt.

Hobbes, Thomas. 1985. (orig. 1661). "Dialogus Physicus." In *Leviathan and the Air Pump: Hobbes. Boyle. and the Experimental Life*, Trans. And Ed. Steven Shapin and Simon Schaffer. Princeton: Princeton University Press. 345–91.

Hodapp, Christopher and Alice Von Kannon 2008. *Conspiracy Theories & Secret Societies for Dummies*. Indianapolis: Wiley.

Hodgson, G. 2005 (orig. 1976). *America in Our Time: From World War II to Nixon: What Happened and Why*. New Jersey: Princeton University Press.

Hoffman, Jascha. 2011. "Q&A Margaret Wertheim: The Outsider Insider" *Nature* 479 (3) November.

Hofstadter, Richard. 1964. "The Paranoid Style in American Politics" *Harper's* November, http://harpers.org/archive/1964/11/the-paranoid-style-in-american-politics/.

Hollyfield, Amy. 2008. "PERSPECTIVE: For True Disbelievers. The Facts Are Just not Enough" *St. Petersburg Times* June 29, http://www.pulitzer.org/archives/8406.

Howden, Saffron. 2012. "Pupils in Dark Over Source of Yoghurt" *The Sydney Morning Herald* March 5, http://www.smh.com.au/national/pupils-in-dark-over-source-of-yoghurt-20120304-1ub5x.html.

Huxley, Thomas Henry. 1911. *Man's Place in Nature and Other Essays*. London: Dent.

Icke, David. 2000. "The Reptilian Brain" *David Icke* May, http://www.bibliotecapleyades.net/sumer_anunnaki/reptiles/reptiles14.htm.

———. 2007. *The David Icke Guide to the Global Conspiracy (and how to end it)*. Ryde, Isle of Wight: David Icke Books.

———. 2013. "Top 10 Illuminati Puppets and Masters of Entertainment" *David Icke* October 27, http://www.davidicke.com/headlines/top-10-illuminati-puppets-and-masters-of-entertainment/.

"In Defense of Food:—An Eater's Manifesto." *Michael Pollan*, http://michaelpollan.com/books/in-defense-of-food/.

"Infowars Activism." *Alex Jones' INFOWARS.COM*, http://www.infowars.com/activism/activism.htm.

Inhofe, James M. 2003. "The Facts and Science of Climate Change", http://www.epw.senate.gov/public/index.cfm?FuseAction=Files.View&FileStore_id=01d83873-cb56-4153-9b8d-f9dd65366b0c.

———. 2012. *The Greatest Hoax: How the Global Warming Conspiracy Threatens Your Future*. Washington: WND Books.

Jane, Emma. 2012. "We're All in the Dark on What's Dished Up" *The Australian* March 8, http://www.theaustralian.com.au/opinion/were-all-in-the-dark-on-whats-dished-up/story-e6frg71o-1226292471863#mm-premium.

———. 2014. "The Scapegoating of Cheerleading and Cheerleaders". In Joel Hodge, Scott Cowdell, and Chris Fleming (eds.). *Violence, Desire, and the Sacred Volume 2: René Girard and Sacrifice in Life, Love, and Literature*. New York, London, New Delhi, Sydney: Bloomsbury. 83–100.

Jaschik, Scott. 2007. "Skepticism of Faculty and Tenure" *Inside Higher Ed* July 12, http://www.insidehighered.com/news/2007/07/12/poll.

Joiner, Robert R., Frederick D. Vidal and Henry C. Marks 1963. "A New Powdered Agent for Flour Maturing" *Cereal Chemistry Back Issues* http://www.aaccnet.org/publications/cc/backissues/1963/Documents/chem40_539.pdf.

Jones, Alex. 2011. "Why Is Alex Jones Still Alive? (To All the Dis-Info TROLLS)" *YouTube* October 3, http://www.youtube.com/watch?v=-R01VF77td8.

———. 2013. "Today on the Show" *Alex Jones' INFOWARS.COM (Live Stream)* July 7 http://www.infowars.com/listen.

Kabat, Jennifer. 2012. "The Rumpus Interview with Thomas Thwaites" *The Rumpus* April 12, http://therumpus.net/2012/04/the-rumpus-interview-with-thomas-thwaites/.

Kant, Immanuel. 1963 (orig. 1784). "Emerging Global Food system Risks and Potential Solutions" In *On History*, Trans. and Ed. Lewis White Beck. London: Macmillan. 3–20.

Kaplan, Jeffrey and Helene Lööw. 2002. *The Cultic Milieu: Oppositional Subcultures in an Age of Globalization*. Oxford: AltaMira Press.

Kay, Jonathan. 2011. *Among the Truthers: A Journey Through America's Growing Conspiracist Underground*. New York: HarperCollins.

Keeley, Brain L. 1999. "Of Conspiracy Theories" *The Journal of Philosophy* 96 (3), March: 109–126.

Kellogg, Michael. 2005. *The Russian Roots of Nazism: White Émigrés and the Making of National Socialism, 1917–1945*. Cambridge: Cambridge University Press.

Kennedy, John F. 1961. "The President and the Press". Address to the American Newspaper Publishers Association, New York City. April 27, http://www.presidency.ucsb.edu/ws/index.php?pid=8093

Kennedy, Shaun. 2013. "Emerging Global Food System Risks". In Wayne Ellefson, Lorna Zach, and Darryl Sullivan (eds.). *Improving Import Food Safety*. Iowa, West Sussex, Oxford: Wiley-Blackwell.

Knight, Peter. 2000. *Conspiracy Culture: From Kennedy to The X-Files*. London: Routledge.

———. 2003. *Conspiracy Theories in American History: An Encyclopedia*. California: ABC-CLIO.

Kruglanski, Arie W. 1980. "Lay Epistemology: Process and Contents" *Psychological Review* 87 (1): 70–87.

Kuhn, Thomas. 1977. *The Essential Tension: Selected Studies in Scientific Tradition and Change*. Chicago: University of Chicago Press.

Lacan, Jacques. 1948. "Aggressivity in Psychoanalysis". In *Écrits: A Selection*, Trans. and Ed. Alan Sheridan. New York: Norton. 1977.

———. 1981. *The Four Fundamental Concepts of Psycho-Analysis*, Trans. Alan Sheridan. (ed.) Jacques-Alain Miller. New York: Norton.

———. 1988. "The See-Saw of Desire". In Jacques-Alian Miller (ed.). *The Seminar of Jacques Lacan. Book I: Freud's Papers on Technique. 1953–1954*, Trans. John Forrester. Cambridge: Cambridge University Press.

———. 1993. "The Other and Psychoses". In Jacques-Alain Miller (ed.). *The Seminar of Jacques Lacan. Book III: The Psychoses. 1955–1956*, Trans. Russell Grigg. New York: Norton.

Laclau, Ernesto and Chantelle Mouffe. 1985. *Hegemony and Socialist Strategy: Toward a Radical Democratic Politics*. London: Verso.

Latour, Bruno. 2004a. *Politics of Nature: How to Bring the Sciences into Democracy*, Trans. Catherine Porter. Cambridge and London: Harvard University Press.

———. 2004b. "Why Has Critique Run Out of Steam? From Matters of Fact to Matters of Concern" *Critical Inquiry* 30, Winter: 225–48.

Lee, Martha F. 2011. *Conspiracy Rising: Conspiracy Thinking and American Public Life*. Santa Barbara, California: Praeger.

Lewis, Tyson and Richard Kahn 2005. "The Reptoid Hypothesis: Utopian and Dystopian Representational Motifs in David Icke's Alien Conspiracy Theory" *Utopian Studies* 16 (1): 45–74.

LifeLiberty Now. 2013. "Obama Reptilian Secret Service Conspiracy DEBUNKED and DESTROYED!" *YouTube* March 24, http://www.youtube.com/all_comments?v=WrDSgW3qSeg.

Limbaugh, Rush. 2012. "Fast and Furious Cover-up: Obama Asserts Executive Privilege to Protect Himself" *Rush Limbaugh Show* June 20, http://www.rushlimbaugh.com/daily/2012/06/20/fast_and_furious_cover_up_obama_asserts_executive_privilege_to_protect_himself.

Luedtke, Mark. 2013. "Government's Corruption of our Food" *Dayton City Paper* June 4, http://www.daytoncitypaper.com/conspiracy-theorist-35/.

Lyotard, Jean-Francois. 1979. *La Condition Postmoderne: Rapport sur le Savoir*. Paris: Les Editions de Minuit.

————. 1987. "Rewriting Modernity." *SubStance* 16 (3): 3–9.

Macey, Richard. 2006. "One Giant Blunder for Mankind: How NASA Lost Moon Pictures." *The Sydney Morning Herald* August 5, http://www.smh.com.au/news/national/one-giant-blunder-for-mankind-how-nasa-lost-moon-pictures/2006/08/04/1154198328978.html.

MacFarquhar, Larissa. 2003. "The Devil's Accountant." *The New Yorker* March 31: 64–79.

Machiavelli, Niccolo. 2005 (orig. 1910). *The Prince*, Trans. N H Thomson. Delaware: Prestwick House.

Manufacturing Consent: Noam Chomsky and the Media. 1992. Film. Dir. Mark Achbar and Peter Wintonick.

Mandel, David R. 2002. "Instigators of Genocide: Examining Hitler From a Social-Psychological Perspective". In Leonard S. Newman and Ralph Erber (eds.). *Understanding Genocide: The Social Psychology of the Holocaust.* New York: Oxford University Press. 259–84.

Mandik, P. 2007. "Shit Happens." *Episteme* 4(2), June: 205–18.

Marcus, George E. (ed.) 1999. *Paranoia Within Reason: A Casebook on Conspiracy as Explanation*. London: The University of Chicago Press.

Marx, Karl and Friedrich Engels 2004 (orig. 1947). *The German Ideology: Part One with Selections from Parts Two and Three and Supplementary Texts*, C. J. Arthur (ed.). London: Lawrence and Wishart.

Mattoon, Mary Ann. 2005. *Jung and the Human Psyche*. London and New York: Routledge.

"McDonald's USA Ingredients Listing for Popular Menu Items." 2013. *McDonalds.com*. May 21, http://nutrition.mcdonalds.com/getnutrition/ingredientslist.pdf.

McGovern, Kieran. 2011. "What are Birthers? And Truthers?" *English Language FAQ*, http://www.englishlanguagefaqs.com/2011/04/what-are-birthers-and-truthers.html.

Melley, Timothy. 2000. *Empire of Conspiracy: The Culture of Paranoia in Postwar America*. Ithaca, London: Cornell University Press.

Mesure, Susie. 2012. "David Icke Is not the Messiah. Or Even that Naughty. But Boy, can he Drone on." *The Independent* October 28, http://www.independent.co.uk/news/uk/home-news/david-icke-is-not-the-messiah-or-even-that-naughty-but-boy-can-he-drone-on-8229433.html.

Milbank, Dana. 2010. "Glenn Beck Is Obsessed with Hitler and Woodrow Wilson." *The Washington Post* October 3, http://www.washingtonpost.com/wp-dyn/content/article/2010/09/30/AR2010093005267.html.

Miller, Boaz and Issac Record 2013. "Justified Belief in a Digital Age: On the Epistmic Implications of Secret Internet Technologies." *Episteme* 10 (2): 117–34.

Minaya, Ezequiel and David Luhnow 2013. "Venezuela Takes Page from Cuban Playbook: Caracas Accuses Washington of Destabilization Plot and

Its "Historic Enemies" of Inducing Chávez's Cancer" *Wall Street Journal* March 5, http://online.wsj.com/article/SB10001424127887323494504578342440377083144.html.

Molière. 1670. *Le Bourgeois Gentilhomme*, http://www.site-moliere.com/pieces/bourgeoi.htm.

Monsters vs Aliens. Film. Dir. Conrad Vernon and Rob Letterman.

Morales, Lymari. 2012. "U.S. Distrust in Media Hits New High" *Gallup* September 21, http://www.gallup.com/home.aspx.

Moss, Michael. 2013. "The Extraordinary Science of Addictive Junk Food." *New York Times* February 20, http://www.nytimes.com/2013/02/24/magazine/the-extraordinary-science-of-junk-food.html?pagewanted=all&_r=0.

"Multidimensional Reptilian Demon Lords." *Reptilian Resistance*, http://www.reptilianresistance.com.

Naegling. 2003. "Sheeple." *Urban Dictionary* October 2, http://www.urbandictionary.com/define.php?term=sheeple.

"New Humanist Magazine." 2013. *New Humanist*, http://newhumanist.org.uk/about.

Niemitz, Hans-Ulrich. 2000. (orig. 1995). *Did the Early Middle Ages Really Exist?* Berlin, http://www.cl.cam.ac.uk/~mgk25/volatile/Niemitz-1997.pdf.

Norris, Christopher. 1997. *Against Relativism: Philosophy of Science, Deconstruction and Critical Theory*. Oxford: Blackwell.

"Obama's Reptilian Secret Service Spotted AIPAC Conference 3 Angles (HD)." 2013. *YouTube* March 18, http://www.youtube.com/watch?v=k2mjs_gdMAI&list=UU8A-0NNgbvSowaC80QqL_aQ&index=6.

Oglesby, Carl. 1976. *The Yankee and Cowboy War: Conspiracies from Dallas to Watergate*. Kansas City: Sheed Andrews and McMeel.

———. 1992. *Who Killed JFK? (The Real Story Series)*. Berkeley: Odonian Press.

"Opinion Polls about 9/11 Conspiracy Theories." *Wikipedia*, http://en.wikipedia.org/wiki/Opinion_polls_about_9/11_conspiracy_theories.

Parsons, Charlotte. 2001. "Why we need conspiracy theories." *BBC News*. September 24. http://news.bbc.co.uk/2/hi/americas/1561199.stm

Parsons, Talcott. 1968. *The Structure of Social Action: A Study in Social Theory with Special Reference to a Group of European Writers*. New York: Free Press.

Phillips, Tom. 2011. "Hugo Chávez Hints at US Cancer Plot." *Guardian*. December 30. http://www.theguardian.com/world/2011/dec/29/hugo-chavez-us-cancer-plot.

Piazza, Jared and Jesse M. Bering 2010. "The Co-Evolution of Secrecy and Stigmatization: Evidence from the Content of Distressing Secrets" *Human Nature* 21 (3): 290–308.

Pipes, Daniel. (with Brian Lamb)1997. "Conspiracy" *C-SPAN Booknotes* December 12, http://www.danielpipes.org/953/conspiracy.

——. 1998 (orig. 1996). *The Hidden Hand: Middle East Fears of Conspiracy*. New York: St. Martin's Press.

——. 1999 (orig. 1997). *Conspiracy: How the Paranoid Style Flourishes and Where It Comes From*. New York: Simon & Schuster.

Plait, Philip C. 2002. *Bad Astronomy: Misconceptions and Misuses Revealed. from Astrology to the Moon Landing 'Hoax*. New York: John Wiley & Sons.

Plato. 1973. "Phaedrus". In *Phaedrus and Letters VII and VIII*, (orig. apx. 370 BCE). Trans. Walter Hamilton. London: Penguin. 19–103.

Pollan, Michael. 2007. "Unhappy Meals" *New York Times* January 28, http://www.nytimes.com/2007/01/28/magazine/28nutritionism.t.html?ei=5090&en=a18a7f35515014c7&ex=1327640400&partner=rssus&pagewanted=all&_r=0.

——. 2008. *In Defense of Food: An Eater's Manifesto*. New York: Penguin Group. Extract published on www.michaelpollan.com, http://michaelpollan.com/wordpress/wp-content/uploads/2010/05/in_defense_excerpt.pdf.

Popper, Karl. 1966. *The Open Society and Its Enemies; Volume II; the High Tide of Prophecy: Hegel, Marx. And the Aftermath*. Princeton: Princeton University Press.

——. 1968. *The Logic of Scientific Discovery*. London: Hutchinson.

——. 2006 (orig. 1972). "The Conspiracy Theory of Society". In D. Coady (ed.). *Conspiracy Theories: The Philosophical Debate*. Aldershot: Ashgate. 13–16.

Rahner, Karl. 1976. *Theological Investigations*, Volume 14. Trans. David Bourke. London: Dartman, Longman & Todd.

Rauschning, Hermann. 1939. *Hitler Speaks: A Series Of Political Conversations With Adolf Hitler On His Real Aims*. London: Thornton Butterworth.

"Reptilian Resistance." *Reptilian Resistance*, http://www.reptilianresistance.com.

Richardson, Robert C. 2007. *Evolutionary Psychology as Maladapted Psychology*. Cambridge, Massachusetts: MIT Press.

Ricoeur, Paul. 1970. *Freud and Philosophy: An Essay in Interpretation*, Trans. Denis Savage. New York: Yale University Press.

Roberts, Mark. "Paranoid Creeps Who, Either Because They Are Off Their Meds or Because They Are Incompetent Intellectual Cowards Who Cannot Defend Their Claims with the Slightest Shred of Evidence or Logic, Resort to Masturbatory Fantasies About the Execution of Mark Roberts" *wtc7lies*, 11th March 2014. https://sites.google.com/site/wtc7lies/semiliterateparanoiacswhofantasizeaboutt.

Roosevelt, Theodor. 1912. "Progressive Covenant with the People" *Library of Congress*, http://memory.loc.gov/ammem/collections/troosevelt_film/trfpcp.html.

Rorty, Richard. 2007. *Philosophy as Cultural Politics*. Cambridge: Cambridge University Press.

Rousseau, Jean-Jacques. 1755. *Discours sur l'origine et les fondements de l'inégalité parmi les hommes*, http://fr.wikisource.org/wiki/Discours_sur_l'origine_et_les_fondements_de_l'inégalité_parmi_les_hommes/Seconde_partie

Rubi, Mark. 2009. "Fast Food Investigation: What are the Real Ingredients of a Big Mac®?" *examiner.com* June 17, http://www.examiner.com/article/fast-food-investigation-what-are-the-real-ingredients-of-a-big-mac.

Rudder, Christian. 2011. "The Best Questions for a First Date" *oktrends* February 8, http://blog.okcupid.com/index.php/the-best-questions-for-first-dates/.

Rumsfeld, Donald H. 2002. "DoD News Briefing: Secretary Rumsfeld and Gen. Myers" *U.S. Department of Defense* February 12, http://www.defense.gov/transcripts/transcript.aspx?transcriptid=2636.

Rushdie, Salmon. 1981. "Calvino" *London Review of Books* 3 (17): 16–17.

Saha, Tushar Kanti. 2010. *Textbook on Legal Methods, Legal Systems & Research*. Delhi: Universal Law Publishing.

Sakai, Kazuo and Nakan Ide 1998. *The Art of Lying*, Trans. Sara Aoyama. New York: Red Brick Press.

Sarup, Madan. 1993 (orig. 1988). *An Introductory Guide to Post-Structuralism and Postmodernism*. 2nd ed. Athens: The University of Georgia Press.

Saunders, Alan and Peter Ludlow 2011. "The Julian Assange Conspiracy: Networks. Power and Activism" *Philosopher's Zone* Radio National transcript. February 26, http://www.abc.net.au/radionational/programs/philosopherszone/the-julian-assange-conspiracy---networks-power-and/2995228.

Schwartz, John. 2009. "Vocal Minority Insists it was all Smoke and Mirrors." *New York Times* July 13, http://www.nytimes.com/2009/07/14/science/space/14hoax.html.

"Science and Engineering Indicators 2012". 2012. *General Social Survey*. National Opinion Research Center, University of Chicago. Appendix table 7–27. Public confidence in institutional leaders: 1973–2010, http://www.nsf.gov/statistics/seind12/append/c7/at07-27.pdf.

Scruton, Roger. 1999. "Whatever Happened to Reason?" *City Journal*, Spring, http://www.city-journal.org/html/9_2_urbanities_what_ever.html.

Sedgwick, Eve Kosofsky. 2003. *Touching Feeling: Affect, Pedagogy, Performativity*. Durham and London: Duke University Press.

Seitz-Wald, Alex. 2012. "Limbaugh: Al-Qaida 'gave up Osama' ". *Salon* September 13, http://www.salon.com/2012/09/13/limbaugh_al_qaida_gave_up_osama/.

———. 2013. "Alex Jones: Conspiracy Inc." *Salon* May 2, http://www.salon.com/2013/05/02/alex_jones_conspiracy_inc/.

Shakespeare, William. 1992. (orig. circa 1604) *Hamlet*, Barbara A. Mowat & Paul Werstine (eds.). orig. circa 1604. New York: Washington Square Press.

Shapin, Steven and Simon Schaffer 1985. *Leviathan and the Air-Pump: Hobbes, Boyle, and the Experimental Life*. Princeton: Princeton University Press.

Sheets, Connor Adams. 2013. "8 Boston Marathon Bombing Conspiracy Theories That Won't Go Away" *International Business Times* April 26, http://www.ibtimes.com/8-boston-marathon-bombing-conspiracy-theories-wont-go-away-1218035.

Sisson, Mark (a). "The Primal Blueprint: Updated and Expanded (Paperback Edition)" *Primal Blueprint*, http://primalblueprint.com/products/The-Primal-Blueprint%3A-Updated-and-Expanded-%28Paperback-Edition%29.html.

Sisson, Mark (b). "Mark Sisson" *Mark's Daily Apple*, http://www.marksdailyapple.com/about-2/mark-sisson/#axzz2VrdXlR7p.

Sisson, Mark (c). "Who is Grok?" *Mark's Daily Apple*, http://www.marksdailyapple.com/about-2/who-is-grok/#axzz2VruFGw2T.

Sisson, Mark (d). "Primal Fuel" *Primal Blueprint*, http://primalblueprint.com/products/Primal-Fuel.html.

Sisson, Mark (e). "The Primal Blueprint Luxury Retreat" *Primal Blueprint*, http://primalblueprint.com/products/The-Primal-Blueprint-Luxury-Retreat.html.

Sisson, Mark (f). "Damage Control Master Formula" *Primal Blueprint*, http://primalblueprint.com/products/Damage-Control-Master-Formula.html.

Sisson, Mark. 2007a. "The Vegetable Conspiracy: Why You Should Avoid Greens at All Costs: How to Get Sick and Die, Part 2" *Mark's Daily Apple* May 3, http://dev.marksdailyapple.com/get-sick-and-die-2/#axzz2VrHilcxm.

———. 2007b. "The Best Way to Get Diabetes: Follow the Diabetes Dietary Guidelines" *Mark's Daily Apple* August 30, http://www.marksdailyapple.com/diabetes-pyramid/#ixzz2VrMujPq6.

———. 2009a. "Is Conventional Wisdom Set in Stone?" *Mark's Daily Apple* September 9, http://www.marksdailyapple.com/is-conventional-wisdom-set-in-stone/#axzz2VrIj9PUd.

———. 2009b. "Is the Stone Beginning to Crack?" *Mark's Daily Apple* September 10, http://www.marksdailyapple.com/is-the-stone-beginning-to-crack/#axzz2VrIj9PUd.

——— (with Jennifer Meier). 2010. *The Primal Blueprint Cookbook*. Malibu: Primal Nutrition, Inc.

———. 2012. "Musings on Specialization and Self-Sufficiency in the Modern World" *Mark's Daily Apple* January 26, http://www.marksdailyapple.com/musings-on-specialization-and-self-sufficiency-in-the-modern-world/#ixzz2VrVmPQXA.

"Skeptical Quotes." *North Texas Skeptics*, http://www.ntskeptics.org/quotes.htm.

Smith, Ben and Byron Tau 2011. "Birtherism: Where it all Began" *Politico* April 22, http://www.politico.com/news/stories/0411/53563.html.

"Sources That Are Usually Not Reliable." *Wikipedia*, http://en.wikipedia.org/
wiki/Wikipedia:V#Sources_that_are_usually_not_reliable.

Spence, Gerry. 2002. *Seven Simple Steps to Personal Freedom: An Owner's
Manual for Life*. London: St Martins.

Spies-Butcher, Ben, Joy Paton, and Damien Cahill 2012. *Market Society:
History, Theory, Practice*. Cambridge: Cambridge University Press.

Spitznagel, Eric. 2013. "Ke$ha Talks Vaginal Exorcism and Dr. Luke Controversy"
Rolling Stone October 24, http://www.rollingstone.com/music/news/ke-ha-
chats-vaginal-exorcism-and-dr-luke-controversy-20131024.

Stahl, Jeremy. 2011. "Where Were You When You First Heard? The Other
Question I asked Myself for the 10th Anniversary of 9/11" *Slate* September
6, http://www.slate.com/articles/news_and_politics/trutherism/2011/09/
where_were_you_when_you_first_heard.html.

"Store." *Primal Blueprint*, http://primalblueprint.com/categories/Store/.

Stout, Jeffrey. 1981. *The Flight from Authority: Reason, Morality, and the Quest
for Autonomy*. Notre Dame, Indiana: Notre Dame University Press.

Strauss, Leo. 1965 (orig. 1950). *Natural Right and History*. Chicago, London:
The University of Chicago Press.

Sunstein, Cass R. and Adrian Vermeule 2008. "Conspiracy Theories." *Harvard
University Law School Public Law Working Paper* 08–03; *University of
Chicago Public Law Working Paper* 199; *University of Chicago Law &
Economics Olin Working Paper* 387. January 15, http://papers.ssrn.com/
sol3/papers.cfm?abstract_id=1084585, 2008.

———. 2009. "Conspiracy Theories: Causes and Cures." *The Journal of Political
Philosophy* 17 (2): 202–27.

Tashman, Brain. 2012. "James Inhofe Says the Bible Refutes Climate Change"
Right Wing Watch August 3, http://www.rightwingwatch.org/content/
james-inhofe-says-bible-refutes-climate-change.

Taylor, Charles. 1992. *Sources of the Self: The Making of Modern Identity*.
Cambridge: Cambridge University Press.

"The Five Worst Cookbooks of 2010." 2010. *Physicians Committee for
Responsible Medicine*. December, http://pcrm.org/health/reports/the-five-
worst-cookbooks-of-2010.

"The Glenn Beck Conspiracy Theory Generator: Fair and
Balanced Paranoia. Delivered on Demand." *about.com*, http://
politicalhumor.about.com/library/bl-glenn-beck-conspiracy.
htm?PS=786%2C362%2C962%2C218%3A10.

The Majestic Documents: Evidence That We Are Not Alone, http://www.
majesticdocuments.com/mission.php.

'The Primal Blueprint'. Primal Blueprint Publishing. http://www.
primalblueprintpublishing.com/books/the-primal-blueprint/.

"theorize." *Merriam-Webster*, http://www.merriam-webster.com/dictionary/
theorize?show=0&t=1369109732.

Thomas, D. M. 1992. *Flying into Love*. New York and London: Bloomsbury.

Thompson, Damian. 2008. *Counterknowledge: How We Surrendered to Conspiracy Theories, Quack Medicine, Bogus Science, and Fake History*. London: Atlantic Books.

Thresher-Andrews, Christoper. 2013. "An Introduction into the World of Conspiracy" *In PSYPAG Quarterly* 88 (September), 5–8.

Thwaites, Thomas. 2011. *The Toaster Project*. New York: Princeton Architectural Press.

Travis, Shannon. 2010. "CNN Poll: Quarter doubt Obama was born in U.S." *CNN Politics* August 4, http://politicalticker.blogs.cnn.com/2010/08/04/cnn-poll-quarter-doubt-president-was-born-in-u-s/.

Trillin , Calvin. 1967. "The Buffs." *The New Yorker*, June 10, 41–71.

Trollope, Anthony. 1873. "The Eustace Diamonds" *The Literature Network*, http://www.online-literature.com/anthony-trollope/eustace-diamonds/.

Turner, F. M. 1974. "Rainfall, Plagues and the Prince of Wales: A Chapter in the Conflict of Science and Religion." *Journal of British Studies* 13: 46–65.

———. 1978. "The Victorian Conflict Between Science and Religion: A Professional Dimension." *Isis* 69: 356–76.

UfoDisclosure 2012. 2013. "White House Officially Responds on President Alien Bodyguards!" *YouTube* March 30, http://www.youtube.com/watch?v=LZXxeFYw7jA.

"U.S. Supreme Court," *FindLaw*, http://caselaw.lp.findlaw.com/scripts/getcase.pl?court=us&vol=378&invol=184.

vampirepoet. 2011. *OkCupid: Forum*. November 4, http://www.okcupid.com/forum?tid=5306216900248969674.

Verified Facts, http://www.verifiedfacts.org.

VintageTVCommercials. 2009. "1975 McDonalds Commercial Two All Beef Patties Special Sauce Lettuce…" *YouTube* March 7, http://www.youtube.com/watch?v=dK2qBbDn5W0.

Volkan, Vamik D., Norman Itzkowitz and Andrew W. Dod. 1997. *Richard Nixon: A Psychobiography*. New York, West Sussex: Columbia University Press.

Warnock, Emery C. 2009. "The Anti-Semitic Origins of Henry Ford's Arts Education Patronage" *Journal of Historical Research in Music Education* 30(2), April: 79–102.

Washington, George. "Letter to George Washington Snyder, October 24, 1798." *The Writings of George Washington from the Original Manuscript Sources, 1745–1799*. John C. Fitzpatrick (ed.). The Library of Congress, http://memory.loc.gov/cgi-bin/query/r?ammem/mgw:@field%28DOCID+@lit%28gw360395%29%29.

Watson, Paul Joseph. 2013. "YouTube Censors Family Guy Clip Which Predicted Boston Marathon Attack: Media Floats Erroneous Claim that Issue is an 'abhorrent hoax' ". *Alex Jones' infowars.com* April 16, http://www.infowars.com/family-guy-episode-predicted-boston-marathon-attack/.

Weikart, Richard. 2009. *Hitler's Ethic: The Nazi Pursuit of Evolutionary Progress*. New York: Palgrave MacMillan.

"Welcome to the RR Movement United." *Reptilian Resistance*, http://www.reptilianresistance.com.

Welch, Claude. 1996. "Dispelling Some Myths about the Split between Theology and Science in the Nineteenth Century". In W. Mark Richardson and Wesley J. Wildman (eds.). *Religion and Science: History, Method, Dialogue*. New York: Routledge. 29–40.

Wertheim, Margaret. 2011. *Physics on the Fringe: Smoke Rings, Circlons, and Alternative Theories of Everything*. New York: Walker & Company.

Wheen, Francis. 2004. *How Mumbo-Jumbo Conquered the World: A Short History of Modern Delusions*. London: Harper Perennial.

"When and Why to Cite Sources." *Wikipedia*, http://en.wikipedia.org/wiki/Wikipedia:INCITE#Inline_citation.

"Who Wants Me Dead?" *Thrive Debunked*, http://thrivedebunked.wordpress.com/who-wants-me-dead/.

"Wikipedia: Size Comparisons." *Wikipedia*, http://en.wikipedia.org/wiki/Wikipedia:Size_comparisons#cite_note-1.

Wile, Anthony. 2012. "Foster Gamble on 'Thrive' the Movie, Its Critics and What Can Be Done to Stop the Conspiracy" *Daily Bell* March 4, http://www.thedailybell.com/3664/Foster-Gamble-Responses.

Williams, Bernard. 2002. *Truth and Truthfulness: An Essay in Genealogy*. Princeton, Oxford: Princeton University Press.

Wilson, Woodrow. 1913. *The New Freedom. A Call for the Emancipation of the Generous Energies of a People*. New York: Doubleday.

Wittgenstein, Ludwig. 1980. *Culture and Value*, Trans. Peter Winch. Chicago: University of Chicago Press.

Wolf, Naomi. 2009. "The Pleasures and Sorrows of Work by Alain de Botton" *The Times* March 20, http://www.thetimes.co.uk/tto/arts/article2404068.ece.

Zaitchik, Alexander 2011. "Meet Alex Jones: The Most Paranoid Man in America is Trying to Overthrow the 'global Stasi Borg state,' One Conspiracy Theory at a Time" *Rolling Stone* March 2, http://www.rollingstone.com/politics/news/talk-radios-alex-jones-the-most-paranoid-man-in-america-20110302#ixzz2YUywjzPy.

Zinn, Howard and Anthony Arnove 2004. *Voices of a People's History of the United States*. 2nd ed. New York: Seven Stories Press.

Žižek, Slavoj. 2013. "Some Bewildered Clarifications: A Response to Noam Chomsky" *Verso* July 25, http://www.versobooks.com/blogs/1365-some-bewildered-clarifications.

Zoglin, Richard. 1986. "What if Oswald Had Stood Trial?" *Time Magazine* December 1, http://www.time.com/time/magazine/article/0,9171,962995,00.html.

INDEX

Note: Letter 'n' following by the locators refers to notes.

KFC (Kentucky Fried Chicken),
conspiracy theories about 21,
63–4
Khomeini, Ayatollah 78
Kirchner, Cristina Fernández de 38
Knight, Peter, *Conspiracy Culture*
2n. 2, 17n. 9, 30–1, 35, 39–40,
45, 55, 74, 85–6, 92, 97, 106–8
knowledge
elite vs. democratic acquisition
of 24–5
generalist, and food/diet 54, 66–7
non-expert, trend toward
legitimation of 60n. 7
paranoid 123
popular 17
production of, and social ethics
25
see also authority, distrust of;
epistemological alienation;
mediation of knowledge;
official knowledge, rejection
of; specialist knowledge,
expansion of
Kollerstrom, Nick 47
Ku Klux Klan 21, 72
Kuhn, Thomas 36n. 3
Kyoto protocol 100

LA Confidential (film) 107
Lacan, Jacques 123
Laclau, Ernesto 119n. 5
Lady Gaga, conspiracy theories
about 115
language, as speaking vs. being
spoken 119–20
Latour, Bruno 25n. 18, 96
Lautréamont, Compte de 114
Lear, Edward 93
Lee, Martha F. 94n. 2, 105–6
Lewis, Tyson 12n. 2
liberal humanism, conspiracy theory
and anxiety about 86–7

Limbaugh, Rush 38, 136
Locke, John 120n. 7
London Bombings (2005) 47
Lööw, Heléne 17n. 10
Ludlow, Peter 27
Lyotard, Jean-François 59

McCarthy, Joseph 21, 40
*McCarthyism: The Fight for
America* 46
McCartney, Paul, conspiracy
theories about 1
McDonald's 62–3, 70
Machiavelli, Niccolò, *The Prince*
26–7, 28
Maduro, Nicolás 38
mainstreaming of conspiracy
theories
as conspiracy culture 106–10
and history of U.S. 98–9
and JFK assassination 106, 107–8
and party politics, conspiracy
theory and 97–8
vs. political rhetoric 99
polls on belief in conspiracy
theories 35, 41
Majestic Documents, The (website) 45
Mandel, David R. 75, 95
Marat, Jean-Paul 8n. 5
Marcus, George E., *Paranoia Within
Reason* 2n. 2
Marx, Karl 58, 67, 68, 119
mass communication *see* Internet;
media
mass consensus, conspiracy theories
and 59
the masses
conspiracist conceit of elevation
above 58
deception of 27
as easily led 5, 7, 17, 23, 58, 60,
64, 82, 112
wisdom of 17, 44

The Matrix (film) 107
media
    balance claims of 48–50
    conspiracy theories about 24, 38, 42, 80
    as fourth estate 6
    influence of, in conspiracies 29–30
    and mediation of knowledge, suspicion of 113–14
    and perception of conspiracy theory as purview of the political right 97
    polls of public trust in 57
    and speed of dissemination of conspiracy theories 96
    technological determinism 8, 43
    see also Internet
mediation of knowledge
    in analytic epistemology 54n. 1
    direct inquiry as still dependent on mediation 135
    and Internet search engines 135–6
    overwhelming mass of information as requiring 53–4
    and the written word, suspicion of 112–14
    see also epistemological alienation
medical and pharmaceutical industries
    conspiracy theories about 24
    doubts about, as real 57–8, 103n. 5
    food pyramid and 66
    polls of public trust in 57
Melley, Timothy, *Empire of Conspiracy* 2n. 2, 17n. 9, 22, 79, 86–7, 100, 102, 105, 117, 121, 124, 125
metanarrative *see* grand narratives
Middle East, conspiracy theories involving 76, 79, 83

    see also 9/11 terrorist attacks, conspiracy theories about
millennial panic 87
Miller, Boaz 135–6
mimetic doubling of conspiracists and debunkers
    alarmism and 3, 4, 22–3, 74
    catastrophic predictions 3, 4, 5, 71–2, 78–80, 133–4
    circular citations 44–5
    cognitive closure, need for 75–6
    connections, tracing 116–17
    and debunkers as integral to conspiracy discourse 7
    defined 4n. 3
    demonisation of the enemy 74, 94–7
    as exacerbating the problems 74–5, 88–9
    explanatory scope 75–6
    formerly addressed only in terms of conspiracists emulating conspirators 72, 73
    framing errors and 49
    grand narratives 55, 74, 75–6, 78, 138
    horseshoe theory and 134
    humour as avoidance of 137
    hunts for hidden connections among groups 4
    infiltration of 'enemy' groups 4–5, 73, 91–2
    injury conflated with willed agency 76–8
    intolerance of ambiguity 75–6
    and isolation from opposing viewpoints 134
    mocking and derision, pleasure gained from 82–3
    and nature of evil 4
    overview 9, 71–2
    pleasures of conspiracy 81–3
    projection and 72
    resistance to the enemy 84–7